MACHINE GUNS

GUNS A PICTORIAL, TACTICAL, AND PRACTICAL HISTORY

To Ginny, without whom this book never would have happened.

MACHINE GUNS

A PICTORIAL, TACTICAL, AND PRACTICAL HISTORY

JIM THOMPSON

GREENHILL BOOKS
LONDON

In this book, American author Jim Thompson provides information about American gun laws. For information regarding firearm regulations outside the United States, consult your local Police Authority.

Machine Guns:
A Pictorial, Tactical, and Practical History
by Jim Thompson

Copyright © 1989 by Jim Thompson

ISBN 1-85367-055-3
Printed in the United States of America

First published in the United Kingdom 1990
by Greenhill Books, Lionel Leventhal Limited
Park House, 1 Russell Gardens, London NW11 9NN

British Library Cataloguing in Publication Data available

Direct inquiries and/or orders to the above address.

Contents

Introduction

There is no shortage of books about automatic weapons. Many of them are quite specialized, and I've probably used most of them here in this summary history. A few stand out, which I not only recommend (see below), but refer to constantly. The main difference between the other historical books and this one is that I am operating on the assumption that anyone who buys this text is interested in actually shooting or owning automatic weapons, or is pondering such an expenditure.

This is not the most comprehensive history ever written on the subject of automatic weapons. Peter Senich, Tom Nelson, and especially George Chinn have pursued the nitty-gritty details, from biographies of the greats to markings of specimens. Their works are far more detailed than any I could even attempt. This book is not intended to be a manual for any of these weapons, for W.H.B. Smith in *Small Arms of the World* covered the classics way back in the forties, and the newer updates—though to some extent neglecting the older guns—continue that process with the more recent models. Where I can, I'm trying to present practical information, enough history to understand the gun's use, and information about the machine gun's best friend and worst enemy—ammunition.

I've interviewed many men who are more knowledgeable than I concerning machine guns; in fact, I don't consider myself an expert on the hardware. However, I've shot more ammunition in the seven months it took me to compile this text than some armies shoot in small wars. I tested bullets I doubt anyone has ever put through a machine gun before. There were many case separations, blown primers, hangfires, and annoyances along the way—and some genuine fine, fun shooting.

Some of these guns were old friends, especially the BAR, with which any decent rifleman can feel deep kinship; such was not the case with other guns. I didn't fire them all. Between my bad experiences with a Chauchat many years ago and some recent bad experiences with 8mm Lebel ammo, I saw no advantage to combining the two. Some of the rarer and more valuable guns covered herein should never be fired under any circumstances since there is that one-in-a-million chance that something could go wrong, and their dollar value— even with a flawless gun and perfect ammo—is just too much to risk for no real gain.

I did not include every machine gun on which I have information, nor even every specimen examined or fired. A GAST or Skoda is unlikely to fall into your hands, and neither ever saw much service. Some genuine oddballs are included here to show the direction of production efforts or because they were superb specimens of an important weapons line. Mostly, though, I wanted to stay on track with guns that are common in the marketplace or guns that are important in one's understanding of a given country's development of automatic weapons.

Most guns are listed under the countries where

1

they were developed, not necessarily where they were built. The primary exception is the Maxim and its variants, developed in the United States and England. Ignored in the States, it is used virtually everywhere else. The Lewis is another such exception.

If you notice what seems to be a prejudice in favor of the older, "classic" guns, your observation is correct. I prefer such guns, figuring that if you try some of the state-of-the-art high-tech polymerized guns in competition, you'll probably prefer mostly older guns, too. That doesn't mean there's anything at all wrong with the newer guns. I suspect they aren't as durable, but then the older guns were often *too* durable, meaning that some have already held up seventy years beyond their point of optimum utility.

I did find myself realigning my favorites somewhat. I enjoyed the HK-54MP5 much more than I expected, shooting well with it. The Sten shoots better than it looks, but sooner or later you have to look at it! The MG42 is an awe-inspiring experience that reminded me of my Yugoslavian M53 SARAC variant, purchased new back in my youth but long since passed on to other owners. The M60 is a better gun than most Class III dealers and shooters give it credit for being, but it is far from being as good as the MG42 and FN MAG, and it costs so much. It's popular on the civilian market due primarily to its use in movies. In general, Hotchkiss guns—which I'd never tried extensively before beginning work on this book—are far better than I had expected, but I still hate carrying them. Generally, the .223 is inadequate for any creature much bigger than a gopher or woodchuck, and most shooters regard it as a high-velocity submachine gun cartridge. I found I enjoyed shooting the AUG, a gun whose compact size and good sights make up for a lot of the cartridge's deficiencies.

You may notice a tendency on my part to debunk certain myths (this is, after all, the *practical* and *tactical* history of the weapons). A lot of propaganda and fiction have been recorded in gun books. A lot of mistakes in research have been made that were misinterpreted, recorded as gospel, and passed down like the folklore of ancient societies. You've heard of the dreaded wooden Dum-Dum bullets, which were made to maim and disfigure U.S. troops during World War II? Dum-Dum was an arsenal in British Colonial India, and the wooden bullets are repeater feed blanks, most commonly used in machine guns. Even the U.S. Army has used them,

though not for some time. They probably would inflict an ugly wound at close range, but used as my Egyptian stocks were, they disintegrate very close to the muzzle or strike the ground within a very few yards. Their use has nothing to do with an enemy's lack of humanity or materials; it has to do with feedways, magazines, and cartridge length.

CREDIT WHERE CREDIT IS DUE

Among the handiest general texts on firearms available, the various *Small Arms of the World* books are not so much histories as they are manuals. The collector should really acquire a copy from the pre-1950 period as well as a more recent edition, since the post-1970 editions delete a lot of information on the older guns.

George Chinn's *The Machine Gun* (U.S. Navy, four volumes) is the greatest reference for the in-depth history of the operating principles of the machine gun. Though the illustrations are dated and some are not very good, the drawings and analyses are superb. The nuts-and-bolts explanations are the best you'll find anywhere, and the biographies of the greats of the machine gun's early and middle years are extremely handy in understanding the military politics of the time. His sketches of I.N. Lewis and Hiram Maxim are especially good.

Exhaustive and detailed, Peter Senich's work, *The German Assault Rifle: 1935–1945,* is one of the few scholarly works that make good collector's guides.

Proof and trademark books, as well as ordnance code/identification books, are tedious to use, but they're essential for any serious collector. Though I used David Byron's *Official Guide to Gunmarks* and the Wirnsberger-Steindler *Standard Directory of Proof Marks,* I still ran into a wall or two. You see, makers sometimes *didn't want* to be identified.

Tom Nelson's superb series on assault rifles and submachine guns offers more information than most people can digest. As is the case with many books in the field, there's more than you might want to know on a few obscure guns and just short of enough on some of the more common or sought-after pieces. However, the books cover a lot of ground very effectively, with a minimum of irrelevant material.

In more specialized books, of which I used more than one hundred, there are rafts of texts on the Thompson, many on German firearms (especially automatic weapons), a ton of British texts (especially Dugelby's *The Bren Gun Saga*), and more than anyone can digest on Communist-Bloc firearms in general, including a lot from DIA and other official agencies (especially *The AK47 Story* and *The Great Rifle Controversy,* both by Edward Ezell). But, try to find good production data or even realistic marking information on Swiss, French, and many Italian weapons (let alone objective analysis), and you're in trouble. A lot of this backgrounding had to be done by contacting old friends and asking them to ferret out odd publications—especially military manuals specific to guns like the Breda M37. Such texts had to be photocopied and translated (usually by someone who also knew nothing about firearms, let alone machine guns).

THE SPECIAL ONES

Twenty years ago, I planned a project for publication that died on the vine. *The Little, Dirty Men* was to be the first—and would probably have been the last—true enlisted man's history of warfare in the twentieth century. More than two hundred interviews were conducted, and I acquired seemingly endless hours of tapes and reams of notes from partisans, soldiers, old fighters from both sides in the Gran Chaco, Spanish Civil War, World Wars I and II, the Israeli conflicts of 1948 and 1954, Korea, and Vietnam. Skirmishes around the world that seldom, if ever, were seriously documented or studied were also included. Though no publisher was interested in that project, the remains of those interviews, plus a few new ones with veterans, covered a lot of details that could not have been gleaned from anywhere else. A lot of the men interviewed are dead now. To them and to those who survive, I render a special thanks.

There are others who were helpful beyond measure in this enterprise, some of whom I discuss specifically in the text. So that you, too, can benefit by contacting these firms, I'm going to list many of them here. Many of the guns in this selection of photos are from the Champlin Fighter Museum's J. Curtis Earl Collection, as are all the fighter aircraft. This museum has the finest collection of fighters and automatic weapons on general public display. The museum's cooperation, especially that of Doug Champlin, was essential to compiling this book. Likewise, fifty or so private collectors, some identified here, dug out their treasured gems to be

photographed or shot. Some of these weapons have gone unfired for forty years or more. The collectors lent their guns—for the purest of reasons, the sheer fun of burning ammo—plus a few to a few hundred leftover rounds. They in fact defined what this book is all about—the fascination with lethal gadgetry, the fun of using it, and curiosity in general.

Here, in alphabetical order, are the firms and individuals whose assistance was most vital in compiling this text:

AWC Suppressors & Systems Technology
P.O. Box 1567
Friendswood, TX 77546

Black Hills Shooter's Supply Ammunition
3401 South Highway 79
Rapid City, SD 57701

Mike Bussard
Federal/Norma Cartridge Company
900 Ehlen Drive
Anoka, MN 55303

Cassi/Sterling, Inc.
4320 Northpark Drive
Colorado Springs, CO 80907

Century International Arms Company, Inc.
5 Federal St.
St. Albans, VT 05478

The Champlin Fighter Museum
Falcon Field
4636 Fighter Ace's Drive
Mesa, AZ 85205

Richard Dietz
Remington Arms Company, Inc.
1007 Market Street
Wilmington, DE 19898

Dynamit Nobel/RWS
(RWS, Geco, and Rottweil ammunition
    and components)
105 Stonehurst Court
Northvale, NJ 07647

J. Curtis Earl
5512 N. 6th Street
Phoenix, AZ 85012

John Falk
Olin-Winchester Group
East Alton, IL 62024

David Fiden
Jerusalem, Israel

Fiocchi of America, Incorporated
Route 2, Box 90-B
Ozark, MO 65721

Val Forgett
Navy Arms Company
689 Bergen Boulevard
Ridgefield, NJ 07657

Gordon J. Gee
Chippewa Falls, WI

Gun South, Inc./Steyr-Daimler-Puch
P.O. Box 129
108 Morrow Avenue
Trussville, AL 35173

Hornady Manufacturing Company
P.O. Drawer 1848
Grand Island, NE 68802

Tammy Kahler
Paragon Sales and Service
P.O. Box 2022
Joliet, IL 60434

Royce Kerbo
Denver, CO

Chris Lares
Chandler, AZ

Hilton LaZarr
Phoenix, AZ

Marty Mandall and Fritz Huls
Mandall's Shooter's Supply
3616 N. Scottsdale Road
Scottsdale, AZ 85252

Merkuria/BRNO, FTC
Argentinska 38
17000 Prague 7
Czechoslovakia

Omark Industries, CCI-Speer
P.O. Box 856
Lewiston, ID 83501

Bob Pollock
Mesa, AZ

Sarco, Incorporated
323 Union Street
Stirling, NJ 07980

Nick Sasso
National Bullet Company
1585 East 361st Street
Eastlake, OH 44094

E.R. Shaw/Small Arms Mfg. Co.
Thomas Run Road & Prestley
Bridgeville, PA 15017

Silver Bullet, Ltd.
Douglas County, NV 89423-9030

Bob Simpson, Simpson, Limited
587 E. Main Street
Galesburg, IL 61401

Springfield Armory/Rock Island Armory
420 West Main Street
Geneseo, IL 61254

Springfield Sporters, Inc.
R.D. #1
Penn Run, PA 15765

C.B. Stern
IMI-Samson/Action Arms/Action Ammunition
P.O. Box 9573
Philadelphia, PA 19124

John Student
North Hollywood, CA

United States Army Ordnance Museum
Aberdeen, MD (Aberdeen Proving Ground)

Miraslav Vucetic
Zagreb, Yugoslavia

Zero Bullet and Ammunition Company, Inc.
P.O. Box 1188
Cullman, AL 35056-1188

If you noticed that the above sources seem to be mostly ammunition suppliers, then you have already discerned a great deal about the machine gun. Over the life of a gun or, rather, over your period of ownership, you will most likely spend more than the gun's value on ammunition—if you shoot much at all. Since ammunition is also the primary source of danger to yourself and your firearm, please note that much of this book relates more to fodder than guns. And that is *not* misemphasis.

How much did I shoot, you wonder? Should I give you that figure in rounds? In fifty-five-gallon drums? In pickup loads? The truth is, four friends of mine who are avid reloaders may not need brass until sometime in the twenty-second century now that I let them have all the brass I shot!

CHAPTER 1

So, You Want to Own a Machine Gun?

There's a sort of murky conventional wisdom that machine guns are somehow illegal. One hears this even from gun buffs. And from the antigun folks who know that they aren't, one hears the general attitude that they sure as hell *ought* to be illegal. Two truths seldom expressed anywhere are that machine guns are *not* illegal in the United States and, as a weapon for illegal activity, the registered machine gun is just about useless. Without proper practice and training, a good shotgun or long-magazined rifle is a much better weapon than anything that's fully automatic.

This chapter is a thumbnail sketch of the ins and outs of automatic weapons ownership. It is not legal advice, but it is *commonsense* advice.

BACKGROUND

Strictly speaking, the National Firearms Act (NFA) and Federal Firearms Act (FFA) provisions dealing with automatic weapons weren't intended to be antigun legislation in the modern sense. The intentions of the taxing and registration provisos were to control gangsters and brigands whose almost casual use of Thompsons and BARs during Prohibition seemed to endanger everyone. Until 1934, there were no federal laws governing machine guns *per se,* though a crazy quilt of state and local laws, some far more repressive than subsequent federal statutes and close to the Gun Control Act of

1968 in their intent, did limit sales in some areas. It was largely the '21 Thompson, a compact gun with a very high rate of fire used in such incidents as the St. Valentine's Day Massacre, that added fully automatic mobility to the thug's repertoire. Serious historians will note, however, that Baby Face Nelson, among others, felt the .30-06 Browning Automatic Rifle was more intimidating; he was a small man and apparently felt he needed a bigger weapon. Other gangsters used Maxims, Hotchkisses, and Colt-Brownings in their criminal sprees, feuds, wars, robberies, and executions. However, it still seems ironic that by the time the bills restricting machine gun use were entered into law, the criminal use of the machine gun had almost come to an end. The serious criminals of the period, particularly of the organized variety, had figured out that the looks and noise of automatic weapons drew entirely too much attention to allow for practical purchase and employment. The police crackdowns and public outcries that followed were also obstacles such criminals had to overcome.

The Gun Control Act of 1968 proscribed automatic weapons transfers, and subsequent Treasury rulings have had the effect of generally tightening restrictions, as have certain ancillary pieces of legislation that have passed since. One also has to deal with a patchwork of state laws (summarized in the following chart, which was compiled by J. Curtis Earl and reproduced here with his permission), some of which can be downright confounding.

STATE LAWS REGARDING MACHINE GUNS

The following is a summary of STATE LAWS regulating the ownership or possession of machine guns, as interpreted from the Federal document "Published Ordinances – FIREARMS, State Laws, Relevant to Title 18, U.S. Code, Chapter 44" Publication P-5300.5   NOTE: This list may or may not be conclusive and is intended only as a reference.

STATE	MACHINE GUNS PERMITTED		Special Requirements to Purchase or Possess — if any —	STATE	MACHINE GUNS PERMITTED		Special Requirements to Purchase or Possess — if any —
	Dewat	Live			Dewat	Live	
Alabama	yes	yes	none	New Hampshire	yes	yes	none
Arizona	yes	yes	none	New Jersey	yes	yes*	*Judge's permit req'd; Dealer OK
Alaska	yes	yes	none	New Mexico	yes	yes	none
Arkansas	yes	yes	Register gun with State	New York	yes	no*	*Manufacture Licensee can own
California	yes	no*	*Dealers can possess	North Carolina	yes	yes*	*Sheriff or Court Clerk permit required
Colorado	yes	yes	none	North Dakota	yes	yes*	*Permit req'd.
Connecticut	yes	yes	State reg. after receipt	Ohio	yes	yes	none
Delaware	no	no		Oklahoma	yes	yes	none
Dist. Columbia	yes	no		Oregon	yes	yes	none
Florida	yes	yes	none	Pennsylvania	yes	yes*	*Curio-Relics only
Georgia	yes	yes	none	Puerto Rico	yes*	no	*Police permit req'd.
Hawaii	no	no		Rhode Island	yes	yes*	*Dealers & Lawmen only
Idaho	yes	yes	none	South Carolina	yes	no	
Illinois	yes	yes*	*Lawmen & Dealers only	South Dakota	yes	yes	State reg. after purchase
Indiana	yes	yes	none	Tennessee	yes	yes	none
Iowa	yes	yes*	*Dealers only can possess	Texas	yes	yes	none
Kansas	yes	yes*	*Dealers can possess	Utah	yes	yes	none
Kentucky	yes	yes	none	Vermont	yes	yes	none
Louisiana	yes	yes*	*Lawmen, Dealers can poss., "War relics" OK to others	Virginia	yes	yes	none
Maine	yes	yes	none	Virgin Isles	yes	?	Permit required
Maryland	yes	yes	Register gun with State	Washington	yes	no	
Massachusetts	yes	yes*	*Permit & license required	West Virginia	yes	yes*	*Permit required
Michigan	yes	yes*	*Lawmen & Dealers can only	Wisconsin	yes	yes*	*Police or Sheriff permit req'd
Minnesota	yes*	yes*	*Curio-Relics only OK	Wyoming	yes	yes	none
Mississippi	yes	yes	none				
Missouri	yes	yes*	*Curio-Relics; Dealers any				
Montana	yes	yes	State reg. required				
Nebraska	yes	yes	none				
Nevada	yes	yes	none				

NOTE: Some Cities and Counties have laws prohibiting or limiting or registering machine guns, but as these are few, they are not listed above. Inquire.

(*) NOTE: MACHINE GUN DEALERS LICENSES ARE NOT DIFFICULT TO OBTAIN.

CURIO-RELIC CLASSED MACHINEGUNS COVER NEARLY ALL MACHINEGUNS MANUFACTURED UP TO AND THRU WORLD WAR II AND CAN BE POSSESSED LIVE IN ALL LEGAL 'LIVE' STATES.

FOR FURTHER INFORMATION ON STATE OR LOCAL LAWS GOVERNING MACHINE GUNS, I SUGGEST YOU CONTACT YOUR LOCAL OR REGIONAL OFFICE OF **BUREAU OF ALCOHOL, TOBACCO & FIREARMS. U.S. TREASURY DEPARTMENT, INTERNAL REVENUE SERVICE.** These people are the most qualified to give you expert advice in this respect. Most often, local law people are just not properly informed, or used biased personal opinions that are misleading or totally incorrect.

Remember!! Your Federal AT&F Agent can be of great help. He is usually knowledgeable and friendly, but some are neither, and plain anti-gun, so . . .

You have nothing to fear by asking. He is **not out to get you.** Just be friendly and courteous and explain your problem intelligently and you will find him cooperative and friendly too . . . . Hopefully.

Next!! Your next best source of information is your lawyer. Have him **read** the law to you. At least make sure he researches the law. He can draw on all kinds of information. JUST DON'T TAKE A QUICK OFF-THE-CUFF ANSWER **IF IT IS NEGATIVE.**

GENERAL PHILOSOPHY

Should you opt to own an automatic weapon, *cut no corners.* Not only should you not break any laws, but you should make a special point of not even coming close to the edge. This is an area where a paperwork error can result in the confiscation of your weapon as well as a lot of red tape and jail.

Acquiring an individual or new dealer's license will usually require, for example, a background check, mug shots, and fingerprinting. If you're wise, you will not only cooperate—and cheerfully, at that—but you'll make sure any and all authorities even peripherally involved are kept fully and completely supplied with any information they request even if it exceeds the absolute letter of the law. This is not a venture in which you want to offend anyone.

This is especially important once the transaction is completed (which may take months) and you actually have your NFA firearm. Transporting your weapon to a range or show will require an unusual level of planning and security.

A case in point: In 1964, my brother and I were transporting a deactivated M1928 Thompson in his convertible down the Causeway in LaCrosse, Wisconsin. A gas-station attendant we knew saw the piece and asked to look at it, and we obliged. A police captain directing traffic almost one hundred yards away saw the attendant and the weapon he was handling. He came over and proclaimed that the Thompson was "illegal." After spending a few minutes showing him where the actuator handle was, demonstrating that the chamber was properly steel-plugged, and showing him the papers on the weapon, he relented a bit and we were on our way.

You need to remember that the registered NFA firearms owner must always be aware that people, especially the police, tend to react instinctively to anything perceived as a "machine gun." That is one reason why I have very mixed feelings about owning handguns or carbines that look as if they were fully automatic, as well as "nonguns" that are exact external, unfireable replicas of automatic weapons. After all, at first glance a law officer isn't going to know whether or not the weapon is fully automatic.

Other than ignorance, one reason you'll seldom hear antigunners lock horns with us over registered automatic weapons is that there simply is no issue. In fifty-four years of registration history, there's apparently been only one crime committed with a registered automatic weapon. In that case, it was a household homicide that could have been commit-

ted with most any weapon. As a sidelight, there was *no* federal legislation whatsoever governing artillery until the GCA 68, and I have seen no research that indicates any criminal involvement with artillery. The weapons are often cumbersome; more important, they cost so much and attract so much attention that they're virtually useless to anyone with any serious criminal intentions.

THE LAW

This section will cover only the basic tenets of federal rules and offer some commonsense advice.

With the exception of those who hold appropriate Curio and Relic (C & R) licenses, NFA firearms can be transmitted via common carrier only between licensed dealers.

Since all federal firearm legislation is based upon taxing power, registered NFA weapons are taxed $200 per individual weapon at the time of this writing. Federal law imposes a tax of $500 per annum for dealers in Class III firearms. For those who wish to become serious collectors, the dealer's license tax is almost a necessity. If, however, one acquires the dealer's license, one is obligated to actually engage in commerce. Therefore, a wheeler-dealer has to have the Class III. The normal tax stamp for individual weapons is paid by the individual consumer only once, but it is assessed at each transaction. The seller is responsible for the tax, which he then passes on to the purchaser. The "03" Curios and Relics License costs $10 per year ($30 for the normal three-year term) and exempts its holder from the shipping limitations on weapons manufactured prior to 1945 or those specifically on the C&R list. It *does not* change record-keeping requirements or exempt the holder from the individual tax stamp on weapons. Deactivated automatic weapons must be registered, but as of this writing, no transfer tax is required.

Generally speaking, individuals applying for a dealer's license have fewer problems and fewer hoops to jump through than individuals seeking to register only one weapon. The record-keeping provisions are exact, however, and these are not laws that can be avoided or circumvented.

For example, if you unlawfully reactivate a registered unserviceable weapon, plan on doing time, losing the weapon, and paying a fine—if you live through the initial raid. There are specific provisions under which such a weapon may be properly remanufactured, and there are some excellent firms doing this work that can literally save you from disaster. With some welding jobs, manufacturers who are licensed to do such work will advise the registered party that the costs of remanufacture would be excessive or would come just short of the illegal act of manufacturing, by hand, a new receiver. This means the party who did the original welding destroyed the crystalline structure of the metal; even if the legalities have been properly served, reactivating such a piece is very expensive and unwise.

There is no such thing as a legal, unregistered fully automatic receiver except one that has been demilitarized. That means it has been cut in pieces and holed. Weapons brought into the country under the old DEWAT (Deactivated War Trophy) programs of the late 1940s to the 1960s are now considered contraband unless they were registered during the 1968-1969 amnesty. While some individuals, including myself, are pushing for another amnesty period that's coupled with a fairly massive publicity campaign, the only act that may now be legally consummated with such a piece is the stripping of all parts and the destruction of the receiver. Surprisingly, the sum of the parts is then often worth more than the total firearm. This may be true even more so in the future, as new restrictions and regulations have been enacted to severely restrict the importation of machine gun parts from abroad.

New automatic weapons can no longer be manufactured or registered, except for the direct consumption of the U.S. government and certain authorized law-enforcement functions. No older units can be imported, save under the same conditions. No new units of any kind can be registered. Some states, notably Delaware and Hawaii, either directly forbid automatic weapons ownership or, like California, make the process so miserable that it is wiser not to even try to begin the paperwork. Indeed, it is not a bad idea to engage an attorney before undertaking step number 1 in many states, and it is essential to seek the general advice of your Class III dealer early on.

Remember that automatic weapons transactions are generally final. In fact, you can't lawfully return such a piece via common carrier, and if the manufacturer still exists, even sending the piece off for authorized repair can be extremely awkward. With recent changes in import regulations, especially restriction of barrel importation (now reversed), it is wise to purchase all the spare parts you'll ever need immediately upon consummating the deal.

It can take 90 to 180 days after your purchase before your registration is complete and the weapon is actually received.

If all this hasn't discouraged you yet, be advised: *Expect further restrictions.* This, should you wonder, is what the antigun lobby would like to put rifle and shotgun owners through, after the handgun bans take effect. Look to identify repressive legislation by the specifics, not by the party label of the sponsor, and react immediately and calmly. Machine gun owners—the legitimate kind, like you—have so far been models of sanity and tranquility. I think maintaining that record is a big step toward assuring our continued (though limited) right to keep and bear arms.

HARD REALITY

Nothing about machine guns is cheap. Very little is easy. Even if ranges are willing to let you shoot, they usually saddle the machine-gun owner with special rules and restrictions. Such restrictions make perfect sense. After all, the machine gunner can devastate backstops or target boards, and if he's marginal with the law or paperwork, he can cause a range lots of paperwork and legal nightmares. The guns themselves require special discipline when it comes to firing and adherence to a cooling and cleaning regime. You do not *need* a machine gun, which means you have to really *want* one.

The brief summary I've presented is only a guideline. Contact your dealer, your local BATF (Bureau of Alcohol, Tobacco and Firearms), or Treasury Department office, or write:

United States Treasury Department
Bureau of Alcohol, Tobacco and Firearms
Literature Distribution Services
P.O. Box 14188
Washington, DC 20044-4188

CHAPTER 2

Learn, Shoot, Clean, Analyze

Rather than have this book thought of as the encyclopedia of the machine gun, I'd like it to be a first-aid manual of sorts, or a consumer guide to automatic weapons. Remember, if you have no valid information, a machine gun is the *last* thing you need.

The following are two good sources of correct manuals for some of the guns described herein: Survival Books, 11106 Magnolia Boulevard, North Hollywood, CA 91601-3810; and William J. Ricca, P.O. Box 25, New Tripoli, PA 18066-0025.

Though the above sources are good, there are nowhere near enough manuals on some of the fairly common guns. You may wind up, as I did, trying to get key sections of manuals translated from Serbo-Croatian, Greek, Chinese, or Japanese—if you're lucky enough to locate the old originals. Reprints often don't exist in convenient languages, either. However, take every rational step to get all the information you can on machine guns in general and your model in particular before you actually attempt to fire any automatic weapon. To me, this advice applies equally to shooting with *all* firearms.

Also, before you pull the trigger for the first time, try to locate a source for parts. You should have a spare barrel on hand, and perhaps a bolt and spring kit, too, plus spare magazines and/or belts. Sarco, Springfield Sporters, and several other companies stock parts for many automatic weapons. If it's a new weapon you're contemplating, often a semi-automatic version is still imported and most parts

are compatible in most versions. The original importer, if he's still around, may well stock parts for the gun. A good source for parts on new and used weapons is Sherwood International Import and Export, 18714 Parthenia Street, Northridge, CA 91324. Generally, though, Sarco has the best parts selection for the less-common weapons.

Barrels may have to be machine-duplicated from blanks, especially in unusual calibers and for the more uncommon guns. I've used E.R. Shaw blanks in the larger outside diameter sizes for quite some time. When allowing a machinist or gunsmith to work on gas-operated guns, be sure he combines the drilling for the gas vent (which technically should be in a groove, not a land) with the threading or rear template in a manner that will position the port precisely so as not to leave sprue or flash in the bore.

It's a good idea to actually examine and shoot the weapon before you lay down your money. Don't be surprised if the importer or manufacturer snubs you when you try to get information. After having written more than fifty magazine articles and two books, I have a list of importers and manufacturers who will not and/or cannot communicate with me! You'll often have better luck approaching another owner or a dealer. This is especially true with machine guns since new receivers can no longer be made for the civilian market and stocks of the importers or manufacturers for general sale are exhausted. Even some of the REMAN/REMIL manu-

Marty Mandall's Finnish Jati, one of very few in the United States.

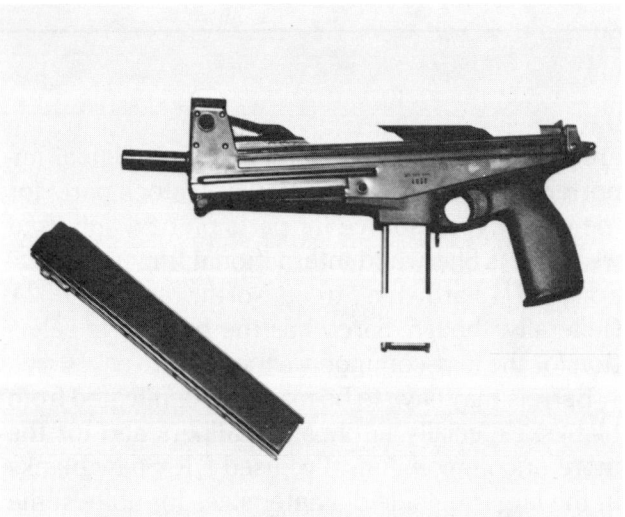

Jati.

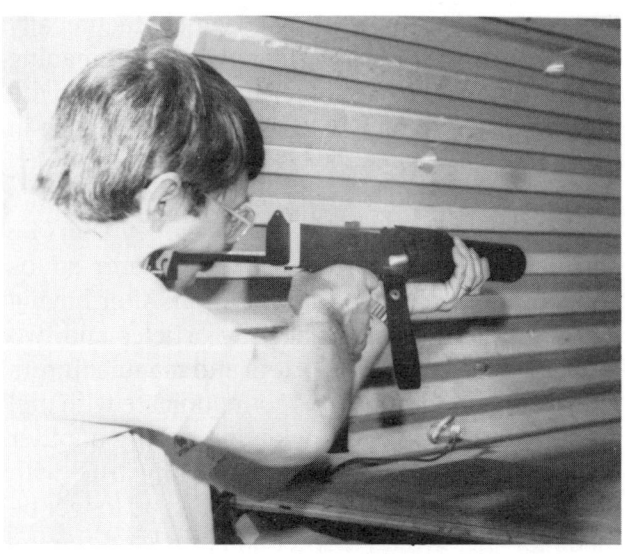

Firing a suppressed MAC-10 at Mandall's.

facturers have no catalog materials on their parts kit guns and don't like to answer written queries, which means you almost have to go there to get any information. That's why books like this one are necessary. Examining and/or shooting a piece depends on developing your own information and intelligence sources, and hoping you find a friendly face somewhere. Or you can go to Mandall's in Scottsdale, Arizona.

Marty Mandall is an escaped New Yorker who runs the most unusual gun shop I've ever seen. He imports SIG (Schweizerische Industrie-Gesellschaft), Bernardelli, and other European products of high quality, though he also stocks more used guns and oddball ammunition than any other storefront you can imagine. If you drop in to window-shop, you can sit down between the Vickers and the Lahti or over by the M1919A4 and ogle the Obregon, the AKs or the SIG P210s. And, yes, he's got all the accessories, barrels, and kits.

All this stuff is at least nominally for sale, though there is a Class III sample or two among the machine guns. For the price of range time, gun rental, and ammo, you can shoot your intended weapon in the downstairs range. Marty applies this fairly hefty fee to the amount of your purchase, less ammo. Let's face it, though, there are very few places that allow you to test not one or two weapons, but even sixteen to forty automatic weapons to help you make up your mind. A lot of times, your decision hinges on what not to buy. The MAC-10 and Uzi are fine guns within their limitations, and heavily publicized in the movies, but most folks who actually test them end up buying something else. The indoor shooting pictures here are from Marty's range, one of few places in the country where you can shoot a machine gun indoors.

To satisfy my curiosity, we ran IMI/Samson 9mm 158-grain subsonic ammo through Marty's suppressed MAC-10 without using any ear protection. I've fired silenced Thompsons (much quieter than the MAC) and rifles with big, beautiful, outrageously priced precision Maxim silencers (quiet, but a loud "crack" from downrange), but I had to satisfy my curiosity about shooting with a modern setup, full auto, indoors. Later, doubling up ear protection by using the cigarette filter jobs and my "Mickey Mouse" ears, my nephew Bob and I tried out the MG42. I must say, shooting in that tunnel causes you to feel a tremendous amount of vibration at 1,200 rounds per minute. At that time, Bob was a machine-gun novice who sampled several SMGs and the BAR at both the high- and low-fire rates. He had no problems, and quickly became comfortable with the guns.

The main thing to remember when shooting a machine gun is to stop shooting when you can't see the target any more and wait until you regain a sight picture. Dust and muzzle blast will obscure your sight picture rather rapidly, so you'll develop the discipline of using short bursts. You don't have to do this with a heavy and secure tripod-mounted gun. You can shoot very accurately and to the same point of impact with a real winner like the ZB-37 even if you can't see every single bullet impact. But it's always more fun and more rewarding to see what you're doing.

Your real problem is finding a place to shoot without getting arrested in the process. Be sure to call any agency that should know you'll be shooting a machine gun; tell them what you're doing and that it's legal in order to avoid any hassles later. Take at least one copy of your ownership papers with you. Many ranges want to check them on the spot, and that's wise from their point of view and yours. Bring your own target boards or stands, and make sure they're approved by the range master. If you're shooting on approved public land—and especially if you're shooting on approved private land—be very sure you do no ancillary damage. Police the area before you leave to make sure it's cleaner than when you got there, and never—never, ever—violate any laws or safety rules.

Prevention is, in effect, "first-aid" for your weapon and begins with inspecting the gun and ammunition (see the following chapter). Right now, though, I'll give you some cleaning and maintenance advice that could save you money, burns, and other headaches. Not surprisingly, it all has to do with ammunition—more specifically, the machine gun's appetite for same.

HEAT, AMMO, AND THE CLEANING PROCESS

It is vital that you always remember that the machine gun changes certain ground rules of shooting because of the simple laws of physics. Burning primer and powder, bullet friction, and the rapidity with which the machine gun initiates the explosions inside its breech magnify heat buildup, which causes metal to be in a state of flux. That state of flux accelerates metal decay, and the porosity that comes with heat and expansion further increases the chance of deterioration. Therefore, *all*

ammunition that's fired from a machine gun for any length of time becomes corrosive or, more accurately, erosive since—in addition to the heat created by explosions and bullet friction—burning powder acts as an abrasive (the more so when the steel with which it is in contact becomes hotter). You can think of powder as burning dirt—which is about what it is at 400- to 500-degree metal surface temperatures. Add very hard bullets and you have a very destructive situation.

Air-cooled guns of any type are essentially guns cooled by time and the natural tendency of heat to radiate in space. Convection around air-cooled barrels is not fictional with such well-designed jackets as those for the Lewis and early Beretta subguns, but it is also not very helpful or very fast in cooling an overheated barrel.

Water is, however. That's why there are water-cooled machine guns. But you needn't lug around seven or eight pounds of water. Instead, do what I've developed the habit of doing: carry a nozzled plastic spray bottle of detergent/water solution. During short breaks and with the muzzle down, squeeze a few sprays of water down the bore. With a gas-operated gun, leave the gas system open for a few seconds while spraying. Spray and dry it separately (it doesn't get quite as hot), but be sure no significant amount of water gets into the gas system. Pass a patch through the bore if time allows in order to eliminate grit and powder residue. Do all this from the chamber end if possible.

In addition to doing a little cooling, you've just done most of the serious cleaning your gun will require, even if you use corrosive ammo. The occasional drink of water, though, is as important to a machine gun as it is to human beings. You could follow with a corrosive or black-powder-style solvent, and then wipe it out. At some point, you should brush the bore as well. Never actually touch a hot barrel. If you must work from the muzzle end, use a non-steel rod or muzzle protector. Be very careful, since muzzle-crown damage is as damaging to a machine gun and its resale value as it is to a rifle or pistol. You don't have to do this while you're shooting, though I must say it will greatly extend your barrel's accurate life.

It is important that you clean your weapon after you're done shooting, especially if you shoot corrosive ammo. But it's a good idea to get in the habit of thinking that all ammunition is corrosive in a machine gun because the heat buildup is much more severe than in slower-firing weapons.

It is also important to lubricate your weapon properly, using lubricants recommended for your operating conditions and temperature. In hot weather, I prefer heavy greases. When shooting M3s and Sten guns—especially when "hot dogging" (shooting from waist)—it's very common to get peppered with hot oil. If you use thin lubricants, this will happen all the time. I use an automotive bearing molygraph grease, and it stays where you put it. Oil doesn't.

WD-40, a very handy short-term lubricant and solvent, has no place at all as a lubricant on semiautomatic or automatic weapons. I saw a gun catch fire once, and the cause was its owner's excessive use of WD-40. The fire didn't last long, and it didn't hurt the gun once we wiped it down and cooled it off. Both WD-40 and Liquid Wrench are very handy working solvents that work well to remove bore crud and caked-on fouling. However, neither the manufacturers nor I can recommend them as lubricants for fully automatic firearms. I can't stress it enough: Do not use WD-40 as a lubricant.

There are men who use unbreakable oven thermometers on their barrels, and I've seen one man shoot a pair of AN M2 .30s with a hose running constantly over the barrels. When you see this, you realize it's smart to either hold burst length down or keep your barrel cool. The "water-flush, brush, then solvent and wipe-down" cleaning technique is an alternative to something even more ridiculous— using my suggested, abbreviated form of the same setup during a shooting session. It forestalls other forms of annoyance and cash outlay, not to mention the nightmare of finding a barrel or having one made for an oddball gun. The decision is yours. But once you've fried your first barrel or two, you may find yourself wishing you'd brought a hose and stuck a thermometer on your barrel.

Watch out for hardened steel bullets. They're found mainly on Czech ammo from the late 1940s and early 1950s (often steel-cased and lacquered), but also on German and some Belgian ammo, and certain types of Soviet rounds from various periods. Usually there are rust flecks on the rounds. The problems are obvious: gas rushing past the bullet base and higher friction coefficients. All of this increases heat at a greater-than-normal rate. Even a pistol shot slowly and deliberately can experience accelerated bore wear when firing this load family. And the higher the velocity, the worse the problem. Firing fewer than one hundred rounds caused serious damage to a friend's P38 in 9mmx19. A machine-gun barrel is more massive, but not necessarily much harder. At 7.92x57JS velocities, 2.5 times as fast, throwaway time might come even earlier, especially when blown down the bore twenty rounds per second.

OPERATIONS AND ANALYSIS

To some extent, the characteristics of the automatic weapon are determined by its operating system, though if the design is good enough, just about any operating system, even the odd ones like blow-forward and long recoil, can be made to work and work well. Gathering information about your weapon is useful in determining the importance of certain parts. In recoil guns, in which the barrel and bolt must together perform a short flight rearward, a barrel must perform both mechanical and ballistic functions. The condition of overall bolt and ancillary parts in blowback guns requires careful attention, especially in delayed mechanisms. Gas guns often employ pistons and plungers inside their gas tubes, and they must be watched for signs of wear or corrosion. None of these little asides are going to cause sudden failures or surprise danger conditions, unless you do something very stupid or the gun is flawed.

This book doesn't cover the mechanical machine guns (such as the Gatling and Nordenfeldt) since their multiple barrels are properly left to the past. Nor does it mention the cumbersome electrically activated systems (such as the mini-gun), which are really no faster than an MG81Z setup and are substantially heavier. They have virtually no civilian application, and make a water-cooled gun look svelte.

The self-operating automatic machine gun has a very simple transfer function; it uses the explosion inside the case—the energy just created—to impart movement to a breechblock or bolt and all other components necessary to feeding and firing the next round. All automatic machine guns use the same root source of energy (expanding gases and their pressure) to initiate activity. The gases are merely used at different points and in different forms to impart energy to the necessary components.

The key problem in all automatic weapons design is assuring a delay period before the breech is opened. If the cartridge is exposed too soon (while there is still pressure in the barrel), the gun or the shooter may be damaged and the cartridge itself may swell to excess or separate. This would cause a jam due to failure to eject and/or failure to feed or clear the feedway. Thus, some sort of delay is necessary. Mechanically, this delay is often referred to as the *null* or *dwell,* though the terms are also applied to the take-up period planned into most weapons before the cartridge imparts any movement. In recoil systems, cams, raceways, and tabs physically lock the barrel and bolt together through at least part of the movement—through the entire aft movement in the extreme case of primitive long recoil systems—but all operating systems eject the fired cartridge at the near rearmost point of the bolt's travel, clearing the feedway to pick up the next round.

Recoil systems thus use the cartridge case itself, the same energy source as in blowback systems, to activate movement of the bolt and barrel. Recoil systems can use long barrels, though barrel weight affects spring tension requirements and can therefore affect the rate of fire.

In blowback systems, only the bolt moves. It is generally delayed sufficiently by bolt mass, spring tension, or some sort of mechanical leverage disadvantage, often provided by springs against surfaces or roller bearings.

Gas systems, as in the Eklund/Ljungmann and most of Stoner's designs, may omit the usual piston assembly common to most guns. They still must tap gas pressure at some point, preferably close to the muzzle or some other convenient point or way, to assure that the bullet—which forms the pressure seal—has left the barrel before the breech opens. As with other systems, some control of timing is important to assure that the bolt does not open too soon. If the port is located close to the muzzle, the problem of timing is already partly solved. In whatever form, gas gushes through the vent and into a tube. It either propels the bolt directly or propels a piston, which in turn is connected to an operating rod or plunger. This rod or plunger then drives the bolt and, subsequently, the entire system. In all cases, it is a spring mechanism of some sort that reverses the action at the appropriate time.

These are the classic explanations of the most common operating systems in automatic and semi-automatic weapons. There are other systems, including blow-forward, in which the breech remains static and the barrel flies forward, thus performing almost all tasks usually initiated and finished in the breech.

Since Maxim, many modern weapons have com-bined systems, especially in aircraft guns. In fact, the MG42 employs all three systems. Gas is trapped, but not vented to the breech, imparting instead extra speed from the cone to the barrel. The recoil stroke, very short indeed, has finished while the bullet is still in the bore; this is why the bolt in the system is roller delayed since it performs part of the function of the bolt in a retarded blowback system.

Many gas guns use blowback as a "to null" boost, though this is far more common in cannon than in the .50-caliber and smaller guns covered in this text. Chinn gives a better and more detailed explanation of these operating systems and their applications in his four-volume set than could be done here. What is important to remember, though, is that pistol cartridges operate at roughly 25,000 to 30,000 c.u.p. (copper units of pressure), with rifle cartridges at about twice that rate. It is these forces that cause the machine gun to act like a perpetual motion machine—until the ammo runs out.

THINGS THAT CAN KILL YOU OR YOUR GUN

Most machine-gun problems begin with sloppy maintenance, including failure to check components that are known to be wear and stress points. The other common cause of problems is ammunition, that which is bad quality or incorrect for a specific weapon. When these factors are combined, the results can be deadly.

Barrel blockages of any kind cause great peril. It seems ridiculous to say it, but before shooting, the bore should be checked for impediments. I habitually run a single patch through each bore *before* shooting. During shooting, though, the main cause of bore impediments is a squib round, especially one in which there is either no powder in the case, or the powder does not ignite or ignites incompletely. Never, ever proceed with shooting on a short recoil round without checking the barrel for obstructions. If there's a bullet a few inches down the bore, you may survive the conflagration, but your barrel will probably have to be cut away and, needless to say, discarded. If the barrel doesn't give, the breech might. I've always been a little superstitious about tubular receivers since they closely resemble a barrel, and that bolt can act like a big steel bullet. Only if the explosion happens in the breech will all this stuff come rearward.

A second control to watch and check carefully is

headspace—that is, the relationship between chamber and bolt. There are such things as manufacturing tolerances, and sometimes they pile up to a point where a shiny new barrel sometimes won't mate appropriately with a particular bolt mechanism. The pounding that machine guns take and the sometimes mechanical wear in recoil guns can cause the chamber to actually distort or change battery position slightly, perhaps leaving the case head unsupported beyond the weapon's design tolerance or too tight against the bolt to allow extractor function.

Short headspace, where the case is not far enough into the chamber, can be solved with a reamer or the headspace adjustment of some guns. Also, some guns move the bolt back and forth or allow its position to be otherwise adjusted. Excessive headspace inserts the case too far, so that the firing pin may pound the case forward upon firing, then allow it to tear back. This can sometimes cause case separations or, depending on the feed system, cause the firing pin to fail to discharge the case at all.

Troubleshooting requires a specific manual to be precise, but misfires, distorted brass, jams, and troubles to which systems are subject are to be looked into immediately. Often, the tendency of a given gun to jam with a given cartridge is due to a weak magazine spring rather than the bent feed lips so often discussed. While shooting an MP40 recently, my one magazine fed the splendid Federal Match 9mm load with alacrity, while the other jammed regularly. With a little finger pressure, I realized that the one with the stronger spring was feeding everything, including CCI Lawman hollow points, whereas the other would gobble up only hardball.

Belts develop frays and tears in fabric areas, bends and dings in nondisintegrating metal units. These usually won't directly cause jams but, if not fixed, they will only get worse. Be sure you have the correct belt or magazine. I once bought a machine gun after carefully preparing my "system" to use it, only to discover it was a far rarer variant than advertised. It would not accept the same, more common feed setup its brethren made famous, though it looked as though it would. It thus spent its entire time in my hands as a doorstop, and might as well have been deactivated.

I have only hit a few highlights here, but the best troubleshooting items are a few simple measuring tools, common sense, and an appropriate manual.

Condition	Cause	Remedy
Fails to fire (cartridge in chamber)	Defective cartridge	Retract bolt and fire
	Weak driving spring	Replace spring
	Fouled weapon	Clean and lubricate
Fails to fire (no cartridge in chamber)	Defective magazine	Replace magazine
	Short recoil	Adjust gas regulator to next larger setting
	Short recoil	Clean and lubricate
Ruptured cartridge (repeatedly)	Excessive headspace, loose barrel, worn bolt	Adjust (may require armorer's repair)
Fails to extract	Dirty chamber	Clean
	Broken extractor	Replace extractor
Fails to eject	Fouled weapon	Clean and lubricate
	Short recoil	Adjust gas regulator
Runaway gun	Short recoil	Adjust gas regulator, lubricate

Some common firing problems and how to fix them.

Keep your gun clean, feed it the correct ammunition, keep a few parts on hand, and make sure that squibs are avoided or solved (you drive them out of the rifling or change to another barrel). Following this advice, you're taking no more chances than you would with a hunting or target rifle.

DEFINITIONS & NOTES

There are a few terms that you'll want to understand before going any further.

DEWAT. Technically, a chamber-welded Deactivated War Trophy, brought in under the old law before GCA '68. The original DEWAT required only a simple write-off form and weren't registered upon transfer in the modern sense. This has all changed. An unregistered DEWAT is now considered contraband, and unless the law changes, it cannot be registered or transferred or, for that matter, owned. About all you can do is strip the gun and hope to find a usable or rebuildable receiver, sell the parts, destroy the receiver, or get some kind of trade deal going. Barrels are tack-welded to receivers on correct DEWATs.

DEMIL. A demilitarized gun is one that has been reduced to "nonfirearms" status, basically by being hacked to bits by a variety of processes from sawing to torching. These need not be registered. Some borderline cases, such as receivers that are internally welded and have multiple holes, are in a gray area, but as more and more of these are confiscated, their status becomes less of an issue.

REMANS or REMOS. These are semiautomatic

weapons that have been remanufactured to fully automatic condition, usually lawfully but sometimes unlawfully. Underground gunsmiths, most of whom are not very good, specialize in doing the illegal ones, primarily in California and Florida, where the drug trade is centered. Their primary customers are folks in the illegal chemical industry. The lawful trade mostly centers around receivers registered and coupled with parts kits prior to the May 1986 ban on the manufacture of new receivers for civilian use. The illegal trade mostly involves MAC-10s, MAC-11s, and Uzis, whereas the legal side of this business includes a lot of new manufactured receivers on which paperwork was completed before the deadline.

Never even look at or consider an illegal weapon. In addition to the legalities involved, most illegal guns are unsafe and unreliable.

REMILS. These are demilitarized guns rewelded after careful realignment on special jigs to allow their recompletion as deactivated weapons or sometimes as actual working ones. It surprises people, but REMILS, properly executed, retempered, and with new parts where necessary, can be excellent, safe shooters. It all depends on who does the work.

REWATS. REWATS are guns that have been reactivated from a deactivated, welded condition and, if they're legal, reregistered as live guns, subject to tax. Properly done, these can be superb guns. Naturally, a new barrel is required, and it is important that the remanufacturer have a good command of metallurgy.

Many shooters like to display their guns at shows, and certainly pride of ownership plays an important part in machine-gun collecting. When barrels may be quickly or conveniently changed, it's often a good idea to either leave the barrel out of the gun—handy with some of the water-cooled jobs, where they look the same with or without a barrel—or secure a worn-out unit, have it plugged (preferably at both ends so the public can see it's plugged), and use that for gun-show display. This helps soothe the public and may discourage potential thieves. A gun in this state is called a "temporary DEWAT."

CHAPTER 3

Ammunition: Where the Explosion Begins

Ammunition is the primary cause of most malfunctions with firearms and is responsible for many accidents. The most common source of bad ammo, and the most dangerous, is the sloppy reloader or, worse still, the reloader who likes to "explore the upper limits of pressure tolerance." Don't even stand next to these guys at the range.

Beware of reloaders who don't use manuals, and be sure to use one or more of them if you reload. In this book and my magazine articles, I talk a lot about bullets, but almost never about exact powder charges. That's because I've never believed what works for me is necessarily right for you, and powder charges are, after all, what kills guns and, sometimes, shooters.

With machine guns, it is bullet design and overall cartridge-length parameters that you need to figure out based on your own gun. Few subguns, for example, will gobble up CCI's 200-grain, deep-dish hollow point (#3965) in .45 caliber, though a '21 Thompson gave me no problems with the load. It is rather short, slops around in the magazine, and can sometimes arrive at terrible angles, especially if a magazine spring is also weak. But the 9mm equivalent, the 115-grain #3614, gave no problems in any gun, and it too is shorter than hardball, flat-fronted, but more tapered along its length.

Rimmed cartridges are especially touchy about cartridge length, at least in box magazines. In a Bren, Remington's 180-grain Core-Lokt #R303B1 shot beautifully, but because of its length, the thick

rims intermingled improperly once in a while, causing simple but annoying jams when the next cartridge in line jumped the rim above. Belt-fed guns using rimmed ammo were no problem regardless of length, but reloads with burrs or dings on the rim would cause odd pickups, again easily cleared. Reloads with several 7.7/.311 Speer and Hornady bullets caused no aggravation of any kind, provided they were within about .007 inches of maximum hardball length. The same 150/174/180-grain bullet selection from Speer and Hornady worked well in the 7.7 Japanese guns. Surprisingly—having been told bullet shape would cause problems as we deviated from sharp points—we had no problems with the round-nosed bullets in either caliber. I use .303 British and 7.7 Japanese as examples here,

CCI Blazer hardball and 9mm hollow points never jammed, but the 200-grain deep dish did in a .45 M1 Thompson (although a nice M1921 shot the latter ammunition flawlessly).

19

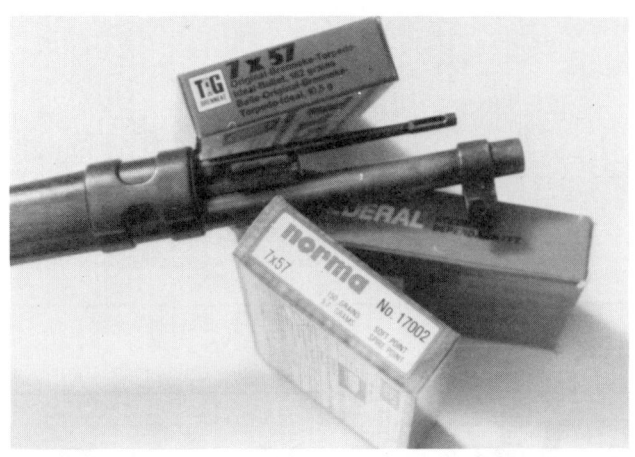

Once in a while, shooting the very best ammunition is fun, even with a machine gun. For reference, however, a wise man first tries it in a conventional firearm.

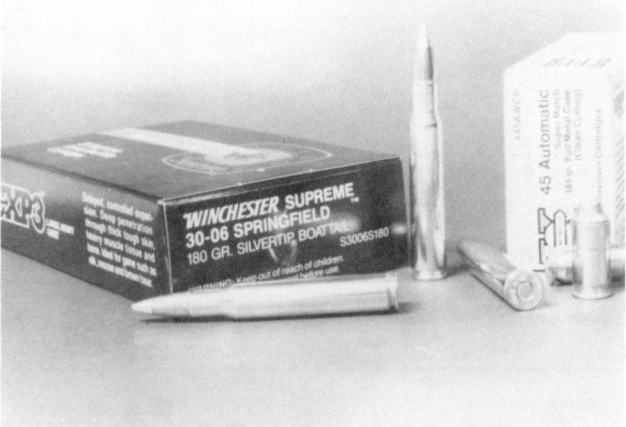

Winchester's "Supreme" 180-grain Silvertip is premium, accurate, and special in every way, and it is devastating downrange to boot. It also feeds fine in everything. The 185-grain jacketed wadcutter, however, would feed only in a commercial Reising M55 and M1921 Thompson.

Federal's budget American Eagle and Match 230-grain hardball are both superb loads. The Match round was dazzling from Mandall's Reising.

Norma's 165-grain power cavity load is below maximum length and flat nosed, but it shot devastatingly well in an MG42, MG34, and an ancient Maxim.

Franchi's 7.63 Mauser *is not* 100% compatible with the 7.62 Soviet round, and won't chamber in most Tokarevs. It works fine in PPs and PPsH guns, and is ideal for Broomhandle Mausers. At this writing, it is the *only* reloadable .30 Mauser in the U.S.

Chinese import ammo, like this 7.62x25mm, is excellent, but it is corrosive and not reloadable with standard deprimer equipment due to the Berdan primers and steel cases.

IMI-Samson's "UZI" ammunition—in .50 caliber, high- and low-velocity 9mm, and .45 "carbine" high velocity— was the only ammo fired in these specialized parameters.

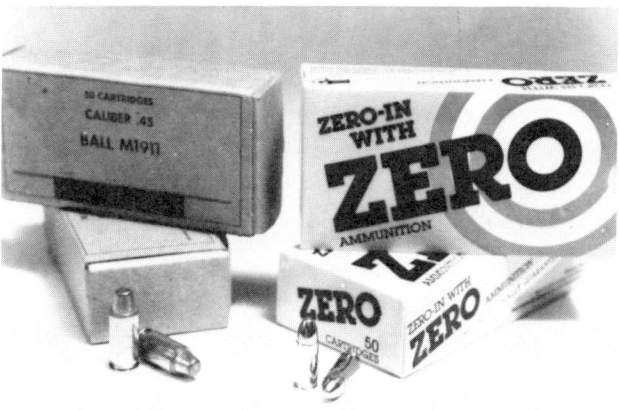

Zero ammunition.

primarily because they're such different cartridges, one a rimmed antique, the other a modern, Mauser-style round. Yet, they are ballistically related and considered "obscure" in many circles.

There are several varieties of ammunition.

Super Premium

Winchester's new Supreme line, Federal Premium, RWS/Geco, some of the target specialty items, and selected items from Remington, especially its elegant R308W7 in .308, a 168-grain Match item that I use interchangeably with Federal's nearly identical 308M. This is great ammunition, period. Every round downrange costs about $1.50—not what you want to use every outing, but a jolly good way to win bets and bragging rights, and to test your gun under absolute optimum conditions.

Commercial Vanilla

From K-Mart or the sporting goods store down the street, this is what comes right off the shelf for hunting. It is usually bought one box at a time, every two years, by fellows with deer tags or dusty pistols at home in a drawer. It's fine, and we're down to 50 to 75 cents per round in rifle calibers, maybe half that or so in pistol—we call 'em submachine-gun—calibers.

Commercial Custom and Reloads

I've tested more of this stuff than I care to remember, and I think some is loaded with charcoal,

dead flies, and match heads. Two bets: If you find one round—that's a single round—that won't chamber or looks weird, never buy the brand again. I recommend Black Hills in all but the H&G #68, but it's pointless in subguns of .45 caliber. I tested all the company's 9mm, .45, and .223 cartridges. Black Hills ammunition is often more accurate than items from the "commercial vanilla" grouping. NBC (National Bullet Company) markets a copperized load in both 9mm and .45 that's handy for subguns, cheaper than jacketed, not as dirty as lead, and shoots well. Zero ammunition was tested in two loadings, a 200-grain SWC (semi-wadcutter) that seemed hard-cast and was from the reload line, and the new 115-grain jacketed hardball. There were no feed difficulties with the semi-wadcutter, which I did not expect, and accuracy was superb with this .45 load, especially from the Reising, which I did expect. The 9mm loading performed well, though near the middle group of test loads in terms of accuracy. Of course, had I done a little more slow, contemplative shooting, the results might have been better.

Commercial Budget

Federal's American Eagle, Winchester's "USA" line, oddments from Remington, Geco 9mm when it's on special at K-Mart, IMI-Samson hardball, the new Yugoslavian imports when Boxer primed—all stuff produced for people who love to shoot but who like the major brands and don't trust reloads. Federal has the most extensive line here, with more on the way. The Yugoslavian stuff in 8mm was among the best fodder for the German guns; the cases were apparently strong enough to deal with SARAC, the

Yugoslavian MG42, and the only loading in that caliber in this price range. This is all good, clean, reloadable stuff, and your price per round drops considerably. Winchester needs to add .30-06 to its budget line. The .45 was excellent. These latter two categories are about due to disappear from the surplus world, and this is the logical place for them to re-emerge.

Reloads

Make sure they are your own or those of a very close friend. I like Winchester's Ball Powders. They clean up easily, were originally designed for automatic weapons, and reduce bore erosion. I also like match bullets in machine guns. Beyond that, I have used more obscure and popular and expensive Speer and Hornady bullets than I even knew existed. I supervised the reloading process—in which I did not physically participate—with a sharp eye toward safety and excellence. I note a couple of loads here using other than ball powders, and they're standard stuff. Other than that, load for a machine gun using the best advice you can get, and that comes from manuals.

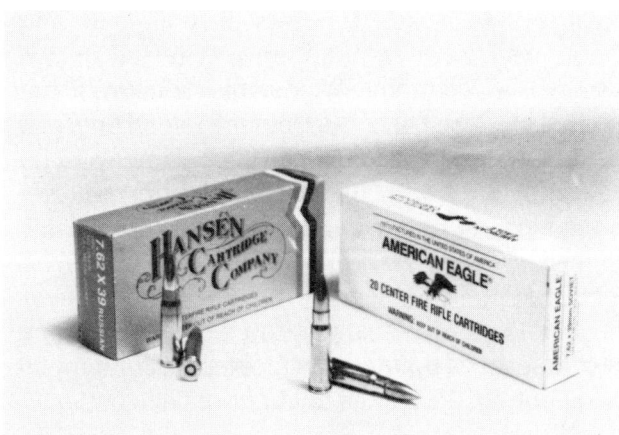

Finally, there are two reloadable, noncorrosive 7.62x 39mm (AK) loads on the U.S. market: Hansen from Yugoslavia and Federal's excellent American Eagle.

Surplus Ammo

For as little as 6 cents a round, you can raise hell and maybe survive. What you need here is a supplier whose information you can trust so that you needn't trust the ammo.

Some of the most pleasant surprises—and most unpleasant ones as well—that I encountered while writing this book revolve around surplus ammo. I have never fired (and probably never will) a good, mint specimen of the original French Hotchkiss in the original 8mm Lebel loading. I have heard good things about the guns and have fired other Hotchkiss types, as well as the derivative, improved Japanese guns, even a .30 M1917 heavy. But two lots of old French ammo that looked pretty good delivered endless flintlock-like hangfires and one squib, with a bullet down the bore. That ammo is now in the possession of the owner who allowed me access to his gun and the Champlin Museum displays. I had similar experiences with one lot of 7.5 French. Forming either case from other brass is a very iffy enterprise. I was advised by the supplier that the ammo was "decorator grade," so I was not especially upset. Still, it was an opportunity missed.

What you need from a surplus supplier is general information. Is the ammo corrosive? Is it Berdan primed? How *old* is it? Does it all shoot? I'll mention certain specific rounds, but the surplus suppliers I use now all give me accurate data, which is how I rate them. I use Sarco, Navy Arms, Paragon, and Century Arms. The surplus market is volatile, so none of the loads I describe here may be on hand by the time you read this. But information counts. And it's on that basis that I buy or don't buy.

Specialty Ammo

I like IMI's idea of special "carbine" ammo with extra oomph, and subsonic ammo for suppressed or silenced guns and for those who like bigger bullets in 9mm. This stuff shoots superbly, isn't expensive, and delivers as promised downrange.

I also like CCI's aluminum-cased, budget Blazer ammo. Keep in mind that aluminum is more porous than brass and dislikes dirty chambers, so use a chamber brush before popping any of these Berdan caps.

With a good barrel, good ammo, a rigid breech, and a steady hand, a machine gun will deliver great accuracy. I seriously recommend using premium ammo for at least a box or two once in a while.

Another recommendation: try to acquire some kind of rifle in the same chambering as your automatic weapon, especially if you shoot surplus ammo. It doesn't have to be anything special, just safe and cheaper than your machine gun. If it's a submachine gun that's the apple of your eye, then a semiautomatic pistol is your companion piece. The idea is to try test loads for safety and accuracy in the less-valuable gun before you take any gambles with the machine gun.

A final note to ammo companies that want to make money: Doing anything for automatic weapons buffs in particular is a mistake, and even we would admit there aren't enough of us to justify a major marketing decision. There are, however, tons of rifles and pistols in the country that are compatible with certain cartridges we'd like to see around. While we appreciate the efforts of Fiocchi, Norma, and others to keep us pampered, decadent American shooters supplied, we'd like someone on the same continent to manufacture the following loads:

1. 8mm Lebel (there are millions of rifles around right now).
2. 7.5 French (thousands around, more coming).
3. 8mm Mauser (a budget load with some real power, please).
4. 7.5 Swiss (can't *something* be loaded for less than one dollar per round?).

ADVICE FOR RELOADERS

Reloaders in particular may have difficulty coming to terms with machine guns. Many military guns use loose chambers, basically headspacing on the extractor or merely allowing room for grit at the sides of the chamber. This is not sloppy manufacture, it's intentional and was obviously done to keep combat guns working under very nasty conditions. It may, however, frustrate the reloader's attempt to reuse his brass a reasonable number of times since the expansion-resizing-expansion cycle will eventually cause brass failures. This is mainly a problem with the belt-fed and light guns of rifle caliber since submachine guns seldom deal with very high pressures. You may find you'll save money in the long run by fabricating a new barrel with a civilian-style chamber. This will also bestow the added benefit of keeping the original barrel unused and therefore undamaged and unworn, thereby retaining the gun's collector's-item value longer. A chamber casting and comparison with SAAMI (Sporting Arms and Ammunition Manufacturing Institute) or other civilian specification will give you an idea how your gun stacks up.

A tight chamber on a gun may demand a very high polish level to extract properly, and experimentation is sometimes necessary to figure out the exact specification for maximum case life and trouble-free functioning. Still, nothing to do with automatic weapons is easy. Should you encounter evidence of excessive brass strain, you'd be wise to work out the details based on your shooting and reloading habits. It may work out cheaper to just shoot surplus ammo and dump your spent brass.

The opposite problem may occur with certain beautifully made commercial guns, especially commercial Maxims, early BARs, and Japanese Type 92s, where the chamber is so precise that reloads fired in another gun and not resized to full length simply won't chamber at all. The two classic options are to locate and confine a brass supply for just that one gun or to resize to full length all loads for that gun. The "other gun"—the one with the more liberal chamber—might benefit from a new barrel, too, solving the problem at its source.

Most of the details regarding specific commercial loads and surplus ammo have been mentioned earlier, but here I will discuss some details of those bullets that worked especially well in given loadings.

.223/5.56mm

Anyone who tells you he's getting good long-range performance from this souped-down varmint cartridge is either doing something very unusual or has a very apocryphal view of what constitutes accuracy. But of the bullets I tried, the following worked out exceptionally well *by comparison:* Hornady's #2278 68-grain BTHP and #2267 55-grain FMJ (full-metal jacket). The former was more consistent with various guns and barrel lengths than most. Speer's #1047 was also a good performer.

6.5 mm

The .263 bullets served several calibers. Owing to most manufacturers' tendencies to steer clear of European military cartridges, almost all wound up living in Norma brass, though we located some Lapua 6.5 × 55mm Swedish. Most of the shooting was done with 6.5 × 50mm Japanese. Raw stock here was generally Norma, which is the basic brass for Federal's American Eagle. The same was equally true of the Italian and Swedish rounds. Not surprisingly, hollow-point boat-tails performed best, with

Only Federal's American Eagle 6.5 Japanese (on Norma brass) proved 100% reliable *and* was reasonably priced in that chambering.

Hornady's superb 140-grain #2633 delivering the best accuracy in fully automatic, semiautomatic, and comparison single shooting at all ranges. Deep downrange, Speer's Spitzer 140-grainer #1441 was almost as accurate and sells for less. Hornady's 160-grain #2640 round-nose was more accurate in heavier guns at great range, though our loads recoiled rather severely in the Type 96 in full auto. The smaller 100- and 120-grain Spitzers in both lines were accurate, and they might be superior where velocity is desirable. However, with the smaller bullets, powder loads in all calibers had to be carefully worked up to assure reliable automatic operation.

7mm

We had some dinged bullet noses in Hotchkiss guns using round-noses in 7 × 57mm. The serious rifle or machine-gun shooter will quickly discover that the Mauser loads, while not quite as accurate out to 400 yards or so as the 6.5s (yes, the Japanese, Italian, and Swedish cartridges are inherently extremely accurate), carry well at great range, shoot tightly, and hit hard. Plus, there is a wonderful selection of bullets, partly owing to the stateside popularity of the 7mm Magnum. The surplus loadings in this chambering are beginning to disappear, so for reliable functioning in machine guns, you need to use expensive factory ammo or reload. And having seventy-five or so bullets on the domestic market from 90 grains or so to 175 grains makes for a nice comfort margin. Military-issue loads ran 139 to 175 grains, and machine-gun loads were usually 150 grains or heavier. Hornady's #2840 BTHP and Speer's #1631 145-grain match bullets both per-

formed brilliantly, with the heavier 162-grain Hornady generally shooting the tiniest bit tighter. Should one have an actual security use for the cartridge, both manufacturers boast devastating soft points, and the boat-tails are generally more predictable. Pay careful attention to gross length/bullet seating in this caliber, where long bullets can cause jams if not seated to suitable depth.

7.7/.303

Here again, there isn't as much bullet choice as one would hope for, and in the magazine guns—mostly Brno-based—cartridge length is critical, especially in .303 Brens. Ideally, about a 185- to 190-grain boat-tail hollow point of issue length and pointed configuration would service these guns exactly. But no such American commercial bullet exists. Therefore, the British round, Speer's #2217 Spitzer, a 150-grain projectile, is ideal for the Bren's curved magazine. This makes less difference with the Japanese round or belt-fed guns, where Hornady's #3130 174-grain round-nose was an excellent and potent shooter.

.308/.30-Caliber

Bullet selection here is so good and data so sound that my notes are superfluous. Suffice it to say, the same 168- and 190-grain bullets that have performed splendidly in match rifles over the years do the same in machine guns, but there are literally no bad performers among the twelve Speer and eight Hornady designs we tested. The round-nosed, 130-grain or less units were handy with the carbine, and the spire-pointed plinkers were run through Kalashnikovs and even subguns with good results.

8mm

This is a bullet size that cries out for either a cheap hardball equivalent or half-jacket economy bullet, and/or some kind of seriously accurate hollow-point boat-tail of 190 to 210 grains. Hilton LaZarr loaded some stiff rounds using the #3238 Hornady 220-grain soft-point, and I ran some through an MG42 with explosive consequences to a rock-loaded box target. I quit shooting the loads because the expensive brass was being seriously dinged (common with German GPMGs) and then tested

Egyptian 8mm surplus experienced some major difficulties, including case separations, failures to ignite, pierced primers, and smashed rims, due to strange primer materials and hard brass.

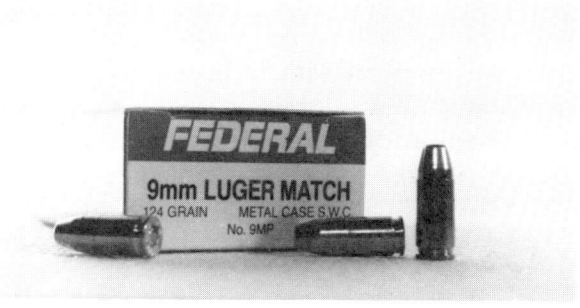

Federal's 9mm Match truncated cone and similarly loaded Hornady #3556 loads were exceptionally accurate and very reliable when using good magazines.

this load with other rifles, with superb accuracy results. American 8mm (7.92 × 57JS) is seriously underloaded and always utilizes a 170-grain bullet, rather light for the bore size. Speer's #2277 150-grain Spitzer is fairly close to military design and configuration, and it should be perfect for mechanical function. Pulled Egyptian bullets worked satisfactorily and were easily pulled since many were not properly crimped in to begin with. The Egyptian load is still too expensive to use in this manner, however; the ammo is satisfactory, at best, dangerous at worst, so pulling the bullets may be the only constructive use for the stuff. The Portuguese and Yugoslavian surplus and the German prewar military from Navy Arms were more consistent in all respects and generally cheaper. Sarco still has some Portuguese surplus as this book goes to press. Nosler markets a 200-grain Spitzer in its "partition" series that might provide good performance for actual security or combat use. Speer's SP #2285 Spitzer, was accurate and powerful. So was the 2283, the best in the 170-grain class, a semi-Spitzer.

9mm

After fifty years or so of pip-squeaky, underpowered, inaccurate, and generally third-rate ammunition, some decent 9mm × 19 "Luger" loaded ammo has hit the American market. This is the most popular pistol cartridge in the world and the only serious submachine-gun cartridge for which guns are still manufactured. Some good bullets and sound selections are also happening statewide. This cartridge performs best with loads close to maximum from

the manuals and bullets of 115 to 125 grains. The ability of a given gun to handle soft points or hollow points of a given design tends to be very individual, though the tapered- or hardball-profile expanding bullets tend to cause no difficulties except with very sloppy, rough guns. We tested every Hornady and Speer bullet in both lines and had no recurring difficulties with most guns. Most of the guns that we had difficulties with, typically the Hornady #3550, a 90-grain hollow point, also had intermittent difficulties with hardball. But the "Match" truncated cones and round-noses do perform much better in terms of accuracy. Running Speer's #4601 through the Hungarian 39M gives one the feeling one can hit anything, and the 9mm Mauser load delivers exceptional accuracy and punch.

.45

Again, you can follow standard pistol advice here, with the additional notation that .45 SMGs have more problems feeding hollow points, due to the sharper fronts, than 9mms in general. Don't be reluctant to try really huge bullets of correct .452 diameter in subguns. Speer's #4683 and Hornady's #4520, both designed for the old Long Colt, can deliver tremendous close-range punch *if* overall dimension/powder space specifications are watched closely and your gun will feed them. But the match-grade 200 to 230s are accuracy champs; in round-nose or SWC configuration, they feed fine. Weigh any pulled bullets in .45, especially if they're mated with brass of unfamiliar headstamp.

As noted, I used Winchester Ball Powder exclusively, save on a few loads noted elsewhere. Friends did the actual reloading, and I busied myself with research. A load that works well and functions a tight Maxim MG08 will blow an '88 Mauser to atoms. And certain actions are better worked with slightly reduced loads. With a bolt-action gun, a lot of reloaders like to work with the upper limits of recommendations. This is not suicide with a machine gun, but remember that improper bullet seating, for example, is more serious with violent machine-gun action than, say, with your bench-rest target rifle. Your parameters are specific to your gun and your own concept of safety. Machine guns are all valuable collector's items, even—though least of all—a Chauchat. A smart reloader will find a load adequate to cycle the action of his gun and to shoot accurately and then work very close to that level. The guns last longer that way, and the shooter is subjected to fewer shocking and painful surprises.

CHAPTER 4

Australia

The Australians found themselves alone and surrounded with the outbreak of war in 1939. By 1941, when the Japanese entered the war on the Axis side, the Australians began mass producing the Austen, a partial Sten copy using MP38/40 style internals, and the Owen. Though 20,000 Austens were built, it was the Owen, with its unusual top magazine, that was the more popular weapon by far. More than 40,000 were produced. The gun was first made because the chances of receiving reliable supplies from England were dicey at best and the United States had only the Thompson to offer in very limited quantities. But the work of Lt. E. Owen was so good that the weapon rapidly became the favorite of Australian personnel, even when other weapons were available.

All Owens were camouflaged in yellow-green and yellow-beige paint from 1943 until 1952, when all the weapons were called in for refurbishment and refit. While the top-mounted magazine was unusual and required offset sights, troops claimed it was less awkward than the side-mounted magazine of the Sten and didn't stick in the dirt when fired from the prone position, as most other magazines did.

The metal skeleton stock may be removed by pressing the spring-latched catch mounted within its forward spars. A simple barrel catch allows the rapid removal of the barrel and front foregrip for cleaning and replacement, though spare barrels were seldom available in the field.

The Owen served well into the 1960s, and a few pictures of the guns in the hands of Aussie troops

OWEN MK1

Name:
Owen

Model:
MK1

Caliber:
9mm

Overall Length:
32 inches

Barrel Length:
9.75 inches

Weight:
9.35 pounds

Type of Fire:
Selective fire

System of Operation:
Blowback

Cyclic Rate (approx.):
700 RPM

Feed System/Ammunition Delivery:
30-round box magazine

Country of Manufacture:
Australia

Manufacturer:
Lysaghts Newcastle Works

Countries of Use:
Australia

Period of Manufacture (approx.):
1941–1945

Period of Service (approx.):
1942–1960s

Primary Service:
Australian armed forces,
World War II–1960s

Primary Tactical Use:
Individual infantry

The Australian Owen MK1 was a super submachine gun.

as late as 1968 and 1969 affirm the Owen's long life and popularity. The Owen inspired the current F1, a cross between the Owen and the British Patchett/ Sterling SMG, still with a top-mounted, though slightly curved, magazine.

CHAPTER 5

Austria-Hungary/Austria

The Schwarzlose is a rarity among heavy/medium machine guns, firing a full rifle-caliber round from a blowback mechanism. This makes for a simple mechanism since only the bolt or breech-block need move, and not in a very complex manner. A huge spring, large mass, or both are required to time the backward movement so that the cartridge case is not compromised by remaining pressure when the breech opens. Schwarzlose used both, using the mainspring as both a shock absorber and firing-pin spring. Blowback also dictates a rather short barrel. An oil pump was employed to lubricate each cartridge case to ease its backward movement.

Andreas Schwarzlose perfected the Model 07/12 around 1902, and it was officially adopted in 1907. By 1912, he had redesigned the gun to eliminate the oiler.

In tests, the gun fired 35,000 rounds with minimal stoppages, all easily cleared, and no apparent loss of accuracy.

The Austrians got especially good results from this gun, primarily, many experts believe, because they allocated much more ammunition to training than other countries.

After World War I, the guns were awarded to various Allied countries as reparations, though Austria retained quite a few, as did Hungary. The Schwarzlose proliferated around the world. The Italians used it during World War II, and the Germans some-

SCHWARZLOSE MODEL 07/12

Name:
Schwarzlose

Model:
Model 07/12

Caliber:
8x50R Mannlicher

Overall Length:
42 inches

Barrel Length:
20.75 inches

Weight:
44 pounds

Weight, Mount:
44 pounds

Type of Fire:
Full auto

System of Operation:
Blowback

Cyclic Rate (approx.):
400 RPM

Feed System/Ammunition Delivery:
Fabric Belt

Country of Manufacture:
Austria

Manufacturer:
Osterreichische Waffenfabrik, Steyr

Countries of Use:
Austria, Hungary, Germany, Italy, Netherlands, Turkey, Denmark

Period of Manufacture (approx.):
1912–1918

Period of Service (approx.):
1912–1945

Primary Service:
Austrian medium machine gun

Primary Tactical Use:
Crew-served and aircraft

Schwarzlose Model 07/12.

Schwarzlose Model 07/12.

Twin Schwarzlose guns on an Austro-Hungarian Aviatik fighter. These guns usually had their jackets stripped for aircraft use.

Detail of the Schwarzlose guns.

Romanian troops deploy their Schwarzlose 07/12, awaiting whichever enemy arrives next. Romanian Schwarzlose guns were probably rechambered to 8x56mmR (M30), since most of them seem to have been marked "07/12 M.30."

Blast tubes through the Aviatik's radiator for its twin Schwarzlose guns.

how acquired quite a few even before the 1938 *Anschluss,* having perhaps acquired them from their former enemies or from Austrian Nazis. The Hungarians kept theirs all through World War II, converting most of their guns to the later, flatter-shooting 8x56R M31 Mannlicher cartridge, a simple rechambering job which, surprisingly, required no new parts or springs.

STEYR MPi 69

Name:
Steyr Machine Pistol

Model:
MPi 69

Caliber:
9x19mm Parabellum

Other Chamberings:
Some 7.65 Parabellum for European police

Overall Length:
Stock extended: 25 inches

Weight:
6 pounds

Type of Fire:
Selective fire by trigger pressure

System of Operation:
Blowback

Cyclic Rate (approx.):
550 RPM

Feed System/Ammunition Delivery:
25- and 32-round detachable staggered-row box magazine

Country of Manufacture:
Austria

Manufacturer:
Steyr-Daimler-Puch

Countries of Use:
Austria and small others worldwide

Period of Manufacture (approx.):
1969–present

Period of Service (approx.):
1970–present

Primary Service:
Ranking personnel, local defense, and vehicle crews

Primary Tactical Use:
Defensive and special operations

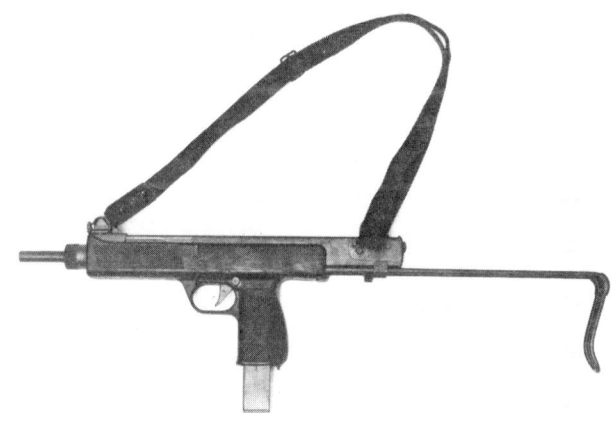

Steyr MPi 69.

This little weapon is a far better shooter than most of the guns that resemble it. Its ejection port, like that of the Uzi, is covered when not actually ejecting or returning from ejection. The magazine is in the grip (using the hand-can-find-hand princi-ple), as it is with the Uzi and some Czech guns. Field-stripping is especially handy. Unlike a lot of submachine guns that look like they'll handle well instinctively, this one really does. The finish uses unique polymers, with a "spackled" look on some surfaces of most export models. This gun is replacing the venerable MP38 and MP40 in Austrian service.

AUG ASSAULT RIFLE

Name:
Assault Rifle

Model:
AUG

Caliber:
.223/5.56mm U.S.

Overall Length:
31 inches

Barrel Length:
20 inches

Weight:
8.5 pounds

Type of Fire:
Selective fire

System of Operation:
Gas

Cyclic Rate (approx.):
675 RPM

Feed System/Ammunition Delivery:
30- or 40-shot transparent polymer

Country of Manufacture:
Austria

Period of Manufacture (approx.):
1977–present

Manufacturer:
Steyr-Daimler-Puch

Countries of Use:
Austria, small lots elsewhere

Period of Service (approx.):
1979–present

Primary Service:
Basic assault rifle, general purpose

Primary Tactical Use:
General-purpose infantry and specialists

A handy bullpup offered with a 1.5X scope in green, black, or camo, this gun also offers ejection flip-flop, as does the French FAMAS-Giat. The gun uses polymers where possible to minimize corrosion possibilities, and its metals are coated with similar concoctions where possible for the same reason.

This little popgun is really a souped-up submachine gun, but it will shoot quite accurately with 55- to 65-grain bullets out to 250 yards or so.

AUG assault rifles.

CHAPTER 6

Belgium

As with most Browning designs, Fabrique Nationale (FN) in Belgium was the sole worldwide marketing agent outside the United States. The initial Model 30 was similar to the American M1922 "cavalry model" BAR (Browning Automatic Rifle) with finned barrel and pistol grip, but the guns were manufactured to fulfill user-country needs. One version, for example, later manufactured in Sweden, used the 6.5x55mm cartridge and employed a curved magazine. Most Model 30 guns were manufactured in .30 caliber or the various Mauser loadings—7mm, 7.65x54, or 7.92. They are easily distinguished from American guns not only by the finned barrel and pistol grip, but by the dome-shaped gas regulator, different magazine, and ejection port cover. An M1932 was designed for and apparently sold to the Japanese in 7.7x58mm, which is interesting since that cartridge was not officially adopted by the Japanese for general issue until 1939. Some of the Japanese models were captured and examined in 1942 and 1943.

The Model D was actually introduced incrementally, and ready for full production when the Germans occupied Liège in 1940. American soldiers and Marines who recall using or seeing BARs with pistol grips and finned barrels are correct; from the time the FN plant was recaptured in 1944, guns in .30 were put into Allied hands as fast as they could

BELGIAN BAR D

Name:
Herstal Browning Automatic Rifle (BAR)

Model:
Model D 1948

Caliber:
7.92x57mm/.30 U.S.

Other Chamberings:
7.65x54mm, 7x57mm, 7.62x51mm (.308)

Overall Length:
47 inches

Barrel Length:
24 inches

Weight:
19.7 pounds

Type of Fire:
Variable-speed automatic

System of Operation:
Gas

Cyclic Rate (approx.):
250–550 RPM

Feed System/Ammunition Delivery:
20-round box magazine

Country of Manufacture:
Belgium, others under license

Manufacturer:
Fabrique Nationale

Countries of Use:
Belgium, Egypt, Latin America, Poland, many others

Period of Manufacture (approx.):
Model 30: 1928-1940
Model D: 1944-1960

Period of Service (approx.):
1944–present

Primary Service:
Military, commercial, and export sales in Belgium and abroad

The Germans used Schwarzlose guns as guard and mobile weapons throughout World War II, apparently in both 8x50mmR and 8x56mmR chamberings. This one is being set up on a captured British Bren Gun Carrier for patrol duties.

The BAR was used by Ethiopia's best troops against the Italians. Though they had no shoes, Ethiopian soldiers had excellent training, superb weapons, and first-rate fighting spirit. The weapon in the center of this photo is a late Model 30, incorporating most of the features of the Model D, including a quick-change barrel. The standard Ethiopian loading was the 7.92x57 JS cartridge.

be made (some were still in storage or use well into the 1960s). Many guns converted to 7.62x51mm NATO are still in active use all over the world.

One Model D BAR shown here bears no national markings at all, and was apparently never a military gun anywhere. It has two barrels and two sets of magazines, working equally handily with the German or American service cartridges. It is also uncannily accurate at its slow fire rate, controlled by a clockwork device quite unlike the buffer used in American rifles. Field-stripping has been streamlined, and trigger assembly removal is far easier than on the original design. The operating rod spring is located in the butt rather than in the pistol slide assembly.

These guns generally sell below American-made BAR variants and are far more serviceable. There are many sight and fore-end variations.

Some guns of a pattern combining features of the Model 30 and Model D were built in Poland and are often called "Radoms." The Germans used these guns (they, too, were in the standard German 7.92 loading) all over Europe, though mostly with second-line troops. The SS *Division Prinz Eugen* had an especially large allocation.

The Japanese employed a BAR marked "M1932," essentially an M30 in the Japanese 7.7mm caliber. Apparently, the original guns were made in Belgium. They were quite rare in the Pacific, but more common on the Asian mainland and in Indochina.

The Germans were inclined to use all they could capture, especially if equipped with 8mm barrels.

The original FN Browning was based on the U.S. M1922, though it gradually evolved into a very different gun. The guns are quite pleasant to shoot, and are especially handy for those wishing to use surplus ammo bargains, which appear in a variety of calibers at unpredictable times. (In .308/7.62x51, the FAL magazine may be used.)

Model D, like all BARs, do break firing pins on occasion (though they are easier to strip than American guns), so it's wise to keep a spare pin or two on hand. I have seen one Model D lettered in Arabic, but without the usual Egyptian crest (which employed semiautomatic, slow, rapid, and safe positions on the change lever). I was told the gun was Syrian. It may have been a small lot order or locally modified.

Like most BARs, the Model D and the Model 30 are quite gentle with brass.

FN FAL

Name:
FN

Model:
FAL

Caliber:
7.62mm NATO

Overall Length:
40 inches

Barrel Length:
21 inches

Weight:
Standard rifle: 9.06 pounds

Type of Fire:
Semiauto or full auto

System of Operation:
Gas

Cyclic Rate (approx.):
700 RPM

Feed System/Ammunition Delivery:
20-round box magazine (10- and 30-round units have been produced)

Country of Manufacture:
Belgium

Manufacturer:
Fabrique Nationale

Countries of Use:
Argentina, Australia, Austria, Belgium, Canada, Chile, Ecuador, India, Ireland, Israel, Libya, Netherlands, Pakistan, Paraguay, Peru, Portugal, South Africa, UK, Venezuela, West Germany

Period of Manufacture (approx.):
1950–present

Period of Service (approx.):
1952–present

Primary Service:
Since 1953, the FAL has been the most popular assault rifle in the Western Bloc

Primary Tactical Use:
Individual infantryman

The *Fusil Automatique Légèr* (FAL) evolved from the SAFN 49 as a 7.92x33mm *Kurz* assault rifle, but upon NATO/U.S. insistence, it was enlarged to accept the 7.62x51mm cartridge. Extensively tested against the U.S. M14, FAL won more often until tests were devised in which the M14 could successfully compete. In 1957, the United States rejected the T48, its version of the FAL, and adopted the M14, whose first-line service with U.S. units was over

within ten years. FAL went on to become one of the best—if not *the* best—full-caliber assault rifles in history. In fact, it is in first-line service in much of the world to this very day.

With the exception of Taiwan, no nation that has obtained funds through the U.S. Military Aid Program has ever bought the M14. FAL has been sold commercially in the same semiautomatic form in which most nations use it for their military establishments.

Gas-operated and designed from its inception for minimal maintenance, FAL has a tremendous reputation for field reliability. Automatic versions are fairly uncommon in the United States, especially in the standard rifle weight.

Among the interesting ancillary features of the FN FAL are the quickly changed top covers. These allow the rapid fitting of special scopes without the need for adapters other than the covers/mounts themselves and without disturbing the iron sights.

Heavy-barrel versions are used in much of the world as squad or fire-team support weapons.

A derivative rifle called "CAL" (*Carbine Automatique Légèr*) has been produced in 5.56mm. As with the G3, there are also folding stock (paratrooper) versions of FAL, and many small variations in fittings, fixtures, and accessories due to orders from many different countries. The entire system is designed to be easily accessorized by top cover changes.

The heavy-barrel variants approximate BAR performance in short bursts and can be match-tuned (a ramp polish job is especially recommended) to produce a stunning level of accuracy in semiauto fire or short bursts.

The gun has been manufactured in Brazil, England, Australia, Argentina, Israel, and elsewhere. Five hundred thirteen guns were made in the United States for testing as the T48. Springfield Armory markets a receiver made in South America with Israeli parts called the "SAR-48," some of which have been converted by Rock Island (Illinois—not the U.S. Armory) to fully automatic fire.

Unfortunately, some countries are now replacing the gun with the short-range .223 rifles.

The FAL is very clean to shoot, and will handle virtually any ammunition of 7.62x51 NATO or civilian .308 configuration without incident. A book the size of this one would be necessary to describe the ammunition I've put through this rifle family, as I have owned five FALs over the last year or so and have developed a certain kinship with the rifle.

I dislike the open sights that are commonly

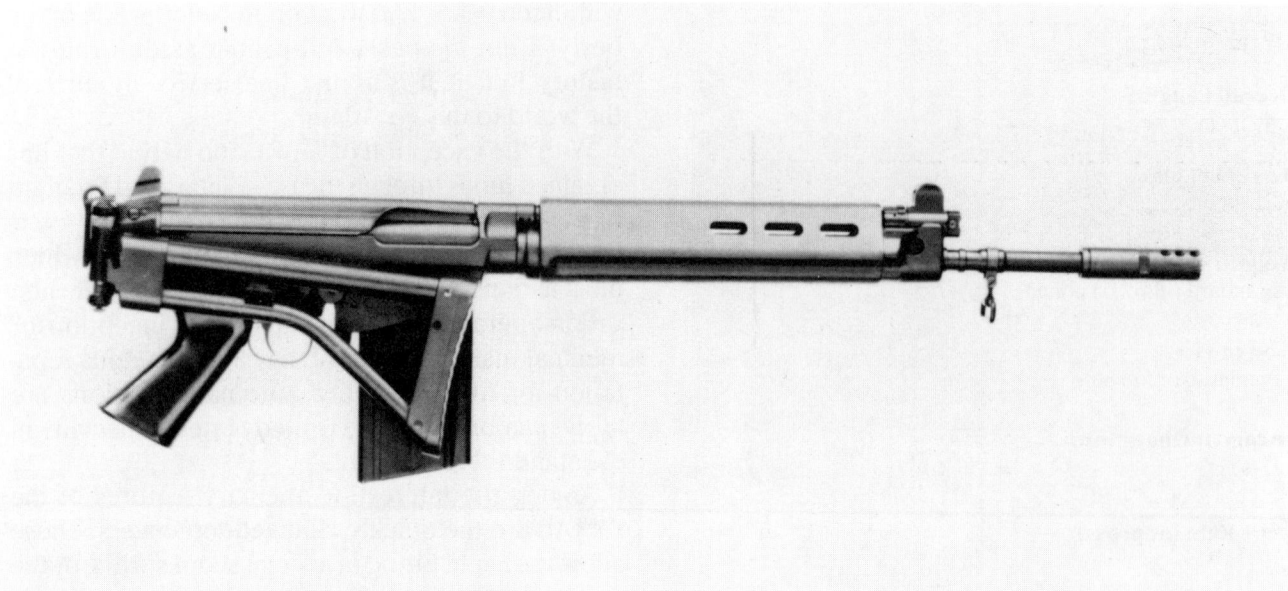

FN FAL with folded stock.

A British-style FAL Paratrooper.

FN FAL

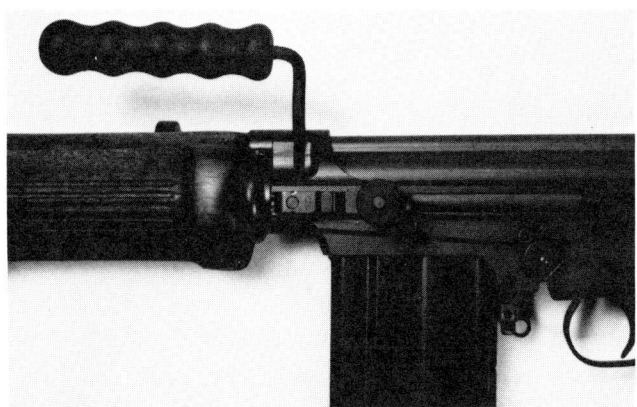

The carrying handle on an FAL HB.

Front sight and gas adjust on an FAL.

Semiauto FAL receiver.

An FAL HB with 6-18X scope.

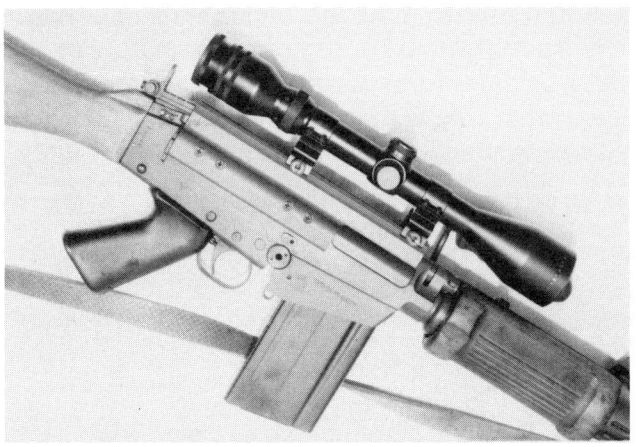

Simmon's Gold Line 3-10x44 "44 Magnum" scope proved handy on the heavy barreled FAL for subdued-light shooting, even without gimmicky gizmos in the viewfinder or gadgets that tend to break. The scope is waterproof, shockproof, and very bright. It stands up well to recoil.

supplied, and usually use scopes, though I have modified the open sights on one rifle with a tiny Redfield aperture and disc.

MAG GENERAL PURPOSE MACHINE GUN

Name:
FN general purpose machine gun

Model:
MAG (*Mitrailleuse d'Appui General*); also M240 (U.S.), L7A1 (UK), and others designators

Caliber:
6.5x55mm Swedish and 7.62x51mm NATO (any cartridge using standard Mauser base and up to .30/06 length may be ordered)

Overall Length:
49.5 inches with flash suppressor and buttstock

Barrel Length:
21.44-25 inches, depending on the version, flash hider type and so on

Gross Weight:
With butt, bipod: 24 pounds
Without butt, bipod: 22.3 pounds

Weight of Mount:
New aluminum mount: 22 pounds (FN supplies adapters for use with many older Browning and other mounts)

MAG GENERAL PURPOSE MACHINE GUN (continued)

Type of Fire:
Automatic only

System of Operation:
Browning gas

Cyclic Rate (approx.):
800–900 RPM (different gas settings and adapter kits can vary rate considerably)

Feed System/Ammunition Delivery:
U.S. MG34- and MG42-style belts of various lengths

Country of Manufacture:
Belgium and others

Manufacturer:
Fabrique Nationale and others

Countries of Use:
More than 20 worldwide

Period of Manufacture (approx.):
1955–present

Period of Service (approx.):
1956–present

Primary Service:
General purpose machine gun

Primary Tactical Use:
Infantry and vehicular use, tripod- or bipod-mounted, mobile, and static

This is probably the finest general-purpose machine gun in the world. The British and Israelis tested this gun against the MG42, M60, and various Soviet guns, as well as others, and this unit was clearly superior in all respects to all except the MG42, which was rejected by both countries due to its high rate of fire in its early form. The gas regulator alone can vary firing rate from 700 RPM to nearly 1100, and add-on kits for special purposes can increase the rate slightly.

Not surprisingly, the gun draws heavily on two of the finest guns of the past, the BAR and the MG42, which have played important roles in Belgian history. The receiver is basically a bottom-locked, beefed-up BAR, and the feed group uses MG42-style scissor arms. The trigger mechanism is much simpler than that of the BAR.

This gun is replacing M60 variants and the short-lived, unsuccessful, and very expensive M-73 tank gun in most U.S. vehicles.

The only gun that many countries consider the Mag's equal in sustained fire is, oddly enough, the earlier belt-fed Browning. In Great Britain, replacing Browning vehicular variants was not considered high priority, though the guns were converted to the 7.62x51mm NATO round.

Sights on these guns vary from none at all for vehicular mounts, where coupled optics are used, to scopes on hefty mounts and traditional tangent-style units, depending on the source of the order. There are also versions with longer and extremely heavy barrels for tanks.

A beefed-up, stable BAR with an extremely heavy barrel is, of course, a guarantee of accuracy, especially when made to FN's exacting standards. Such guns can deliver minute-of-angle accuracy when used with short or moderate bursts at the slow rate. Some spotting guns feature semiautomatic operation, which would be an interesting and probably legal match rifle with a few modifications. These guns are very gentle with brass, much like the BAR.

CAL Paratrooper.

SAR 48 guns.

CHAPTER 7

China

Only the Chinese still cling to the folding bayonet on standard rifles. It adds about twelve ounces to the AK, putting this variant's weight at almost ten pounds. Similar Soviet or Eastern European rifles of the "M" (stamped, welded receivers) are about two pounds lighter, similarly stocked.

This specimen was actually captured in Vietnam.

KALASHNIKOV TYPE 56

Name:
Kalashnikov Assault Rifle

Model:
Type 56 (Chinese)

Caliber:
7.62x39mm

Country of Manufacture:
China and allies

Chinese Kalashnikov Type 56.

CHAPTER 8

Czechoslovakia

In 1924, Václav Holek introduced the world's most significant rifle-caliber light machine gun, still sometimes called the Model 24 in Europe. In 1926, governments began adopting it. An improved but almost identical version was introduced in 1930. Since then, this weapon or its variants have been used officially by twenty-four countries, and many others have copied it unofficially.

The weapon contained no brand-new features, but its top-mounted magazine, slick gas operation, precise drum sight, comparatively handy size, and overall high quality, combined with a fairly easily changed barrel, made it a unique package. The British adopted a version of the gun which the

Czechs called ZGB V33. The British called it the "Bren," combining Brno, the arsenal city of its conception, with Enfield, where the production setups were completed.

The Chinese call this weapon and all those resembling it the "Type 41." This specimen was one of many thousands ordered by the Chinese from the late 1920s until the Kuomintang government evacuated the mainland in 1947 and 1948.

The gun was copied in many countries, especially Japan. A tripod mount was available in the gun's early days. These guns are still issued in Yugoslavia and Iran and are likely in reserve in the arsenals of many other countries. Spain still uses

ZB Vz-26

Name:
ZB

Model:
Vz-26 (Model 26)

Caliber:
7.92mmx57(JS)

Other Chamberings:
Virtually all rifle cartridges
1924–1950s

Overall Length:
45.8 inches

Barrel Length:
23.7 inches

Weight:
20.3 pounds

Type of Fire:
Full auto

System of Operation:
Gas

Cyclic Rate (approx.):
500 RPM

Feed System/Ammunition Delivery:
30-round box magazine,
some 40-round mags

Country of Manufacture:
Czechoslovakia

Manufacturer:
Zbrojovka Brno (ZB)

Countries of Use:
Czechoslovakia, Germany, and many
other European countries

Period of Manufacture (approx.):
1926–1950s

Period of Service (approx.):
1926–present

Primary Service:
Worldwide export sales

Primary Tactical Use:
Individual infantryman

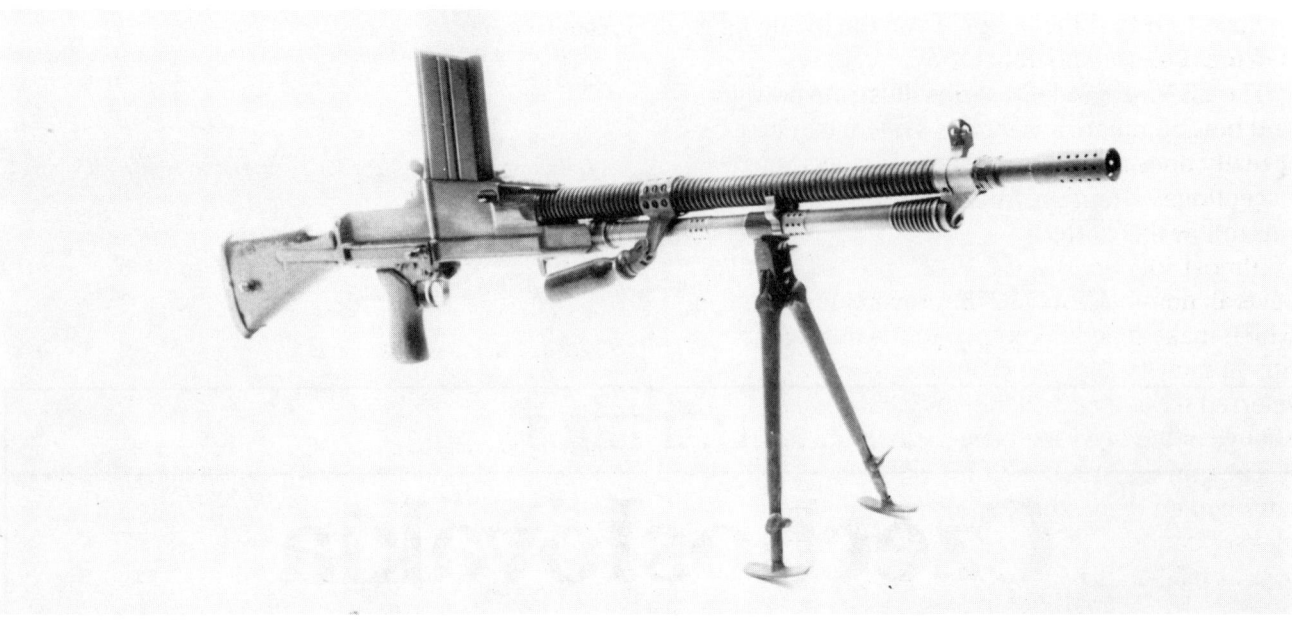

ZB Vz-26.

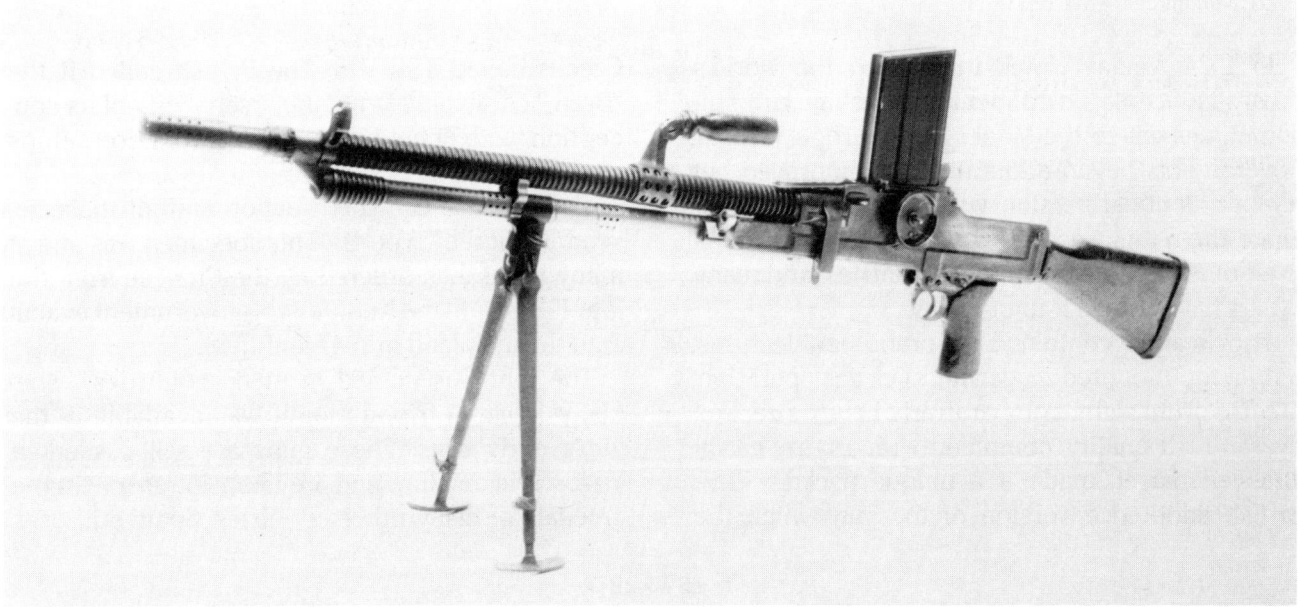

ZB Vz-26.

original guns, and also built the FAO, a direct copy. Most of these guns have been converted to 7.62x51mm CETME and/or NATO, and are still in service. Many of them have been converted to accept a belt and reel-filled drum.

This weapon and its various clones are "cornerstone" weapons, far better than the cheaper, more lightly built weapons that are replacing them. Even as late as the 1980s, Defense Intelligence Agency weapons manuals note that if such a gun and sup-

ply of ammunition can be secured, they are accurate and high-quality weapons.

Presuming a good barrel, the Vz-26 series is extremely accurate and very reliable. The weapons are not especially fussy about ammunition. In testing, I was able to load a magazine to its 30-round capacity with six different loads of varying lengths and power, chugging away with no incident whatever. Rate of fire and the sound seemed odd, for the low-powered and shorter U.S. commercial rounds seemed to retard the action. Even the brittle Egyptian brass caused no difficulties.

The ZB Vz-26 and -30 series illustrate how good and how complete a weapons system can be when it really does nothing at all new, save demonstrate exceptional attention to detail. Most Czech weapons follow this pattern.

Almost identical to the Vz-26, the Vz-30 utilizes several nominal internal improvements, none of which make much difference to the gun's functioning. In fact, by the late 1930s, the gun was usually referred to as the Vz-26/30, though the parts interchange of the two receivers is very limited.

The gun was produced for China in .30-06, and later copied there, shipped all over the world in the Mauser calibers, and listed in Merkuria/Brno catalogs as late as 1956.

ZB Vz-37

Name:
ZB medium/heavy machine gun

Model:
Vz-37 (Model 37) or ZB 53 (Called "Besa" in England and "MG37(t)" in Germany)

Caliber:
7.92x57JS

Other Chamberings:
All Mauser rifle cartridges, .30-06 U.S., others

Overall Length:
43.5 inches

Barrel Length:
26.7 inches

Gross Weight:
Original ZB: 55 pounds; some versions weigh as little as 41 pounds

Weight of Mount:
Long-spar tripod mount with AA adapter: 45.2 pounds

Type of Fire:
Dual-rate automatic (a very few were selective fire)

System of Operation:
Gas

Cyclic Rate (approx.):
Slow: 375–450 RPM
Fast: 650–750 + RPM

Feed System/Ammunition Delivery:
Metal-linked, with 100- or 225-round capability, or special canvas belts

Country of Manufacture:
Czechoslovakia

Manufacturer:
Zbrojovka Brno, various British arsenals (primarily England and BSA)

Countries of Use:
Germany, England, some Latin American countries, many others

Period of Manufacture (approx.):
1937–1950s

Period of Service (approx.):
1937–present (possibly still in use)

Primary Tactical Use:
Vehicles, normal medium and heavy machine gun fixed- and sustained-fire roles

This gun was sold in small quantities by the Czechs well into the 1950s, and though few countries used it as a standard infantry weapon, it tends to pop up all over the world. Photographed as recently as 1987 in Lebanon, the Vz-37 (ZB 53) probably has been converted to 7.62x51mm (NATO).

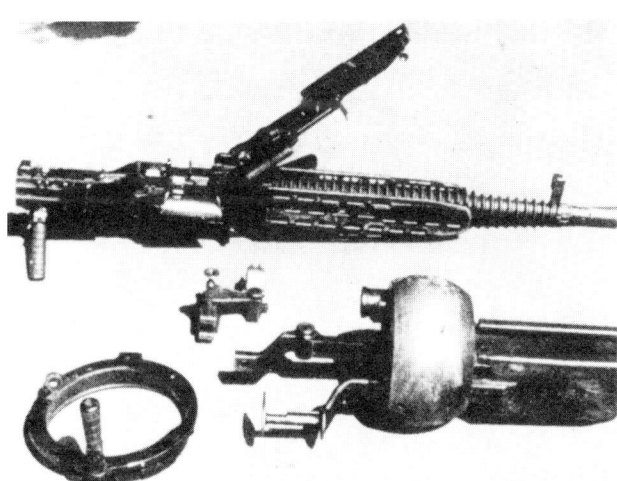

Both sides like the superb Czech medium machine gun, finding it especially handy in vehicles. This is the German setup for Czech Model 35 and 38 tanks, used on all fronts until 1944.

For sheer pride of bullet placement and reliability, there's no finer shooting experience in the machine gun world than the big Vz-37. There's nothing light about it, especially the enormous barrel, but the entire action is exceptionally stable. The Vz-37 will shoot like a precision match rifle, treat your brass tenderly, and just generally act in an entertaining manner. That said, it is a moose to move, and parts are getting hard to find. Fortunately, the ZB seldom requires a new part. No other air-cooled gun will hold accuracy in bursts as well as the Vz-37, and the massive 26.7- to 29-inch barrels, depending on the version, last quite a long time.

Primarily designed by Václav Holek, the gun combines some new features and a lot of conventional wisdom. Actual breech operation is by gas, but the barrel recoils fully with each cycle, firmly locked to the breechblock mechanism for a time for safety reasons and to smooth the action and spread stress. The cartridge to be fired is actually detonated shortly before the full forward end of the stroke, and serves to seal the breech. The gas system opens the breech after the firing cycle. Though this procedure sounds awkward, it greatly reduces wear on the gun and mount; it is correct to say the gun is "gas activated, recoil retarded."

Another odd feature of the Vz-37 is the use of the trigger-guard body as a cocking piece. Most versions place a cocking catch thumbpiece on the left side of the apparatus, the depressing of which allows the forward thrust of the trigger-guard body to cock the action, clicking the sear into engagement. The guard body is then pulled back and the trigger is in the firing position. You're ready to fire, presuming you loaded a belt. Even if you didn't do so, pulling a tab through from right to left readies the gun for firing (on most guns—a very few vehicular guns reversed the feed group entirely). Most versions employ a grip safety and a manual safety as well.

The British Besa (letters derived from combining Brno and BSA) is basically a Vz-37, though parts interchange is limited. The British gun retained the standard 8mm (7.92x57JS) chambering for use in tanks, but some versions of the gun are almost clones of the original; others, however, are quite different. The Germans called the gun the MG37(t) and used enough of them to print their own manuals and manufacture the entire gun as well as individual parts. Many of the German-owned, Czech built and designed PzKPfW 35 and 38(t) tanks used in campaigns until about 1943 utilized these guns

in a form very similar to the Besa. Few scholars—and even fewer hobby historians—realize that a good portion of German tank strength and armament came from Czechoslovakia, and that, generally, Czech medium weapons were highly prized by German troops. In point of fact, the Germans had no medium machine gun capable of anywhere near the sustained fire of the Vz-37 except, of course, with the Czech gun itself. It is partially for this reason, and also because of the high standard of training and lavish detail equipage of the Czech Army, that many historians speculate on the results of a 1938 war between Czechoslovakia and Germany, had the Munich agreement not prevented the conflict. One thing for sure: the Czech Army's equipment and tactics were far better and more modern than those of the Polish Army sixteen months later.

The Czechs continued to market the gun after World War II, offering to furnish it in a bewildering variety of cartridges, even including in their listings several rimmed types and virtually all the Mannlicher cartridges as well as the U.S. .30-06. Most likely, however, any guns delivered were in the usual Mauser cartridges. The Brno/Merkuria literature even suggests the system could be adapted to various belt systems, though, again, how far this actually went is subject to speculation.

I've only fired two weapons from this family, and accuracy was of a level I am reluctant to describe lest someone doubt my veracity. One of these weapons was mounted with an immense scope of about five power, similar to the Soviet DsHK units, running the image through several turns via a prism to keep the line of sight above muzzle blast. This was apparently a standard Meopta product. Using RWS ammo with TIG and TUG bullets—expensive at $30 or more per box of twenty, but sporting accuracy better than most anything else in the German service loading—a little fine adjustment led to groups in full-automatic fire that looked like 12-gauge shotgun slug impacts (twenty to thirty rounds in well under an inch).

These guns would be prohibitively expensive to produce today. They were never cheap, which is why they are uncommon today. However, since they're admittedly ugly and have none of the "show biz" following of many far less efficacious automatic weapons, even the high prices currently charged undervalue the gun. The ZB Vz-37 is the finest shooting air-cooled medium machine gun ever made.

Vz-61 SKORPION

Name:
Skorpion machine pistol

Model:
Vz-61 (Model 61)

Caliber:
7.65 short (.32 ACP)

Overall Length:
Stock extended: 20.55 inches
Stock folded: 10.62 inches

Barrel Length:
4.5 inches

Weight:
2.87 pounds

Type of Fire:
Selective fire

System of Operation:
Blowback

Cyclic Rate (approx.):
700–800 RPM

Feed System/Ammunition Delivery:
10- or 20-round staggered row box magazine

Country of Manufacture:
Czechoslovakia

Manufacturer:
Zbrojovka Brno

Countries of Use:
Czechoslovakia, others (in small numbers)

Period of Manufacture (approx.):
1961–present

Period of Service (approx.):
1961–present

Primary Service:
Vehicle crews, paratroopers for individual defense

Primary Tactical Use:
Individual, close-in defense and police work

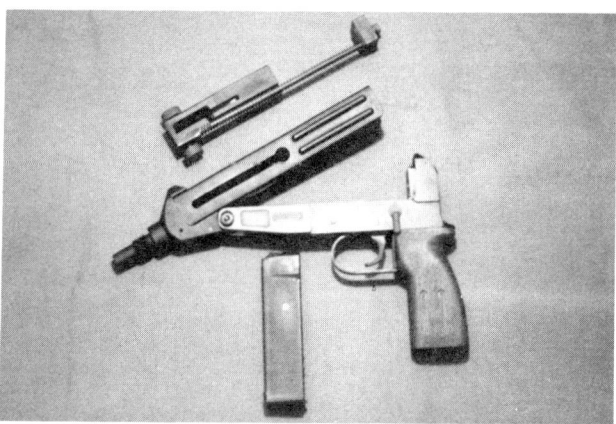

Armitate International of Seneca, South Carolina, is producing a 9mm semiautomatic version of the Skorpion. In full automatic, however, the little .32 ACP cartridge is very handy at close range.

Like the Mini-Uzi and the MAC-11, this true machine pistol proves that less is more. The Vz-61 is the first new design to be initiated in .32 ACP since the early 1930s. Though the cartridge is often inadequate when it comes to killing a human being with a single shot, especially at long range, these new guns in reduced size and reduced power loadings are designed to hit someone very close, and more than once. They're easy to handle in the compact confines of armored fighting vehicles and discourage people from trying to use primitive but effective antitank techniques like those the Russians often employed in World War II—pouring gasoline through the tank's vision ports, for example. No need for a match. If the crew is at all intelligent, they'll leave. This is how one acquires extra armor, for free! And the Czechs and Soviets are aware of how a tank's blind spots can be exploited. APCs (armored personnel carriers) are even more vulnerable, yet moving even a carbine around to dispose of someone on a roof can be incredibly awkward. Thus came the Skorpion.

A luminescent night sight and a silencer are issued for this weapon, handy both for clandestine operations and the normal tasks for which the gun was designed. The cartridge is ideal for both sets of tasks, and the silencer is not very large.

CHAPTER 9

Denmark

The basic breech mechanism of the Madsen consists of a rectangular steel frame that slides on the ribs in the main body of the gun. A breechblock rests inside this frame, pivoting at the rear so that it can only work in a vertical plane. This is similar in concept to the ancient Martini rifle except that there are three positions: locked, dropped, or raised. Vertical movement is controlled by a curved feed arm attached to the left hand side of the box.

This is a long recoil gun, in which the barrel and breech are locked together for the complete aft horizontal cycle. The tight breech tolerances are a prescription for heavy recoil, jams due to damaged brass, and lots of problems. However, the Madsen was so well made that most of these problems didn't come up regularly. The U.S. Army purchased sample lots for testing and found the gun to be basically satisfactory. Because it had some ammunition problems, however, the army rejected it, as well as all the other guns it tested.

Almost every country in the world used some of these guns, though no major power ever adopted it. Photos exist of German, Austrian, Italian, and British troops using it in World War I. The Japanese had some chambered for their 6.5mm round, though there is no information as to how large the

MADSEN M1902/04

Name:
Madsen

Model:
1902/04

Caliber:
7.92mmx57JS

Other Chamberings:
.30 U.S., .303 British, 7.65x54mm, 8mm Lebel, 7.5mm French, and others

Overall Length:
46 inches

Barrel Length:
19 inches

Weight:
22 pounds

Type of Fire:
Full auto

System of Operation:
Long recoil

Cyclic Rate (approx.):
400–450 RPM

Feed System/Ammunition Delivery:
25-, 30-, or 40-round box magazine

Country of Manufacture:
Denmark

Manufacturer:
Madsen or DISA (Dansk Industri Syndicat)

Countries of Use:
Many worldwide

Period of Manufacture (approx.):
1902–1950s

Period of Service (approx.):
1902–1960s

Primary Service:
Militaries of many countries worldwide since 1902

Primary Tactical Use:
Individual infantryman, aircraft, vehicle

Madsen M1902.

Madsen M1902.

lot was. Records cited in Chinn's *The Machine Gun* indicate models were ordered by thirty-one countries. Other countries merely bought off the shelf or arranged for adaptations to someone else's version. Madsen no longer produces firearms.

Given a supply of good magazines and quality ammunition, the Madsen was reliable and reasonably accurate, though it shared fairly brisk recoil characteristics with other long recoil guns. A few variants offered selective fire, and these were sometimes fitted with scopes. Save for the shape of the charging handle, it is difficult to discern from a distance even the approximate vintage of a Madsen since the 1904 model is not much different externally from the Madsens of the 1950s. There were water-cooled guns, and a few with heavier barrels, but these guns are now extremely rare.

MADSEN M50

Name:
Madsen

Model:
Model 1950 (M50)

Caliber:
9mm

Overall Length:
Stock extended: 31.25 inches
Stock retracted: 20.8 inches

Barrel Length:
7.8 inches

Weight:
6.95 pounds

Type of Fire:
Full auto or semiauto (selective)

System of Operation:
Blowback

Cyclic Rate (approx.):
550 RPM

Feed System/Ammunition Delivery:
32-round box magazine

Country of Manufacture:
Denmark

Manufacturer:
Madsen

Countries of Use:
Many South American and Asian nations

Period of Manufacture (approx.):
1950–early 1970s

Period of Service (approx.):
1950–present

Primary Service:
Smaller countries of South America and Asia

Primary Tactical Use:
Individual infantry

An inexpensive, mass-produced submachine gun that makes heavy use of stampings and castings, but is of uncompromised quality in its overall construction, the Madsen has had an excellent reputation since its introduction in 1946 and subsequent modification to this pattern in 1950. The receiver, which is really a "container," is made of two pieces that are hinged together at the rear, enabling the weapon to be easily opened for cleaning or repair.

Like many modern submachine guns, a grip safety is employed.

Madsen M50.

CHAPTER 10

Finland

The design of the M31 is virtually identical to that of the M26 Lahti, except for chambering, and the 1926 date is given here simply to establish the age of the original design, first used in 7.65mm Parabellum. Versions were made with and without the large barrel change lever ahead of the fore-end, and many M26 guns were converted to M31 standard.

This short section represents two countries of manufacture (Finland and Sweden) and two versions of the same weapon. The Suomi is listed under Finland despite the fact that Finnish Suomis are far less common stateside than Swedish guns, but it is difficult, of course, to file a gun whose name

means "Finland" under another country!

Suomi is not well known to modern submachine gun aficionados, though it should be, for it is the very best of the full-power subguns in terms of delivering accurate fire at rapid rates. Made of the finest materials in all its versions, it is beautifully made and evidence of the detail design reflects the eleven years Aimo Lahti worked on the weapon.

The Suomi is the very first SMG whose cocking handle didn't reciprocate with the bolt. It is the first submachine gun—and perhaps the only one—that's designed primarily for operation above the Arctic Circle, and the combination of tight and

SUOMI M31, M37-39

Name:
Suomi (translation: "Finland")

Model:
M31 Konepistooli (Finnish),
Kulspruta 37-39 and 37-39F

Caliber:
9x19mm Parabellum

Other Chamberings:
7.63mm Mauser and 7.65mm Parabellum

Overall Length:
M31: 34.25 inches
M37-39: 31.1 inches

Barrel Length:
M31: 12.2 inches
M37-39: 8.16 inches

Weight:
M31: 10.6 pounds
M37-39: 9.9 + pounds

Type of Fire:
Selective fire by trigger pressure

System of Operation:
Blowback

Cyclic Rate (approx.):
775–920 RPM

Feed System/Ammunition Delivery:
70- to 71-round drum; 25-round
two-row or 50-round quadruple-row
box magazines

Countries of Manufacture:
Finland, Sweden

Manufacturer:
Madsen (Denmark), Husqvarna (Sweden),
Hispano-Suiza (Sweden)

Countries of Use:
All Scandinavian countries, Switzerland,
Spain, and many others in small
numbers

Period of Manufacture (approx.):
1930–1945

Period of Service (approx.):
1926–well into the 1960s and probably
up to the present

Primary Tactical Use:
Individual infantry

loose tolerance, huge but unobtrusive controls, and exceptional finish on mating surfaces of moving parts reflects that mission. Though never manufactured in the numbers of many other small arms, the Suomi had an extremely profound impact on submachine-gun design worldwide and was the impetus behind the Soviet push to submachine guns in the thirties and forties. At one point, the British had decided to adopt a version of the gun, though they ultimately decided in favor of the Lanchester and then the Sten.

The primary difference between the Swedish version shown and the standard Finnish gun is in barrel length, though the Swedes also manufactured the gun as 37-39F with the original length tube. The Swedes also tweaked the buttstock upward, converting the gun to a straight-line configuration, thus reducing its vertical bulk and further damping recoil effect. The Suomi in all its forms, however, is an accurate, easy-to-handle, sturdy, and exceptionally reliable weapon.

Its length, bulk, and strength make it one of the few submachine guns that is usable for buttstrokes in hand-to-hand combat, and many Finnish guns show evidence of having been used for exactly that purpose. On the northern front, around Lake Ladoga in the Leningrad area, the Germans preferred the Suomi over the MP40 and other German guns, largely owing to its excellent cold-weather performance. Needless to say, the Soviets felt the

A typical Finnish soldier of the Continuation War period—during which Finland fought on the Nazi side—armed with a Suomi M31.

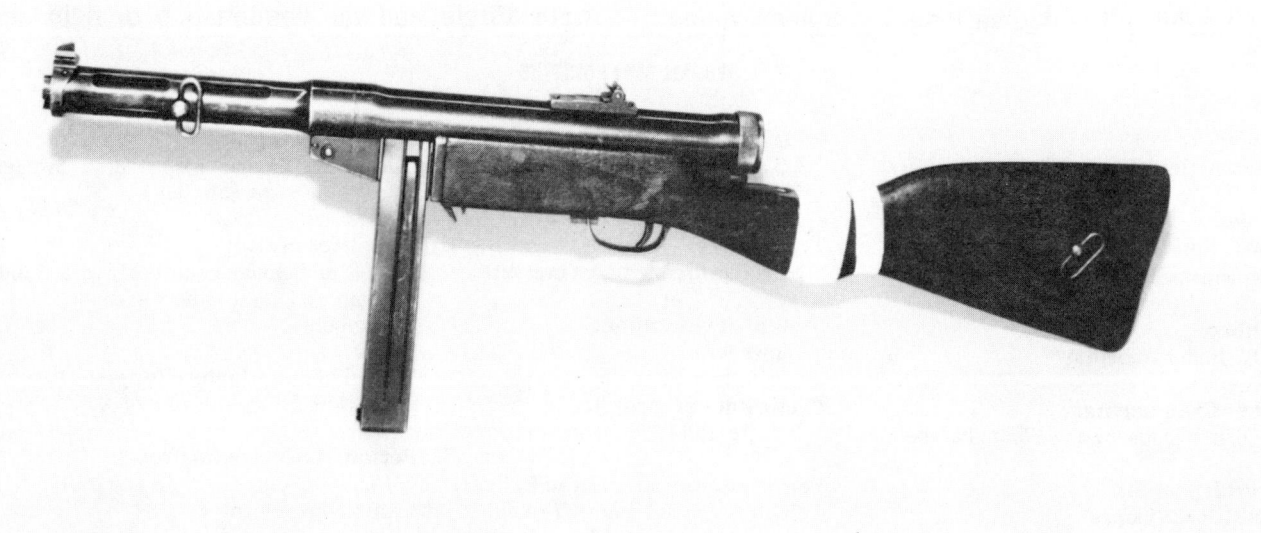

Suomi M37-39.

Firing a Suomi M37-39.

same way about the Suomi, but seldom seized many. They did produce a Russian-language manual on the gun, and some pictures of ski troops seem to show the guns, or what appears to be a much larger version of the PPD 40 or PPsH. It is more than likely, however, that the guns are Suomis. The poor quality of pictures complicates much historical research, especially when at least 40 percent of the firearms-related photos I found while preparing this book were incorrectly captioned by the "experts" of the period.

These weapons will tolerate more ammunition length and bullet design variation than any other 9mm submachine gun. My current list of loads and bullets includes almost everything in the Hornady and Speer line, including some very exotic hollow points and WC/SWC configuration cast bullets, and the Suomi seems to gobble up everything with alacrity. I have yet to experience a jam with a Suomi and have gotten into the habit of running Federal's new Match truncated-cone round through the Suomis and making artsy designs at about thirty-five feet. The three-shot finger-spread triangle design quickly got boring. One hundred-yard shooting is especially easy with the Finnish originals. Only the Reising is as much fun for trick shooting, and it doesn't shoot as fast. I have tried the most radical bullet designs—flat-front wadcutters—only with a newish 25-round stick magazine, but they should work well from the drum. I would be reluctant to get fancy with the 50-round box, not because of any

problems I've encountered with it, but because if the ammo bounced around inside sufficiently, the magazine might have to be disassembled.

The Suomi greatly influenced the design of the Swedish K/45 Carl Gustav, though the tube of the newer gun contains what is essentially a Sten mechanism. Indeed, the first "K" guns were set up to use the Suomi 50-round box magazine. In the mid-fifties, most of the Suomis still in service (nearly all those not sold off as surplus) were modified to accept the later K/45 36-round magazine.

Hefty by modern standards, the durable Suomi in all its forms is a joy to shoot. Unlike some subguns, it functions fine with fairly weak ammo and even better and faster with brisk high-velocity or heavy bulleted loads like IMI's specialized rounds.

KALASHNIKOV RPK

Name:
Kalashnikov light machine gun

Model:
RPK

Overall Length:
40.9 inches

Barrel Length:
23.2 inches

Weight:
With empty 40-round box: 11 pounds
With empty drum: 12.3 pounds

Type of Fire:
Selective fire

System of Operation:
Kalashnikov direct gas

Cyclic Rate (approx.):
550–650 RPM

Feed System/Ammunition Delivery:
40- and 50-round curved box magazine

Country of Manufacture:
Finland (Soviet design)

Manufacturer:
Valmet

Countries of Use:
Communist Bloc nations, Finland, many neutrals

Period of Manufacture (approx.):
1960s–early 1980s

Period of Service (approx.):
Mid-1960s–present

KALASHNIKOV RPK (continued)

Primary Service:
Small-unit support automatic weapon

Primary Tactical Use:
Squad automatic weapon

Kalashnikov RPK.

This photo depicts the Finnish Valmet version of the RPK, the Kalashnikov light machine gun that replaced the RPD in most Warsaw Pact countries. Featuring a chrome-lined barrel and the sturdy, often-copied Kalashnikov action, the gun is quite stable but short on range.

As always with this cartridge, the mid-range accuracy with 120- to 130-grain bullets was amazing. Yugoslavian, Chinese, and Federal American Eagle ammo all produced superb results out to 250 yards or so.

The gun has been made in other Eastern bloc countries, and a similar, upsized weapon in .308/7.62x51mm, known as the Zastava M65/AK, is sold on the U.S. market in semiautomatic form that's made in Yugoslavia. Mitchell Arms imports these guns.

Israel makes a similar gun, the Galil, but in .223/5.56mm.

The Finnish guns show a finer finish and more attention to detail than the Kalashnikovs, but shoot about the same as the Russian weapons.

The gas system remains unmodified, and many standard AK parts—including magazines, in a pinch—may be used easily.

CHAPTER 11

France

The Hotchkiss heavy guns were sold worldwide in a variety of calibers. Even the U.S. Army used Hotchkiss guns in World War I, purchasing 5,255, mostly in .30-06, to outfit at least twelve divisions. These guns, externally almost identical to the gun shown here, were usually referred to as M1917s. The Hotchkiss was one of the most reliable early-generation air-cooled machine guns, proving capable of relatively astonishing feats of sustained fire.

Adapted by Benet and Mercie from an original design by an officer of the Austrian Army, Captain Baron von Odkolek, the Hotchkiss firm purchased all patents and rights for a single price, paying no

HOTCHKISS M1914

Name:
Hotchkiss heavy machine gun

Model:
1914

Caliber:
8mm Lebel, rimmed

Other Chamberings:
6.5mm Japanese, .30-06, .303 British; there is some evidence that the gun was produced in 7.62x54R for the USSR

Overall Length:
51.6 inches

Barrel Length:
31 inches

Weight:
55.7 pounds

Weight, Tripod:
60 pounds

Type of Fire:
Full auto

System of Operation:
Gas

Cyclic Rate (approx.):
600 RPM

Feed System/Ammunition Delivery:
24- or 30-round metallic strips or 250-round "belts" of strips

Country of Manufacture:
France

Manufacturer:
Hotchkiss at CIE

Countries of Use:
Bolivia, Brazil, France, Japan, Mexico, Spain, U.S., U.S.S.R.

Period of Manufacture (approx.):
1913–1930s (production was very slow after World War I)

Period of Service (approx.):
1914–1950s (similar, earlier Hotchkiss guns were in service before 1914)

Primary Service:
World War I through World War II in French and various foreign armies

Primary Tactical Use:
Crew-served heavy machine gun

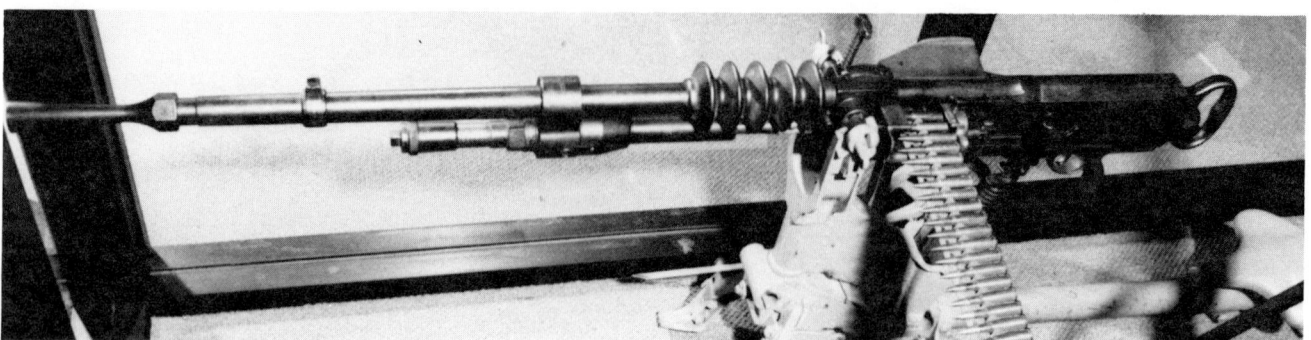

Hotchkiss M1914.

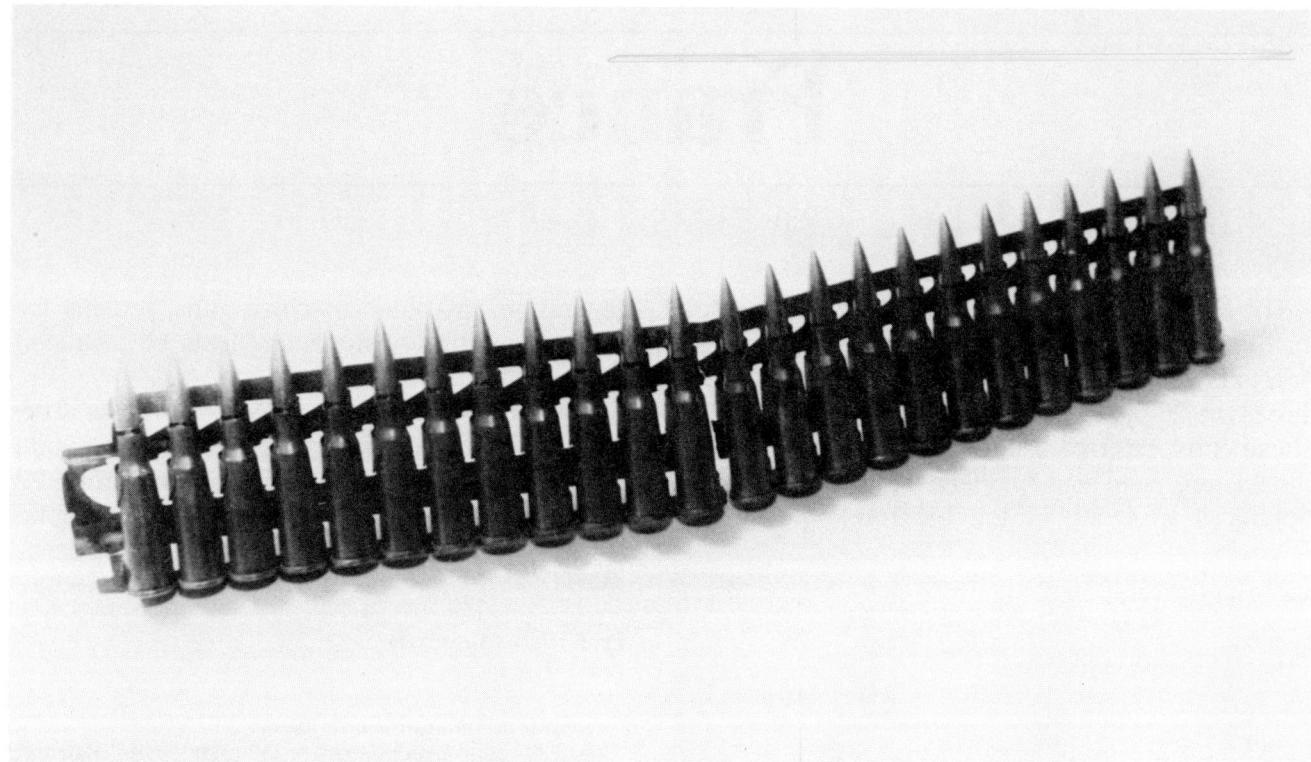

An 8mm Lebel feed strip for the Hotchkiss M1914.

royalties on the subsequent enormous production.

Many early machine-gun designs sought to avoid the fabric belts of the period for reasons that seemed sound at the time. It seemed belts would fray and snag, and gun mechanisms might have difficulty pulling the longer units up into the feedway. All these factors did occur to some small extent, but the metal feed strips were by no means foolproof.

Perfected by about 1900, the Hotchkiss was preferred to water-cooled guns in France's North African and tropical colonies. The gun was tested in 1900 by the Ordnance Board, and after just over four minutes of continuous firing, the entire barrel was glowing red-hot from the doughnut-shaped

cooling rings to the muzzle. Given five minutes to cool, firing resumed until nearly 5,000 rounds had been shot. One of the board's members was John T. Thompson, and he and many others were persuaded by these elaborate tests—which *did not* lead to procurement—that there was indeed a future for the air-cooled machine gun.

The Japanese based all their medium and heavy guns on the Hotchkiss and actually improved the original design considerably.

The Hotchkiss served well after World War II, until the AAT 52 gun was available in quantity. While the Browning was the more common transitional gun, the Hotchkiss was in use well into the era when

France attempted to subdue the Vietminh in what France regarded as colonial Indochina (Vietnam).

A Hotchkiss can be fun to shoot, and it is almost as accurate as a belt-fed Browning. One problem, though, is flintlocking—hangfires that make any and all shooting miserable, dangerous, and disappointing. Flintlocking is caused by using bad old French surplus ammo. The 8mm Lebel load is one that someone (perhaps in the United States or Sweden) should load in quantity and thereby make some money. That load is not just for Hotchkiss guns (which are quite rare) since there are hundreds of thousands of Lebel and Mannlicher-Berthier rifles in the United States that could use this cartridge.

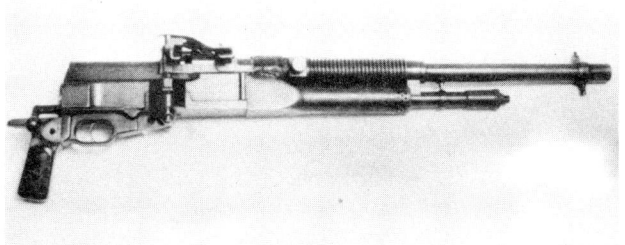

The heavy barrel of the Hotchkiss Light series made it usable as a vehicular and flexible aircraft gun. It was marketed worldwide in many calibers. This is a M1924 in 7mm.

A Hotchkiss MK1 aircraft machine gun (left) compared to a U.S. Lewis gun.

HOTCHKISS MK1

Name:
Hotchkiss aircraft machine gun

Model:
MK1

Caliber:
.303 British

Type of Fire:
Select, full or semiauto

System of Operation:
Gas

Cyclic Rate (approx.):
550 RPM

Feed System/Ammunition Delivery:
Tempered metal strip holding 9, 14, or 30 cartridges

Country of Manufacture:
England

Manufacturer:
Enfield, England

Countries of Use:
England, France, Japan, and many South American and other countries

Primary Service:
Military aircraft machine gun

Primary Tactical Use:
Aircraft, either cowl-mounted or free

The Hotchkiss gun was difficult to synchronize to cowl mounts, though such synchronization was done early on; Garros contrived his deflector device for the Hotchkiss. French ammunition tended to experience primer hangfires, however, resulting in severe timing problems and an occasional lost propeller blade no matter how precise the actual synchronization device. The MK1 was used in moderate numbers as a free or flexible gun, but mostly even French aircraft were standardized on British-style armament and ammunition.

At one time or another, this machine gun was sold in just about every rifle cartridge of the period. Essentially, it is a standard light Hotchkiss with no buttstock. Similar guns were used in vehicles well into the fifties and sixties, primarily in South America. The gun was also license-built in Great Britain, chambered for the .303 British cartridge, but it seems to have seen French service at some time in its life.

This is a credible gun, but not a spectacular one.

Being inherently muzzle-heavy helped keep muzzle shake to a minimum but made the gun clumsy to carry when dismounted. As a flexible gun in air-craft, the combination was a rather excellent one.

HOTCHKISS MODEL 1914

Name:
Hotchkiss light machine gun

Model:
1914

Caliber:
7x57mm

Overall Length:
46.75 inches

Barrel Length:
23.5 inches

Weight:
26.8 pounds

Type of Fire:
Full auto

System of Operation:
Gas

Cyclic Rate (approx.):
600 RPM

Feed System/Ammunition Delivery:
Metallic strip

Country of Manufacture:
France

Manufacturer:
Hotchkiss and CIE

Countries of Use:
Brazil, France, Greece, Mexico, Spain, U.S.

Period of Manufacture (approx.):
1912–1930s

Period of Service (approx.):
1912–late 1940s

Primary Service:
World War I

Primary Tactical Use:
Infantry

Laurence V. Benet, an American, took over the management of the French Hotchkiss firm in 1887, when B.B. Hotchkiss, also of American birth, died at the helm. Working with his assistant, designer Henry Mercie, a design series of automatic weapons was created that served many countries in

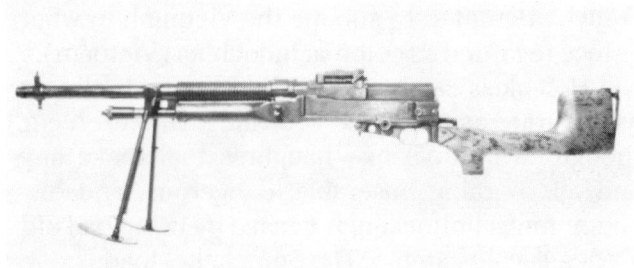

Hotchkiss M1914 light machine gun.

both world wars. In United States, in fact, this gun is known as the Benet-Mercie.

The cammed fitting/barrel extension into which the bolt turns for locking is the *fermeture nut.* The cocking handle is at the rear of the receiver and has to be pulled back about six inches and forced for-ward to activate the weapon. Once forward, it has to be turned to the select mode of fire or safe. The gun fed from feed strips, usually of twenty-four rounds in the early models.

The 7x57mm gun was sold worldwide, especially to cavalry establishments, which appreciated the fact that the gun could be carried in a saddle scab-bard. It was ordered and used by the Brazilian Army.

Like all the Hotchkiss light guns, this weapon is nose-heavy but handles rather well once it is actu-ally being fired.

CHAUCHAT MODEL 1915

Name:
Chauchat C.S.R.G.

Model:
1915

Caliber:
8mm Lebel rimmed

Overall Length:
45 inches

Barrel Length:
18.5 inches

Weight:
19 pounds

Type of Fire:
Full auto

System of Operation:
Long recoil

Cyclic Rate (approx.):
250 RPM

Feed System/Ammunition Delivery:
20-round open-sided, curved box magazine

Country of Manufacture:
France

Manufacturer:
Bayonne Ordnance Plant

Countries of Use:
Belgium, Greece, and U.S.

Period of Manufacture (approx.):
1914–1921

Period of Service (approx.):
1915–1920s (some saw service in France in World War II)

Primary Service:
World War I service with Belgian, French, Greek, and U.S. forces

Primary Tactical Use:
Individual infantryman

The Chauchat was the primary light machine gun of the U.S. Army during World War I. General Crozier had a vendetta against Isaac N. Lewis and/or his gun, was swayed against Hotchkiss variants by a single incident in New Mexico, and proceeded to inflict this abomination on American troops. The navy ignored him, and though he tried to compel the marines to use the "Sho-Sho," they found ways around those orders. Air personnel wanted nothing to do with the Chauchat, but nine American divisions wound up armed with these guns before sailing to Europe. From January to April 1918, some 37,864 such guns, either in 8mm French Lebel or the even worse .30-06 U.S. M1918 edition, were delivered to our troops.

The best that can be said for the Chauchat is that it was available in great numbers and may have taught our troops much about automatic weapons tactics. One of the main things they needed to know was to have plenty of them available since the odds were that a good percentage would not function. The French, Belgians, and Greeks used the Chauchat for a longer period of time, and it's likely they had even more trouble with the gun. Prevalent malfunctions were parts breakage, feed jams, cartridges stuck in the chamber, and, occasionally, a gross failure of the receiver tube, a simple piece of cheap commercial tubing with only nominal reinforcement. Early guns made in tightly controlled military arsenals seem to have performed better, but by 1916, the gun was subcontracted to firms that seem to have been concerned only with getting the guns out the door as cheaply as possible. Refinement in the mechanism and engineering are nonexistent, and true parts interchange is absent.

The gun uses the long-recoil principle in its most primitive form, wherein basically the entire mechanism reciprocates fully with every shot, a guarantee of heavy recoil even at the comparatively slow rate of 250 to 300 rounds per minute. The impact and inertia of everything moving to the rear

Chauchat Model 1915.

French troops tenuously cling to a shell hole in no-man's-land, hoping to discourage German counterattacks with their Chauchats.

guarantees a heavy kick and aim disruption. Therefore, the Chauchat was also very inaccurate.

I've fired only one Chauchat in my life, and I have no interest in repeating that effort. A friend dug up a mint, registered specimen, complete with a splendid coat of dark-green paint, standard French finish. Back then, Remington still produced the 8mm French cartridge, and we had procured a couple of boxes. No one was much impressed with the gun, though it functioned satisfactorily for about thirty rounds. Bored, we went on to other things, discovering only upon cleaning that it had broken its receiver reinforcement after only those few shots. In the interest of safety, its owner had the part welded and the green paint touched up. He had the gun deactivated, despite having paid the $200 transfer tax, and changed the registration.

Whether a well-built Chauchat would have worked is really irrelevant. The gun's French title, *C.S.R.G.,* denotes *Fusil Mitaileur Chauchat Sutter-Ribeyrolle-Gladiator.* The only aspect of the gladiator legend of which this piece reminds most researchers is the mournful salute: "Those who are about to die . . ."

The Chauchat was based loosely on an old Frommer design, but it was compromised by the haste with which it was converted to mass production and the inherently weak concepts employed in order to do so. This is one of the few guns whose deactivation doesn't seem to trouble most enthusiasts at all. In fact, these guns probably should be welded on principle alone.

FRENCH LEWIS MODEL 1914

Name:
Lewis aircraft machine gun (French)

Model:
1914

Manufacturer:
St. Etienne

Except for the manufacturer's name on the side, this extremely rare French Lewis .303 aircraft gun could easily be mistaken for virtually any other aircraft model Lewis gun. As Chinn reveals, however, the French not only built the gun, but they did much research for the guns and their mounts. The French decided on British cartridges as the standard for their air force, though they also produced a ground version of the Lewis gun in 8mm Lebel, known as the Model 1922, after the war. French Lewis guns are so rare, however, that many authorities either do not mention them or presume there never was such a weapon.

This particular gun was owned by Charles Nungesser, France's third leading ace, who scored forty-five victories. He brought this gun to the United States after World War I, along with his Hanriot fighter, and participated in a barnstorming flight demonstration tour across the country. He was killed attempting one of the first transAtlantic flights.

Part of an extensive collection, the gun and air-

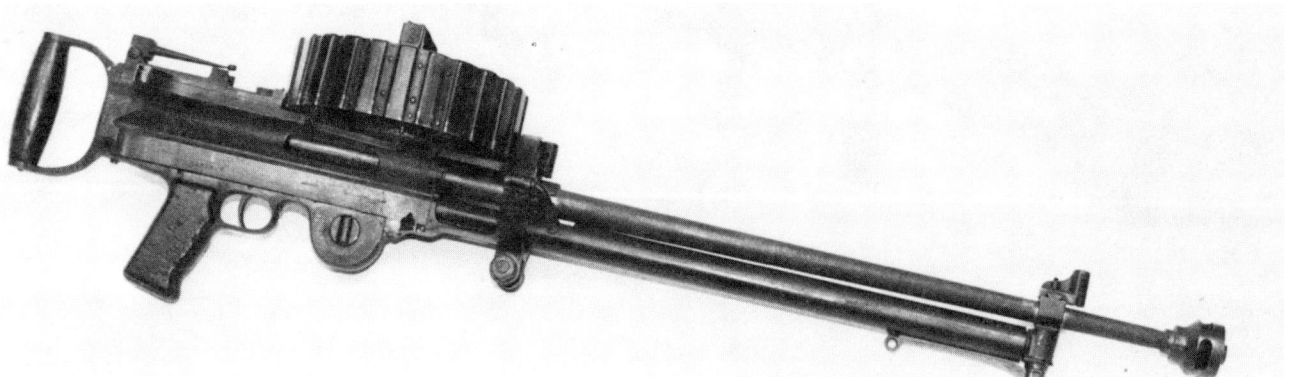

French Lewis Model 1914.

craft ended up in the hands of Col. G.B. Jarrett. The gun was later sold to the Tallmantz collection, remaining there after the aircraft was sold. Curtis Earl purchased it from Tallmantz. This French Lewis, which may be the only example of its kind in the world, now resides in the Champlin collection in Mesa, Arizona.

The gun was produced in France by at least two makers, the giant St. Etienne Arsenal and the Darne firm of shotgun fame. Darne went on to produce a much cheaper and lighter aircraft gun under its own name during World War I. This gun is related to the Lewis shown here only in the sense that Darne appreciated all the difficulties in making a superb product like the Lewis, determined the machine processes were pointless, and promptly set out to produce a gun equally functional, but infinitely cheaper.

CHATELLERAULT MODEL 24/29

Name:
Chatellerault

Model:
1924/29

Caliber:
7.5mm

Overall Length:
42.5 inches

Barrel Length:
19.7 inches

Weight:
24.5 pounds

Type of Fire:
Semiauto and full auto

System of Operation:
Gas

Cyclic Rate (approx.):
500 + RPM

Feed System/Ammunition Delivery:
25-round box magazine

Country of Manufacture:
France

Manufacturer:
MAS

Countries of Use:
France

Period of Manufacture (approx.):
1929–1940 and some post-World War II

Period of Service (approx.):
1929–1960s (some undoubtedly still in service in former French colonies)

Primary Service:
Post-World War I through 1955 with French forces

Primary Tactical Use:
Individual infantryman, fixed defenses in the Maginot Line, and armored vehicles

Chatellerault Modele 1924/29 was modeled after the Browning Automatic Rifle that incorporated one of the excellent features of the Czech light machine guns, a top-mounted magazine (the magazine holds twenty-five rounds). Though of excellent design, it was not without development problems owing to the cutting of metallurgical corners, and its development was in fact quite protracted. By 1931, though, the gun and its new 7.5mm cartridge —very similar to and based upon the German 7.92mm round—were in service. A heavier version, the M1931 machine gun, is still in service in numbers. The 24/29 was very popular with French troops and may still be held in reserve. Development of this weapon was a matter of some urgency, for it was intended to replace the Chauchat.

In service, the weapon proved extremely reliable and easy to use. The French have traditionally relied heavily upon short-term conscripts, so weapon simplification was an important consideration. The

A French conscript awaits the end of *Sitzkreig* in 1940, his Chatellerault Model 24/29 by his side.

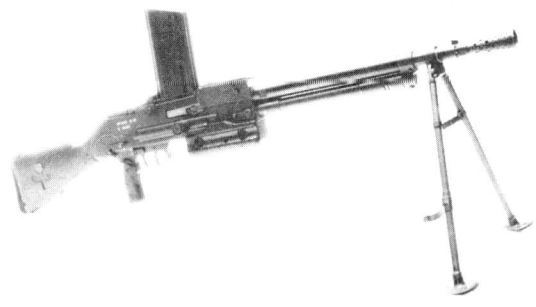

Chatellerault Model 24/29.

gun has two triggers, a forward one for single shots and a rear one for fully automatic fire. The gun was fitted with a gas regulator, the adjustment of which could be used in conjunction with buffer tension to vary cyclic rate. German static defense units in France employed quite a number of these guns during World War II, many of which were seized during the war and reissued to the Free French.

DARNE MODEL 1931

Name:
Darne aircraft machine gun

Model:
1931 aircraft

Caliber:
7.7mm (.303 British)

Overall Length:
41.5 inches

Barrel Length:
27.75 inches

Weight:
18.5 pounds

Type of Fire:
Full auto only

System of Operation:
Gas

Cyclic Rate (approx.):
1200–1700 RPM

Feed System/Ammunition Delivery:
Steel belt link

Country of Manufacture:
France

Manufacturer:
The Darne Company

Countries of Use:
Brazil, France, Serbia, and Spain

Period of Manufacture (approx.):
Late 1920s–1940

Period of Service (approx.):
1931–1940

Primary Tactical Use:
Military aircraft personnel

Chinn mentions that the Darne factory was one of the most outmoded and dimly lit in the world. And the Darne aircraft machine gun was somewhat like that as well. The company bragged that the weapon did not contain a single forged part and sold it cheap. It stressed the fact that the gun was expendable, suggesting modular installations that could be pulled for service, a procedure that was lavish for the times except for the cost of the Darne, which was very low. Though the Darne is a cheap-looking product, it worked quite well. Shown here is a 1930s version, though the guns were in use primarily during World War I. Somewhat ironically, the company's most famous products were high-grade sporting shotguns, famous the world over for their quality construction and slender, graceful lines.

Because the Darne is made in France and similar in appearance and general layout to a Hotchkiss, it is often presumed that the Darne is merely a Hotchkiss copy. Though some early models accepted Hotchkiss feed strips, the similarities end there. The feed system is especially unique and efficient. Two claws attached to the gas piston pull an incoming round from the feedway after the round's dislocation from the link by a cammed device that moves the cartridge back by pushing on the bullet's nose. The claws also prop the round at a 45-degree angle, with two fingers coupled to the piston, without releasing its hold. The primary action takes place while the piston is in the powerful thrust-back stroke, where there is plenty of surplus energy. This also allows a short reciprocating bolt movement, partially accounting for the high rate of fire.

The guns were sold to the French government in 1931 for 700 francs, the equivalent of $28. This is about the then-current U.S. market price of a reasonable single-shot rifle. Between 1918 and 1931, the company sold at least 11,000 guns. Most parts and some guns were produced in an even more primitive factory facility in Spain.

Cheap though the guns were, the British tests of Darne guns went very well. In 1941, when the British government took over an order of French G-36 Wildcat fighter planes, it would have used the Darne guns for which the aircraft were fitted had there been an adequate ammunition supply.

Who contracted for the Darne guns and who actually used them is not exactly known. The specimen shown is chambered for the .303 British round, and bears no national markings at all. There may have been considerable sales to Latin American countries, as well as Sweden, Finland, and the Soviet Union. Any Darne gun that's to be fired, especially the very rare ground versions, should be slugged and chamber-cast. The guns are not neces-

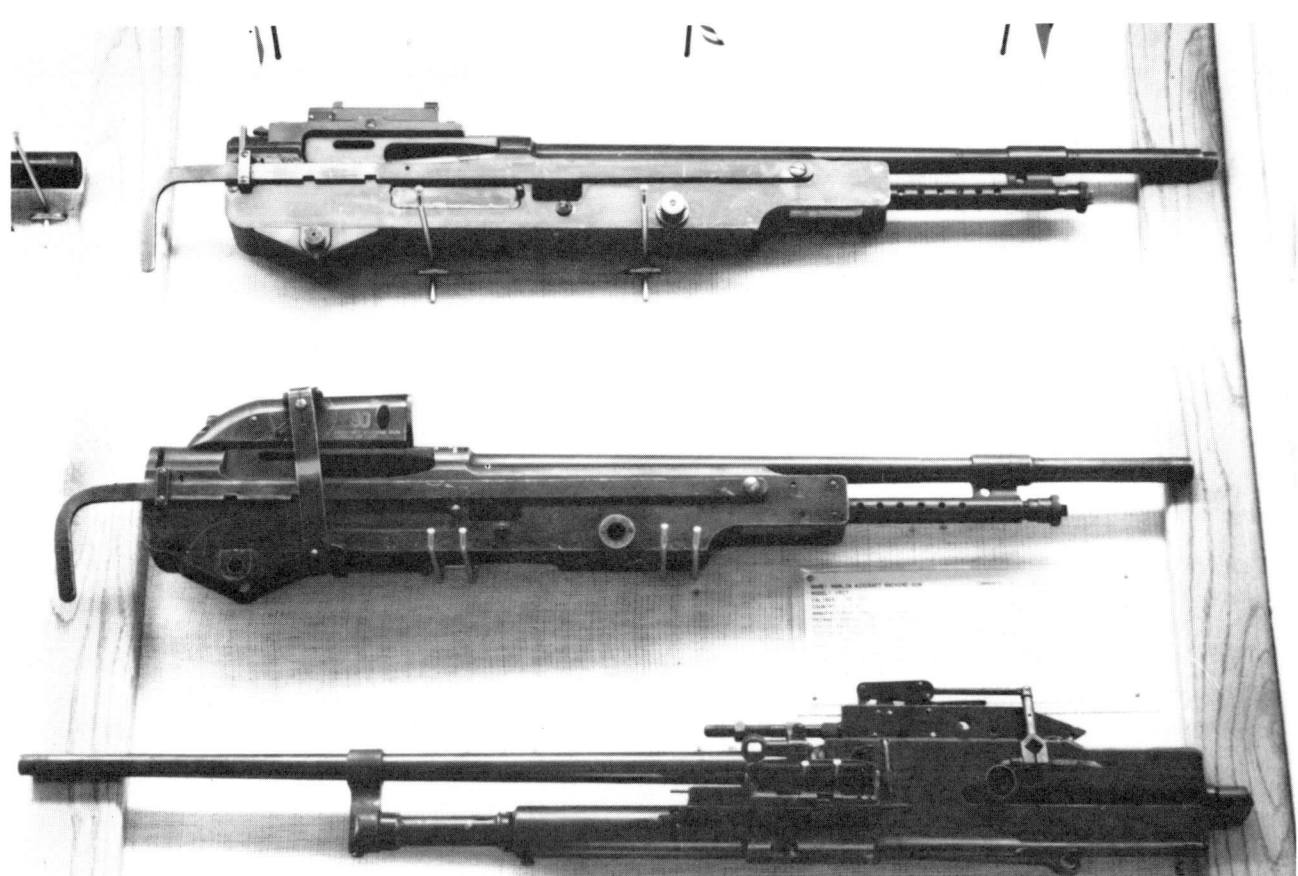

Darne aircraft machine gun (bottom) compared with two Marlins.

sarily of the calibers for which they are marked, and this "mismarking" seems to have been intentional since there were many insurrectionist movements occurring between 1919 and 1940. The Darnes were marked as a legitimate purchase and then altered or waylayed en route in order to avoid boycotts and bypass legal entanglements. Whether a customer, manufacturer, middleman, or agent contrived such plans is unknown, but the fact is that Darne guns show up mismarked all over the world.

At a time when typical aircraft armament was comprised of two or three rifle-caliber machine guns, the Darne firm proposed "packages" of up to twelve modularized guns and one or more cannons for strafing and interceptor use. No one was interested in such a package then; unfortunately, the concept was way ahead of its time. The Darne is not particularly accurate, though the ground guns might have been more accurate than the aircraft models. This difference was intentional since the hose-pipe technique so pointless with ground guns was very useful in air-to-air combat or strafing, especially with very fast firing multiple-gun installations.

MAS MODEL 38

Name:
MAS

Model:
M38

Caliber:
7.65mm French *longue*

Overall Length:
24.8 inches

Barrel Length:
8.8 inches

Weight:
6.3 pounds

Type of Fire:
Full auto

System of Operation:
Blowback

Cyclic Rate (approx.):
700 RPM

Feed System/Ammunition Delivery:
32-round box magazine

MAS MODEL 38 (continued)

Country of Manufacture:
France

Manufacturer:
MAS, St. Etienne

Countries of Use:
France

Period of Manufacture (approx.):
1938–1942; some post World War II

Period of Service (approx.):
1938–present

Primary Service:
French and German occupation forces during World War II

Primary Tactical Use:
Individual infantry

The French .32 (7.65mm Long) round was never taken very seriously for use in handguns, but the controllability of the cartridge in a submachine gun was very handy. This controllability is one reason why this old weapon is still being used by French antiterrorist gendarme units. The MAS M38 is most unusual in that it has a folding trigger and a bolt that travels on an angular path. At the time, this was thought to reduce recoil and make for a more reliable, shorter throw action. The weapon may be conveniently fired with one hand; it cannot be fired with the shoulder stock removed.

The combination of its features makes this model easy to control and reasonably accurate, even in fairly long bursts. However, the supply of ammunition—or rather, the lack of it—is such that, offered an opportunity to shoot this gun recently for the first time in twenty years, I had to decline. I could dig up only fifteen rounds of ammunition and, knowing French ammunition as I do, I had no confidence any of it would fire reliably or well since it bore 1946 to 1948 manufacture dates.

AAT 52

Name:
General purpose machine gun

Model:
AAT 52

Caliber:
7.5mm French M1929

Other Chamberings:
7.62x51mm NATO

Overall Length:
Stock extended: 45.9 inches
Stock retracted: 38.6 inches

Barrel Length:
Heavy barrel: 24.7 inches
Light barrel: 20.9 inches

Weight:
With heavy barrel: 21.7 pounds
With light barrel: 23.28 pounds

Type of Fire:
Automatic only

System of Operation:
Delayed blowback

Cyclic Rate (approx.):
700 RPM

Feed System/Ammunition Delivery:
Extendable 50-round nondisintegrating metallic belt

Country of Manufacture:
France

Manufacturer:
Bayonne, others

Countries of Use:
France, former French colonies, some Third World countries

Period of Manufacture (approx.):
1952–late 1970s

Period of Service (approx.):
1952–present

France's attempt at a general-purpose machine gun, the AAT (Arme Automatique Transformable) 52 is quite reliable, but it seems to have been almost a spiteful swipe at compatibility within NATO, not only retaining the French cartridge, but introducing a new belt setup at the very worst time.

The belt and feed systems are copies of the MG42, but different enough so that the MG42 belt won't function in the AAT 52.

These guns provide only nominal delay and tremendous violence in the action. Case separations and swelled heads are very common. Given this and the eccentricities of French ammunition—plus the total lack of new ammo in the United States—this gun is perhaps the worst possible investment for a hobbyist.

FAMAS-GIAT

Name:
Assault rifle/carbine

The MAS Model 38A is always firing downhill. It was actually an excellent and reliable gun.

Model:
FAMAS-GIAT

Caliber:
.223/5.56mm U.S.

Other Chamberings:
7.62x39mm Soviet in planning stages

Overall Length:
29.8 inches

Barrel Length:
19.2 inches

Weight:
7.7 pounds

Type of Fire:
Selective

System of Operation:
Delayed blowback

Cyclic Rate (approx.):
900–1,000 RPM and 3-shot burst control

Feed System/Ammunition Delivery:
25-round box magazine

Country of Manufacture:
France

Manufacturer:
MAS-GIAT (semiautomatic imported by Century Arms)

Countries of Use:
France, former French colonies, some neutral Third World countries

Period of Manufacture (approx.):
1978–present

Period of Service (approx.):
1979–present

Primary Tactical Use:
Individual assault weapon

This is one of the few infantry weapons with reversible feed/ejection, especially handy for left-handers, and important in these foreshortened bullpup designs.

Innovative, the FAMAS is a natty little package of plastic and steel, basically a bullpup-design submachine carbine with primitive but almost invulnerable sights. The "stock" is also the handle, and the general look of the design is very weird, but businesslike and very handy.

Wisely, the French have designed the gun for straightforward maintenance and maximum flexi-

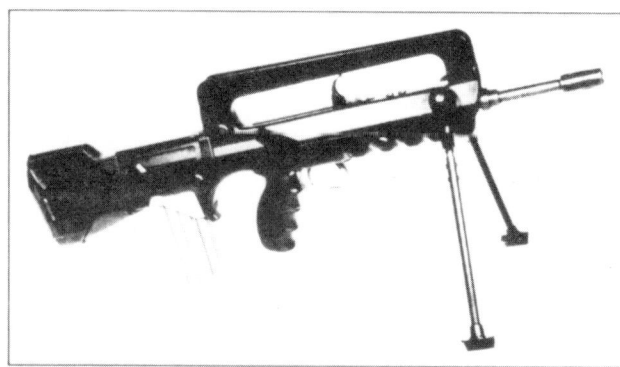

FAMAS-GIAT.

bility, the flip-flop capability of the ejector being especially nice and especially necessary in a bull-pup, wherein the action lies close to the shooter's face, with the magazine at the rear and behind the pistol grip.

The main beef against bullpups, heavy game rifles, or toy gallery guns has always been that men worry about objects exploding next to their faces. This isn't vanity; it's instinct. It is as relevant now as it was with the British EM2 in the forties.

CHAPTER 12

Germany

Hiram Maxim made the automatic machine gun practical. Smokeless powder—the final component needed to take the machine gun from the tenuous prototype stage to mechanical acceptability—came along in the mid-to-late 1880s in several countries simultaneously. These powders were not, of course, truly smokeless, though they were much more so than was black powder.

The great advantage in rapid-fire weapons was not merely concealment, but the reduced fouling and increased visibility that the more uniform, controlled burning rates guaranteed. (Incidentally, only the British regularly used Cordite, a nitroglycerine-based powder often put up in cords or strips. Neither U.S. nor German weapons contained Cordite, although its use was fairly common in British small arms and heavy weapons until the forties.) Maxim used a rotating cam and breaking toggle, whose function was that of the human knee joint in absorbing shock, and which activated reciprocation on his gun. He was thus harnessing energy that was formerly wasted.

Born in Maine in 1840, Maxim was a man of easy genius, who conceived of and built many different inventions. Before concocting his fully automatic gun, he had converted a Winchester to self-loading operation. In his 1885 gun, the cartridge, barrel, and breech were briefly locked together when the first manually loaded cartridge ignited and again at the beginning of each ignition. On detonation, the barrel, breech, and cartridge moved a short distance back while locked together, the breech mechanism imparting its power after separation to a strong fusee spring and then dumping the spent cartridge. When the bolt was fully back, the extended fusee reversed the thrust, thus repeating the process. The toggle setup timed and controlled the mechanism. At the time, critics noted that the metal-reinforced fabric belts were fragile and that the gun would consume enormous amounts of ammunition. The latter analysis was more true than the former, but these objections were minimal compared to the tactical criticisms.

Infantry and cavalry officers found the machine gun difficult to take seriously. The British and others who used the gun against locals in various colonial wars and expeditions found it could cut down the opposition with alacrity, especially when the troops were attacked frontally without cover. The military geniuses of Victorian Europe, however, surmised that "civilized" troops knew the "weaknesses" of the automatic machine gun, would use close cover effectively, and thus overrun the latest mechanical panacea with ease and abandon. That was the theory. Statistics of casualties, however, would prove that there were flaws in that theory.

Naval officers had no such pet theories to test. They knew from their experience with Gatlings and other mechanical rapid-fire weapons, that two threats, the boarding party and the torpedo boat, would respond to the use of rapid-fire weapons. In the sure knowledge that he who survives to get to the battlefront is most likely to succeed on the offensive, the navies of the world, without much commotion or controversy, purchased Maxims for virtually all major warships. By the turn of the century, virtually every major warship in the world carried both rifle-caliber machine guns and the Maxim "pom-pom" guns in calibers up to and beyond 37mm.

It is true, of course, that virtually every nation on the planet also purchased some Maxims for its army. Some then copied the Maxims, improving or simplifying them along the way. A few countries sought and received licenses for local manufacture, while others just went ahead and made as many as they liked. Even France and Italy, feverishly evolving machine-gun designs of their own, ordered Maxim commercial variants to their specifications. So did Austria and the United States. Not surprisingly, the United States showed the least enthusiasm for the Maxim, ordering the smallest quantities of any country (see the U.S. M1904); though one Maxim model was adopted, it never was ordered in any serious quantities. Germany, however, field-tested and adopted several variants, issuing the guns as standard and manufacturing them commercially before the turn of the century. It revised the design again in 1908, continuously refining it until the end of World War I.

The high quality of the early commercial Maxim guns is of a level seldom seen in military firearms. The outside surface of the side plates—an extraneous measurement area, for nothing of mechanical importance happens there—generally retains parallelism to plus or minus .001 inches, and is often even better than that. The dovetail fit of the water jacket/receiver interface is so precise that it seems the bronze is plated onto the steel. The guns were very expensive, of course, but well worth their cost, as the durability of water-cooled guns—especially robust ones and particularly the Maxim—is legendary.

The gun shown here belonged to a famous American mercenary, who used it in several wars. The "S" over the chamber usually meant *schwere,* the German word for "heavy," and the gun was probably rebuilt in Germany sometime during its life. The gun may at one time have been chambered for 8x64S or some similar loading. Purchased in a pawn shop by J. Curtis Earl in a stripped condition after disappearing from the Burnham Estate properties, the gun was lacking many parts. Since no one is quite sure of the gun's original configuration and since

commercial Maxim parts are even more rare than the guns themselves, many German World War I–vintage parts had to be used to complete the weapon. An original bronze fusee cover couldn't be located, though the gun is now found in the Champlin Fighter Museum, where it is presumed that an original fusee cover will be found or, more feasibly, that a facsimile will be cast in the correct size and finish.

At the time the gun shown here was manufactured, most machine guns still rode on wheeled mounts, though tripods of various types came along very quickly. The fact that this model was used until just before World War I suggests that it probably did most of its shooting from a Vickers-Maxim style tripod that is similar to the ones shown here supporting Vickers guns. Not only were the tripods lighter and smaller, but they allowed the gun to sit lower, generally making it less artillery-like than the wheeled mounts. Since the automatic machine gun was lighter than its mechanical predecessors, the heavy carriages were unnecessary anyway.

MAXIM M1889 and M91

Name:
Maxim

Model:
M1889, M91

Caliber:
.303 British, 7.92x57JS, 7mm Soviet, many others

Overall Length:
47 inches

Barrel Length:
28 inches

Weight:
66 pounds without water

Type of Fire:
Full automatic

System of Operation:
Recoil

Cyclic Rate (approx.):
300–450 RPM (with 300 standard)

Feed System/Ammunition Delivery:
Fabric belt

Country of Manufacture:
Germany (originated in Great Britain)

Manufacturer:
Vickers & Sons, Simpson & Company, Suhl, Waffenfabrik, Colt, Maxim-Nordenfeldt, Maxim, Hatton Garden

Countries of Use:
Most countries used this gun or similar ones in some applications.

Period of Manufacture (approx.):
1888–early 1900s

Period of Service (approx.):
These guns served well into the twentieth century all over the world.

Primary Tactical Use:
Fixed fire base, crew-served support

The Germans adopted their first Maxim before the turn of the twentieth century; by 1908, they had trimmed the original somewhat and devised the sled mounting that became so well known during World War I. It is probable that this weapon has the distinction of having killed more men in combat than any other firearm. It was also the primary device that decided the shape of the World War I battlefield, an arena in which the old adages about offense winning battles and the best defense being a good offense were formulas for suicide. Until the tank came along to cross the messy no-man's-land, it was he who moved most boldly who bought his own defeat. Indeed, the very term *no-man's-land* was coined because the long-range, carefully sited,

sustained-fire, water-cooled machine gun established the terrible one- to three-mile wastelands of World War I that even today often look as if they had been churned in some giant food processor.

The machine gun, especially the Maxim, forced and enforced stalemate. Artillery, poison gas, land mines, barbed wire, and accurate, long-range rifle fire made the stable lines a nightmare. Statistics from all sides indicate that far more men were killed or injured by artillery during World War I than from any other cause. However, the other arms were able to do their terrible work because men dared not move from the trenches; the machine gun made the trenches prisons and any point beyond their perimeters a death trap.

Hiram Maxim was an American. Like many creative men, he had considerable difficulty working for someone else. However, he took part in any number of important technological advancements and achievements, though most of his early ones were unrelated to firearms. Like most firearms inventors, he was a hardworking, extremely practical man who looked at problems and saw solutions. By 1885, his experiments led to a working and practical recoil-operated automatic machine gun. With the invention of clean-working smokeless powders in 1886, the single-barreled, rapid-fire, mechanically

Maxim M1889.

automatic machine gun became a practical proposition. Maxim's use of a toggle joint (whose function was similar to that of the human knee) as the primary reciprocating element in an automatic gun can only be called a stroke of genius. The design spread stress, minimized receiver length, and demonstrated the importance of elegant but simple and sturdy solutions to straightforward equations.

By 1890 or so, Maxim set up shop in England. A short-lived merger with the giant Nordenfeldt concern helped turn the guns out in tremendous quantities by the standards of the times. A large gun known as the pom-pom came out around this time, in addition to guns like the M1889. Though the machine gun was rather controversial among the more sophisticated armies of the world, the general feeling being that "civilized" troops could overcome them with steel nerves and *élan de corps,* the navies of the world had no such narrow inclinations. By the turn of the century, *every* navy owned large numbers of Maxims.

The Maxims were the answer to two problems: boarding parties (previously dealt with by Gatlings or grapeshop or other interim measures) and torpedo boats, which were cheap, swift vessels that endangered the most splendid capital ships with their powerful self-propelled explosives. Just before the turn of the century, a .75-caliber gun was also devised for various navies.

In 1888, Maxim joined with Albert Vickers in a new venture, Vickers Sons and Maxim, Limited. Vickers assisted him with lightening the gun to 40.5 pounds by the 1904 model, though, ironically, some customers persisted in specifying the heavier jacket and receiver of the older models. The 1904 issue was the first gun to bear the name *Vickers* along with *Maxim.*

Maxim eventually adopted British citizenship, as he felt he had been rejected in his own country. There are several ironies regarding Maxim and his guns. The British Vickers M1915 was, in fact, a carefully lightened and reengineered Maxim. When Germany began the war in 1914, she took the field with 50,000 Maxims on order or on hand. The Russians, too, had two or three variants of the guns in their infantry. Even the French used the Maxims in considerable numbers, though most were older naval guns or were used in defensive positions far from the front. The United States at the time had fewer than 1,000 machine guns in its army, 282 of them Maxims.

It was Kaiser Wilhelm himself who provided the greatest impetus to Germany's conservative army, still very much a product of the cavalry era. After a demonstration at Spandau, he said, "That is the gun! There *is* no other!" He proceeded to order that the guns be procured and that the army find ways to use them, which it did.

MG08

Name:
MG08

Model:
1908

Caliber:
7.92mm

Overall Length:
46.25 inches

Barrel Length:
28.25 inches

Weight:
40.5 pounds without water

Weight of Mounts:
sled mount: 83 pounds
tripod mount: 65.5 pounds

Type of Fire:
Full auto

System of Operation:
Recoil

Cyclic Rate (approx.):
450 RPM; with muzzle booster, 500 +

Feed System/Ammunition Delivery:
Cloth belt

Country of Manufacture:
Germany

Manufacturer:
Deutsch Waffen und Munitions Fabriken, AG, Berlin; also Spandau and Erfurt arsenals, J.P. Sauer, and Simpson and Company (mostly prewar) in Germany, and Waffenfabrik Herstal in Belgium

Countries of Use:
Germany and its allies

Period of Manufacture (approx.):
1908–1918

Period of Service (approx.):
1908–1930s (later in many other countries)

Primary Service:
World War I Germany; very limited use during World War II

Primary Tactical Use:
Infantry heavy machine gun

The *Machine Gewehr* 1908, a simplification of the original Maxims, is the second revision of the '08. It eliminated some extraneous machining, bits of brass, and the odd accessory receptacle that had grown unjustifiable.

The '08's long barrel and sturdy water jacket were intended to provide range at least as good as that of the rifle, and the sights were perhaps even better. A telescope and a variety of periscopic optics were also available. The Maxim's sustained fire capability was superb and, though it is extremely heavy by today's standards, its range and burst capability are far better than those of today's machine guns of similar caliber. The long barrel endows the gun with somewhat higher velocity than that of today's guns of rifle caliber, meaning the trajectory is quite flat.

The Treaty of Versailles specifically forbade the manufacture of the Maxim on German soil, and severely limited the numbers available to Germany's peacetime *Reichswehr* Army of one hundred thousand and the domestic *polizei*. Still, a considerable number of the guns were stashed, some of which were sold to other countries; others appeared very late during World War II. Germany was compelled to deliver all the Maxims that were contraband to the Allies, who mainly reconditioned and resold them all over the world. Vickers in particular manufactured a streamlined tripod and new fusee cover for the guns, converted many to 7mmx57 Mauser, 7.65x54mm Mauser, and other calibers, and sold them worldwide. Considerable numbers probably remain in Latin America to this day.

This gun was often equipped with a muzzle booster, a gas gush-back device that accelerated the barrel's movement and sped up the overall action to increase the rate of fire by about 100 to 175 RPM. When used with this device, recoil and shimmy were considered a problem. Therefore, to stabilize the gun, a strap was normally rigged across the "pan" between the two front legs of the *Schlitten 08* mount. A tripod was created around 1916 to supplement the sledge mount. The Germans also used Maxim-type weapons captured in the field, including old English- and Belgian-made guns, which they sometimes adapted to the German mounts.

The MG08 is remarkably durable, reliable, and more accurate than many match rifles. The belt-feed system is not picky about gross ammunition length, provided the length is not more than .01 inches longer than standard. Shorter bullets work fine. Ammunition power will change the rate of fire, and weak ammo will sometimes work only with a well-lubricated action. Powerful ammo speeds up the action; adjusting the fusee spring can compensate, but the effect is still there.

A Maxim tested for this book had a new barrel built on a Shaw blank and put 220-grain Hornady or Speer handloads into a half-inch hole all day at one hundred yards. The gun is also easier on brass than most semiautomatic rifles. Though this gun featured very tight headspace and was over seventy years old, it was virtually mint. Still, even fairly beat-up Maxims deliver more than credible accuracy. They are heavy, though, which is why various air-cooled concoctions were always being advanced, tested, and, mostly, forgotten.

The MG08 employed considerable brass and bronze trim until 1916. Even after that time, machine work remained first-rate, state-of-the-art metallurgy.

The sled mount was designed for times when the

MG08.

MG08.

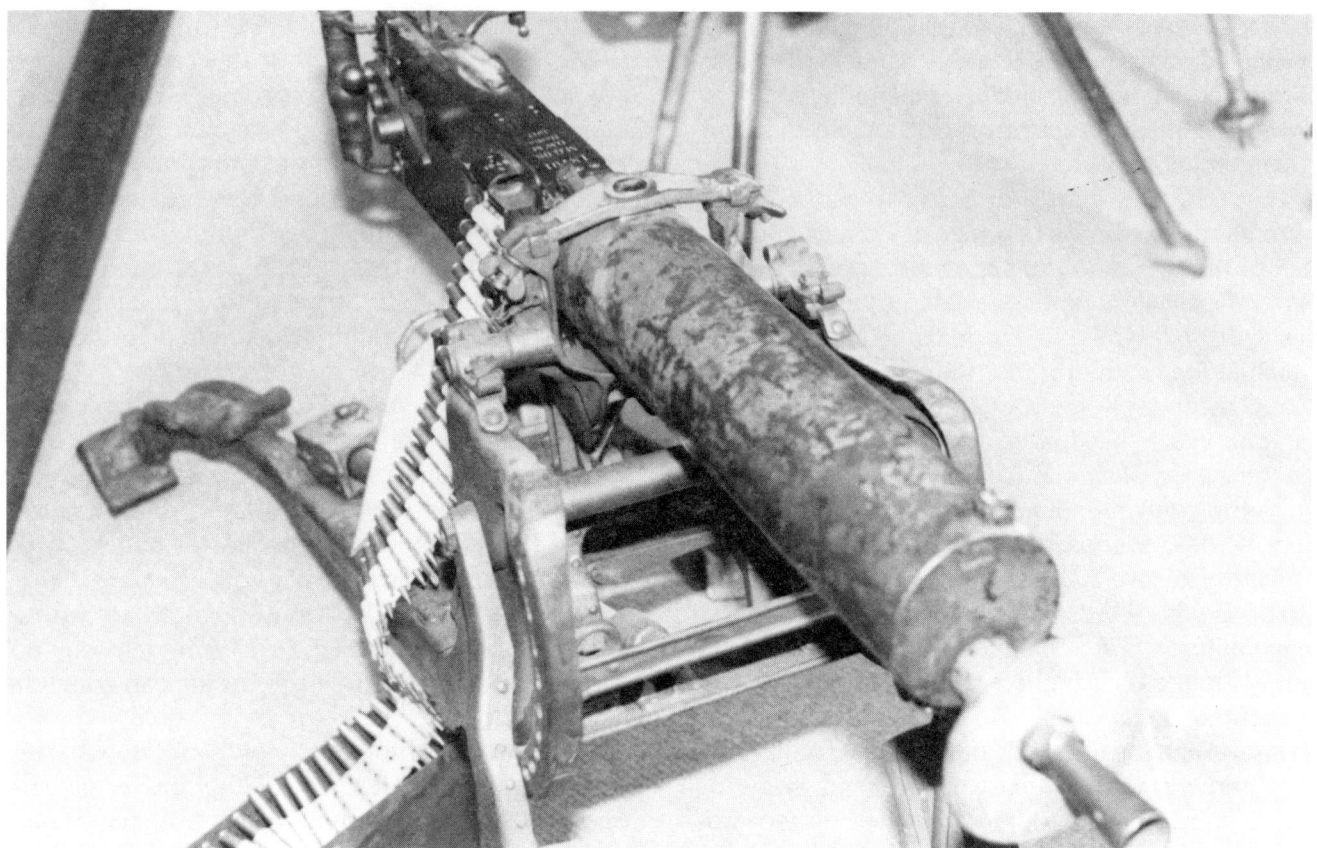

A standard MG08 Maxim on a sled mount with camouflage finish and muzzle booster.

gun had to be moved quickly, and it could be flattened out for carriage by two men. Cynics claimed the Germans would then often cover the gun with a blanket smeared with red paint to give the impression they were moving wounded. Still, the mount was exceptionally stable, which kept the inherent downrange accuracy tight, greatly extending the usable range of fire. No medium or general-purpose machine gun made today will shoot with a Maxim or, for that matter, with any of the better water-cooled machine guns of a few generations ago.

The Maxim was used in intelligent, interlocking nest setups to completely frustrate enemy movement with cross-fire. In flat country with good fields of fire, each "nest" was often comprised of two guns. Two to four nests would interface in a manner designed to cover an area perhaps half a mile across and one thousand to two thousand meters deep. Support personnel would move to ditches, trenches, and holes as things heated up, often employing MP18s and MG08/15s, as well as rifle fire, to further knot up the field. Going into such a maelstrom, even with smoke and some ground cover, meant casualties of 50 to 90 percent.

On the Eastern Plains, German troops stand ready behind a flank nest of two MG08 machine guns.

PARABELLUM LMG 14

Name:
Parabellum

Model:
Aircraft LMG 14

Caliber:
7.92x57JS

Overall Length:
48.25 inches

Barrel Length:
28 inches

Weight:
21.6 pounds

Type of Fire:
Auto only

System of Operation:
Derivative: Maxim recoil (toggle)
Mechanical: Short recoil

Cyclic Rate (approx.):
650–750 RPM

Feed System/Ammunition Delivery:
Special linked or standard Maxim belt, usually contained in a reeled drum

Country of Manufacture:
Germany

Manufacturer:
DWM

Countries of Use:
Germany and its allies; Turkey

Period of Manufacture (approx.):
1911–1917

Period of Service (approx.):
1911–1918

Primary Tactical Use:
Aircraft (some use as ground weapon)

An extremely rare weapon today, the Parabellum might have become what the Maxim became. The Germans, however, were not as well set up to produce this faster-firing, lightened version of Maxim's design. And because of its lighter mechanism, there seem to have been more breakages. But it was this gun and the light Maxim that, together with Tony Fokker's synchronizers, brutalized Allied air forces in the 1915 to 1916 "Fokker Scourge" of legend.

A 1909 specification asked DWM to produce prototypes of an aircraft weapon that would be lighter than the MG08. Designer Karl Heinemann inverted the toggle to break upwards and carefully lightened internals; by around 1911, the gun was producing quality results in flexible installations. The LMG 14 was the flexible model. Most fixed forward-firing guns were called "14/17," though they are externally similar. Eventually, partly owing to the higher rate of fire, the Parabellum was mostly relegated to the flexible role by 1916.

Some early synchronizers had problems with high rates of fire, and many historians think that several German aces (among them Max Immelmann) expired by shooting themselves down. The Parabellum, often fitted with scope optics, was then relegated to bombers, scouts, and airships, and was often used on double mounts as an antiaircraft gun. Many of the ground and observation balloon guns were water-cooled, not because weight was such a factor, but because sustained fire was.

DREYSE MODEL 1915

Name:
Dreyse

Model:
Model 1915 (modified 1912)

Caliber:
7.92mm

Overall Length:
48 inches

Barrel Length:
28.25 inches

Weight:
39 pounds with original bipod; pedestal adds 5 pounds

Type of Fire:
Full auto

System of Operation:
Short recoil

Cyclic Rate (approx.):
700 RPM

Feed System/Ammunition Delivery:
Cloth belt

Country of Manufacture:
Germany

Manufacturer:
RM&M

Countries of Use:
Germany, Portugal, Turkey

Period of Manufacture (approx.):
1912–1918 (these dates are for this version; the Dreyses per se had entered limited production by 1910)

DREYSE MODEL 1915 (continued)

Period of Service (approx.):
1910–1918; until at least the 1930s in some other countries

Primary Service:
World War I

Primary Tactical Use:
Infantry

German guns tend to be known by names other than those of their actual designers and/or manufacturers. For example, the mechanism of the Dryse M1915, externally similar to the Bergmann heavy machine guns in some respects, was patented by Louis Schmeisser in 1907, and rights were assigned to *Rheinische Metallwarn und Maschinenfabrik, A.G.* (RM&M), Düsseldorf. The gun was named in honor of Johann Nikolaus von Dreyse, founder of the Dreyse weapons concern and designer of the needle gun.

The main distinguishing features of the gun involve the mechanical accelerator and a three-claw apparatus on the mainspring housing to withdraw rounds from the belt. These claws make it almost impossible for the belt to cause jams by misaligning ammunition. The breech lock is commonly known as the "oscillating" or "pivoting" type, and is pinned at the bottom of the barrel extension. It swings down for unlocking as the rear portion rides a ramp on the recoil stroke. Used in various early air- and water-cooled incarnations, the guns worked well, but were overshadowed by the MG08.

Inherent cyclic rate was higher than that of the Maxim, and the early guns worked well. However, the Model 1915 and much of the subsequent new production failed, largely because the company cut many metallurgical and machining corners to pro-

Dreyse Model 1915.

Dreyse Model 1915.

duce the new "light machine gun." Many older M1910 and M1912 guns were also "converted," which meant that a band was fitted around the water jacket to hold a primitive bipod similar to the one on the Maxim 08/15. No shoulder stocks were fitted, and the guns were supplied with the usual spade grips and a pedestal for the rear of the gun which looked rather like an oversized automobile engine valve. The gun shown here seems to be a conversion from an earlier production run. Needless to say, the combination was extremely awkward, and most of the guns were "reconverted" to the heavy configuration.

Any Dreyse in a water-cooled configuration is extremely rare, no matter what the model, since virtually all the guns existing in Germany after the war were converted to air-cooling as MG13s. They were sold to Portugal in 1938 after brief service as training guns in Germany.

MG08/15

Name:
MG08/15

Model:
1908/1915

Caliber:
7.92mm

Overall Length:
56.5 inches (approx.)

Barrel Length:
28.4 inches

Weight:
39 pounds with water

Type of Fire:
Full auto

System of Operation:
Recoil

Cyclic Rate (approx.):
450 RPM

Feed System/Ammunition Delivery:
Cloth belt

Country of Manufacture:
Germany

Countries of Use:
Germany and its allies

Period of Manufacture (approx.):
1915–1918

Period of Service (approx.):
1915–1918 (The gun was also used much later outside Germany, especially as an aircraft gun, and also saw use with the *Weimar Reichswehr*, 1919–1933. There was some intermittent and specialized use in the Nazi era, and many were reintroduced to the Volksturm Wehrmacht very late in World War II.)

Primary Service:
World War I Germany

Primary Tactical Use:
Infantry light machine gun

With a much trimmed Maxim receiver, the "Light" Maxim MG08/15 was not really light, but it was certainly more portable than the MG08. It could be used with the conventional belts of 250 rounds or with an open-sided drum canister with a reel containing 50 rounds. Water cooling was retained on most of these guns, though an air-cooled version was also produced.

The bipod was awkward and in the wrong place, but it was very solid. Some were fitted with a crude "vertical grip," but these—apparently intended to encourage firing while walking—seem to have been discarded.

Used aggressively in conjunction with large quantities of storm troopers armed with 32-round snail drum pistols and MP18-I submachine guns, these weapons were quite effective in the Spring Offensive of 1918.

The general construction of the gun encouraged its use from the prone position, though there were mounts contrived for the gun. After World War I, many were refurbished and sold to other countries, especially by the Allied powers, who got them as reparations. Many of these were in loadings other than the German 7.92x57mm. There were also unusual pedestal bases and tripods advertised with the guns, though it seems that few, if any, were actually delivered.

The design of the Light Maxim was also the basis for the German aircraft guns, many of which were only converted 08/15s with air-cooling jackets instead of water containers.

These guns were used long after World War I all over the world, even in Germany, especially in multiple antiaircraft mounts in secondary positions. It was their water cooling and, thus, their capability for sustained fire that made them convenient.

The capability for sustained fire made the 08/15 a handy gun, though it was never as mobile as its air-cooled contemporaries. Even today, the 08/15 can outshoot most modern light machine guns, do so

Maxim MG08/15.

longer, and break less frequently. For all these reasons, it became a viable alternative to a heavy/medium machine gun in defensive roles and in offensive roles where sustained fire was required. Like the '08, the guns were often used in two- and three-gun cross-fire setups, and were used in local support of heavy machine gun installations for serious defensive fire, especially late in the war. Confronted with such interlocking networks of death, the tank became essential for any forward movement.

SPANDAU MODEL 1908/15

Name:
Spandau light machine gun

Model:
1908/1915

Caliber:
7.92mmx57JS

Overall Length:
55 inches

Barrel Length:
28 inches

Weight:
33 pounds

Type of Fire:
Full auto only

System of Operation:
Recoil

Cyclic Rate (approx.):
550 RPM

Feed System/Ammunition Delivery:
Fabric web belt

Country of Manufacture:
Germany

Manufacturer:
Spandau Arsenal and many others

Countries of Use:
Germany and its allies in World War I

Period of Manufacture (approx.):
1915–1918

Period of Service (approx.):
1915–1918 (This weapon was used in some applications by other countries much later.)

Primary Tactical Use:
Military aircraft machine gun

Adapted for air use by substituting a light, ventilated shell for the cooling jacket of the 08/15 ground gun, the Light Maxim was often muzzle-boosted and reworked at the breech end to provide a higher rate of fire. Other versions were manufactured with only a very slender circulating sleeve around the barrel for both ground and air use.

While referring to the standard MG08 ground gun as a "Spandau" is at least nominally incorrect, this weapon was developed at the giant Spandau Arsenal near Berlin. The aircraft version, in particular, really does have its roots there, though the proper term for the gun is *Light Maxim*.

The Light Maxim and the Parabellum, primarily mounted on Fokker Eindeckers, were the guns of the "Fokker Scourge" of 1915-1916. Tony Fokker did not invent the synchronizer to allow shooting through the propeller's arc; he "discovered" it among earlier Schneider patents that were granted but had not been acted upon before the war. Other synchronizers had been designed in Russia and France and also were not acted upon since the military authorities of the period before and even early in World War I saw no real practical use for the airplane in warfare. Many saw no use for the machine gun.

The mechanism of the aircraft guns never really delivered quite the rate of fire desired, though the Germans kept tinkering with it to speed it up. In the end, however, they realized reliability was more important than speed, and beyond changing springs and muzzle boosters, the mechanism was not modified much. Oddly enough, the Germans used every Belgian and British Lewis they could seize to supplement the Maxims with outboard or high-mounted guns, and some of the seized guns showed up very late in World War II in the hands of the *Volksturm* (home guard) organization.

The light guns were made at Erfurt and Spandau arsenals; by Simpson and Company, DWM, J.P. Sauer

Two Spandau Model 1908/15 machine guns mounted on a Fokker D.VII.

A Fokker Dr.1 triplane with two Spandau 1908/15 machine guns.

A Fokker DVIII with two Spandaus.

and Son; and under contract or captive conditions in Austria and Belgium. Sometimes, light Maxims—and often, MG08s—will be seen with the names of other manufacturers on the fusee cover or top plate, but this usually indicates the gun was rebuilt in the postwar period or completed by another manufacturer for export sale from seized German guns or parts.

These guns saw a lot of use after World War I, both in Europe and abroad, and were rebarreled to the usual assortment of calibers where and when necessary. They were used during World War II by many different troops, but seldom in much quantity and never as an actual aircraft gun. Many of these guns, if not most, were converted to a type of interim medium machine gun, often with their water-cooling jackets restored. They appeared often as guard guns in concentration camps.

Like all Maxims, the 08/15 Aircraft was accurate and reliable, if heavier and bulkier than later guns. In the old-fashioned over-the-cowl installation, bulk was an important factor since it obscured forward visibility.

Most of these guns shown here, as well as all of the fighter aircraft, are from the Champlin Fighter Museum collection in Mesa, Arizona.

SPANDAU MODEL 08/15 "AIRSHIP"

Name:
Spandau light machine

Model:
1908/1915 "Airship"

Overall Length:
48.7 inches

Barrel Length:
28 inches

Weight:
38 pounds

Manufacturer:
J.P. Sauer and Son; Suhl

This is the Light Maxim 08/15 in its "airship" configuration, wherein the buttstock was excised and a spade grip added for use from post mounts in the gondolas or "tubs" of zeppelins and barrage/spotter's balloons. This model was also frequently employed as an antiaircraft gun.

Unlike most aircraft Maxims, this variant retained its capability for water-cooling.

MP18/1

Name:
MP18/1

Model:
18/1

Caliber:
9mm

Overall Length:
32 inches

Barrel Length:
7.9 inches

Weight:
9.2 pounds

Type of Fire:
Full auto

System of Operation:
Blowback

Cyclic Rate (approx.):
400 RPM

Feed System/Ammunition Delivery:
Snail drum of 32 rounds

Country of Manufacture:
Germany

Manufacturer:
Bergmann

Countries of Use:
Germany

Period of Manufacture (approx.):
1917–1918 (This weapon was illegally assembled and modified well into the 1920s.)

Period of Service (approx.):
1918–1930s (mostly in modified form)

Primary Service:
German infantry and German/continental police units

Primary Tactical Use:
Individual

One of Germany's innumerable "military secrets" designed to sweep enemy armies from the field of battle, the MP18 was introduced to combat with the storm troopers of Offensive 1918, beginning in March of that year. The gun worked well enough, but the attack—designed to use fresh troops from the east to end the war with one great effort—failed.

Hugo Schmeisser designed the MP18/1 to use the

MP 18/1.

An MP 18/1 and Luger pistol, showing the similar 32-round snail drum.

32-round snail drum common to the Parabellum (Luger) pistols already in army use. The MP18 also borrowed its barrel from the artillery Luger of the period. It was a brilliant and durable design, though the complex drum caused some problems. After the war, most of these weapons were refitted with a new magazine collar that was to use a stick magazine. Though labor-intensive to produce by today's standards, the entire piece was designed for rapid and efficient production; it was much cheaper than the 08/15, yet very handy for short-range shooting. This was the first real submachine gun, though the Villar Perosa was later developed into one.

Of relatively massive construction, this gun is a good shooting proposition with good ammunition. However, the value of unmodified originals is such that it is very important to assure ammo quality in order to avoid blowups.

FG42

Name:
FG42

Model:
1942

Caliber:
7.92mm

Overall Length:
37 inches

Barrel Length:
20 inches

Weight:
9.9 pounds

Type of Fire:
Selective

System of Operation:
Gas

Cyclic Rate (approx.):
750 RPM

Feed System/Ammunition Delivery:
20-round box magazine

Country of Manufacture:
Germany

Manufacturer:
Kreighoff

Countries of Use:
Germany

Period of Manufacture (approx.):
1942–1945

Period of Service (approx.):
1943–1945

Primary Service:
World War II Germany

Primary Tactical Use:
Airborne units and Luftwaffe infantry

Invariably regarded as an aberration by scholars of the period, the FG42 (*Fallschirmjäger Gewehr,* or "Paratrooper Rifle") is remembered in a somewhat different manner by the American, Indian, and British soldiers who had to face it in the Arnhem/Eindhoven and Monte Cassino operations. In the hands of well-trained troops, this rifle was extremely intimidating. It was sometimes the standard weapon with paratrooper and *Luftwaffe* (air force) infantry units. In one battle, Luftwaffe troopers from a signals school in Holland armed themselves with FG42s mixed in with MG42s and MP40s and harassed British and American troops attempting to secure and move across two bridges, between which the Germans were trapped. The Allied commanders involved reported they were dealing with several companies, most likely heavy weapons specialists. Yet, the total number of Germans captured or killed was thirty-seven. Reason: properly coordinated short bursts from a group of men carrying full-caliber automatic rifles can deliver an intimidating sound and volume of fire.

This FG42 employed a straight-line stock to help control recoil. The Germans copied the concept of the American Johnson Light Machine Gun, though as Chinn points out, it was the Lewis that inspired the gun, and the bolt mechanism was very similar in function to the Lewis. The gas port was adjustable. The bayonet and bipod were largely decorative, but the compensator was fairly effective. Like the Johnson, the weapon fired from an open bolt in full-automatic mode and the closed bolt in semi-automatic.

The original design work was done by Rheinmetall-Borsig and the Luftwaffe Weapons Development Branch. Kreighoff produced the original version, however, and constantly complained about inefficiencies in the design and manufacture method. This weapon is the "refined" or "perfected" FG42. Kreighoff built virtually the entire production batch of both models, perhaps 4,700 to 7,000 weapons. For a short time, owing to all the weapons captured between May and September 1944, the Western Allies believed this weapon was being produced in huge numbers. That was never the case.

Since the primary purpose for its design was the demand by the *Fallschirmjager* (paratrooper) units of the Luftwaffe for full range and firepower in a selective-fire weapon with minimal size, considerable accommodation was made in the sighting equipment. The precise post sights can be folded down, and several different quick detach/attach mounts were designed for the compact 4-power scope Gw ZF 4.

Made of high-strength strategic materials at a time when Germany was close to collapse, the FG42 was an extremely expensive and elaborate weapon to produce. Some stampings were used, but they were used in a manner that required much expensive machinery, led to a high level of rejected parts, and still required work after fabrication. The barrels were swaged into the receivers by a very powerful press mechanism in order to assure great rigid-

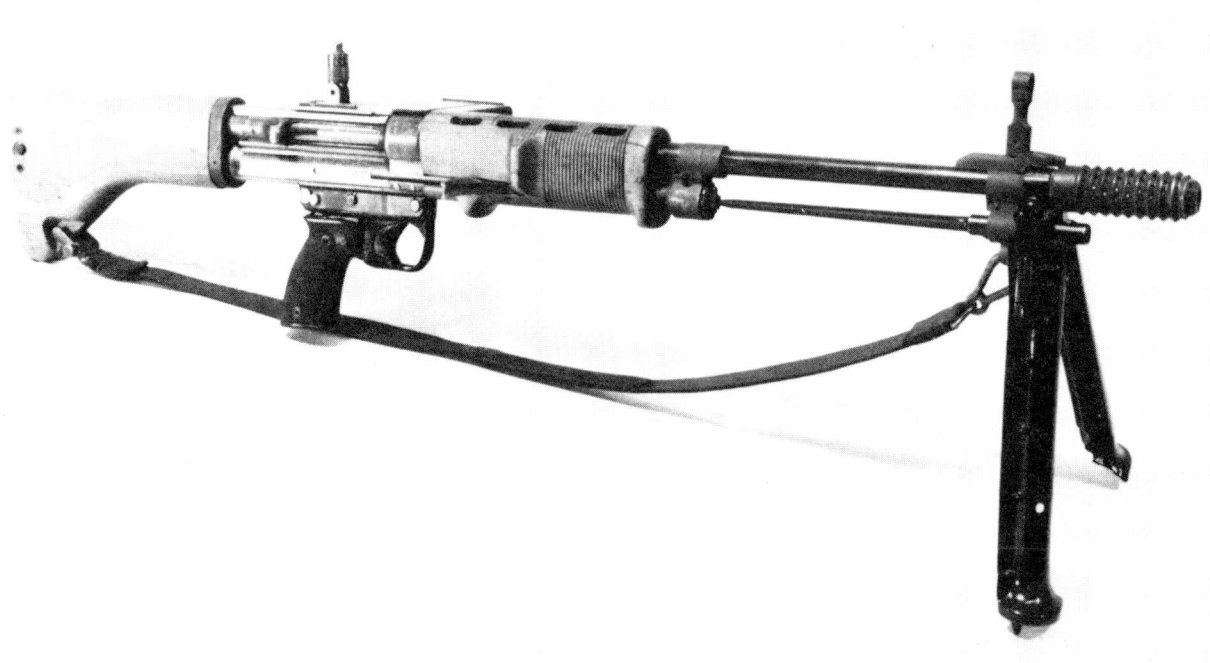

FG42.

ity. This is one reason the rifle is more accurate than its barrel length and military purpose would seem to indicate. The stock utilizes a compression/slide/spring mechanism to reduce recoil and keep it from forming a climbing, positive arc for several rounds.

This weapon had a great impact on American ordnance designers, who used a very similar version of its operating system in the M60 machine gun. Even casual observers notice that the M60 looks rather like the FG42.

It is rather ironic that the one time this weapon was used in an actual airdrop scenario was the futile and abortive Ardennes operation of December 1944 during the Battle of the Bulge, in which most of the paras involved came close to starvation and none got an opportunity to join the battle.

The FG42 design underwent almost constant evolution, for the original model was almost impossible to manufacture, especially under the deteriorating conditions in Nazi Germany. The gun was also rather fragile, a problem that was never entirely rectified. There probably were more FG42s made than the 5,000 figure usually noted since the Allies captured about that many in Italy and France alone.

MP43/44

Name:
MP43/44

Model:
Assault rifle

Caliber:
7.92x33mmK

Overall Length:
rifle: 37 inches

Barrel Length:
rifle: 16.5 inches
Vorsatz J: 14 inches

Weight:
rifle: 10.8 pounds
Vorsatz J: 3.5 pounds (approx.)

Type of Fire:
Selective fire

System of Operation:
Gas

Cyclic Rate (approx.):
500 RPM

Feed System/Ammunition Delivery:
30-round box

MP43/44 (continued)

Country of Manufacture:
Germany

Manufacturer:
Merz and Haenel

Countries of Use:
Germany, Czechoslovakia

Period of Manufacture (approx.):
1943–1945

Period of Service (approx.):
1943–1945 (later in Czechoslovakia)

Primary Service:
Military/infantry

Primary Tactical Use:
Individual infantry

The MP43 is the world's original medium-caliber assault rifle. Actually in a transitional form, most collectors call it the "MP43/44" or "StG44" (Assault Rifle 1944) in less dicriminatory texts, which is more properly the title only of rifles so marked. The rifle was intended to provide good punch and accuracy out to 400 to 500 yards, with a close-in selective-fire capability roughly the equal of a submachine gun.

The curved-barrel device was one of several round-the-corner devices that seemed very mysterious when captured late in the war. However, German tank and assault gun manuals from the later part of the war refer to these as *Krummlaufer Winkelschusser* ("bent mover angle shooter," literally) or *Vorsatz* ("plan") units with various code letters. Though the German instructions are very elaborate, the actual use of the device was quite simple. The Hetzer, late IV/70, JagdPanzer, and other assault guns and tank destroyer vehicles had large, flat roof areas and several blind spots. These curved-barrel device fit through simple ball mounts to deal with close-in infantry that could not be directly observed or fired upon. The bent barrels were fairly efficient, well thought out, and the alternative to a much more expensive and elaborate additional turret. They did wear out very rapidly at the curve and the trajectory would deteriorate, but at the 10- to 25-yard ranges where they were primarily used, trajectory deviations were not of major concern. The devices did deform bullets, especially as they started to wear, but not as much as the more radical ninety-degree version.

These devices appear to have actually seen combat service in the East, where Soviet infantry was inclined to jump atop the vehicles and pour the jerry cans of gasoline from the topside wells down into the slots around the episcopes. It was seldom necessary to ignite the gasoline since the crews usually abandoned the vehicle as soon as they could. This is why some Soviet divisions were largely armed with German vehicles.

MP43 with curved-barrel device.

This compact, versatile rifle was the last of a series of rifles designed for the German 7.92x33mm *Kurz* ("short") reduced-power cartridge developed by Polte. As such, it is the most influential rifle of its era, for it inspired all medium-power rifles, including the Soviet AK series, HK93s, FN CALs, and even the less-powerful, shorter-ranged, more-expensive American AR-15/M16. All the features of this rifle—gas operation, gas piston above the barrel, clever and quick scope setup, large magazine capacity, straight-line stock, sheet-metal construction, and the industrial fabrication methods used to make it—have become standards for military weapons worldwide.

This weapon is also marked "MP44"; a slightly different version is the MP43, though it is functionally the same rifle as the StG44.

These rifles were quite effective, but they were not produced in sufficient quantities to make any difference in the war. They did see extensive use in Russia and in Belgium and Germany in late 1944, but they were the exclusive weapon of very few units.

These guns evolved and the ammunition was tested as the result of a competition between Walther's MKb42(W) and Haenel-Schmeisser's MKb42(H), the latter actually providing the basis for production guns.

The weapons shoot much better than they look. The ammo on the market as this book goes to press consists of some German ammo loaded in the fifties for the *Bundesgrenzschutz* (border police) and odd lots from Yugoslavia and Czechoslovakia. The ammo is steel-cased, reliable, and sells for about

Although the MP43/44 was not much lighter than the guns it replaced, its medium-sized round and low recoil allowed even 12 to 16 year olds to handle it with alacrity.

StG44

Name:
  StG44

Model:
  Assault rifle

StG44.

thirty-five cents a round in small lots. I tested some and got good accuracy. Back in the sixties, an MP44 "remil," ugly and green but fitted with the correct scope, proved quite capable of two-inch groups at 100 yards, much better than I expected.

There is some talk that many of these guns have been modified to semiautomatic operation and have found their way into the United States. Even if such was the case and a few million rounds of ammo followed them to the United States, the round would be difficult to promote. Someone could make serious money loading a lot of this ammo from trimmed 7.62 NATO brass. It is a decent, medium-game round. The ammo has been loaded in Spain, Belgium, Czechoslovakia, and elsewhere, and most of the prototype work-ups on the FAL and CETME were done using the 8mm Kurz (7.92x33mm) round.

MP28/II

Name:
Bergmann (revised model) submachine gun

Model:
MP28/II

Caliber:
9mm

Overall Length:
32 inches

Barrel Length:
7.8 inches

Weight:
8.8 pounds

Type of Fire:
Selective, semiauto or full auto

System of Operation:
Blowback

Cyclic Rate (approx.):
450–600 RPM

Feed System/Ammunition Delivery:
20-, 32-, or 50-round box magazine

Country of Manufacture:
Germany

Manufacturer:
Haenel

Countries of Use:
Various South American and European countries, including Germany and its allies

Period of Manufacture (approx.):
1927–mid 1930s (later in Spain)

Period of Service (approx.):
1928–1945

Primary Service:
Commercial sales in Europe and South America. Also used during Spanish Civil War.

Primary Tactical Use:
Individual

The original MP18/I was a hurry-up job, using a stock artillery Luger barrel and snail drum, but the mechanism was very sound. Most of the original guns still in Germany after World War I were converted to stick magazine loading in the 1920s by fitting a new magazine housing. The MP28/II came equipped this way, along with a simplified firing mechanism. It was also used to raise money for Germany by way of heavy export sales. It was produced in several loadings other than the standard 9mm Parabellum, and was copied in Spain, Belgium, and probably other countries as well. Haenel licensed the Belgians to produce the MP28/II, thereby avoiding the Versailles Treaty Commission, and the Belgians adopted the gun in 1934.

The Bergmann established a good reputation for reliability, and was used in the Spanish Civil War, the Gran Chaco wars, and all over Asia, Europe, and

MP28/II.

Latin America. The gun went out of production before World War II began, but the British were by then producing their own copy, the Lanchester.

M30 "BROOMHANDLE"

Name:
Schnellfeuer Mauser "Broomhandle"

Model:
M30 (M712)

Caliber:
7.63mmx25 Mauser (.30 Mauser)

Overall Length:
Pistol only: 12.25 inches
With stock: 25.5 inches

Barrel Length:
5.5 inches

Weight:
2.75 pounds
With stock: 3.93 pounds

Type of Fire:
Selective

System of Operation:
Recoil

Cyclic Rate (approx.):
700–800 + RPM

Feed System/Ammunition Delivery:
Clip/detachable 10-, 20-, 40-round box magazines

Country of Manufacture:
Germany

Manufacturer:
Mauser

Countries of Use:
China, Germany, Spain, Yugoslavia, some countries in Latin America, and others

Period of Manufacture (approx.):
1930–1938

Period of Service (approx.):
1930–? (Some are still in use by Latin American police units.)

Primary Service:
China in the 1930s

Primary Tactical Use:
Military sidearm/police

The original Mauser "Broomhandle" 1896 was never adopted by any nation as a first-line military weapon, yet it probably saw more use during World War I than a lot of weapons that were. Heavily promoted on the commercial market, the pistol was ex-

M30 "Broomhandle."

pensive, but it was seen just about everywhere, though seldom in great quantity. Winston Churchill carried one in the Boer War, and all versions sold well in the Far East and Latin America. They were commonly captured in just about every conflict— by all sides—after about 1905.

By the late 1920s, Astra and other companies had begun to cut into Mauser's market by underselling and introducing true machine pistols with detachable magazines. These proved very popular among police units, who found that the mere sound of machine-gun fire could disperse surly crowds of angry peasants. While Mauser's designers were initially cool to the idea, these were lean times in Europe, especially in Germany, and no market could be given up without a fight. Thus, the old design was beefed up a little bit—it was already far sturdier than most handguns—and the sear/disconnector redesigned to allow selective fire. The rate of fire was very high, owing to the light moving parts, and varied considerably according to ammunition power. Little could be hit after about the third shot in fully automatic fire, and keeping bursts short demanded a gentle touch of the trigger.

The M30 became quite popular with the SS and SA, members of which procured additional pistols after the Nazis came to power in 1933 and 1934. Yugoslavia, China, and other countries ordered considerable quantities, and quite a few of the pistols found their way to the Soviet Union before World War II.

The gun is far more usable with the shoulder stock, and it can be quite accurately used as a semiautomatic carbine. However, doing so makes the pistol much more cumbersome.

Incidentally, the .30 Mauser cartridge was quite potent and had superb penetration qualities. The Soviets used basically the same cartridge in their pistols and submachine guns, and liked it because of its flat trajectory. The .30 Mauser cartridge will penetrate more body armor than any current standard pistol cartridge, given comparable bullet composition.

MP35/1

Name:
Bergmann

Model:
MP35/1

Caliber:
9mm

Overall Length:
33 inches

Barrel Length:
7.8 inches

Weight:
9 pounds

Type of Fire:
Semiauto or full auto

System of Operation:
Blowback

Cyclic Rate (approx.):
650 RPM

Feed System/Ammunition Delivery:
24- or 32-round box magazine

Country of Manufacture:
Germany

Manufacturer:
Junker & Ruh

Countries of Use:
Germany

Period of Manufacture (approx.):
1933–1944

Period of Service (approx.):
1934–1945

Primary Service:
Waffen SS in World War II

Primary Tactical Use:
Individual infantryman

From prototypes developed by Schultz and Larsen in Otterup, Denmark, a submachine gun, the MP35/1, was introduced by 1934 that bridged the gap between the earlier Bergmann designs and the MP40 series. Adopted by and/or copied by several countries, it was made in a long-barreled version as well as the standard version.

Unlike the earlier Bergmann guns, the MP35/1 was actually designed by Theodor Emil Bergmann and his engineer, Muler, though it was first built in Germany by Walther and later by Junker and Ruh, exclusively for the SS.

Guns virtually identical to this one will be found marked "MP34," the company's original designation. Sweden marked its version as the M/39.

These well-made and strong guns feature an integral compensator and a quick-change barrel. They are also unique in that they feed from the right side.

One unusual feature of the MP35/1 is that it was cocked and activated just as one operates a Mauser turn-bolt rifle. Once secure, it was stationary when firing, and extraneous matter could enter only through the ejection port.

MPS1-100

Name:
Solothurn

Model:
MPS1-100 (Steyr-Solothurn)

Caliber:
9mm

Overall Length:
33.5 inches

Barrel Length:
7.8 inches

Weight:
8.6 pounds

Type of Fire:
Full auto

System of Operation:
Blowback

Cyclic Rate (approx.):
500 RPM

Feed System/Ammunition Delivery:
32-round box magazine

Country of Manufacture:
Switzerland and Austria

Manufacturer:
Steyr

Countries of Use:
Germany, Austria, Switzerland, Chile, El Salvador, Portugal, China, Japan, and others

Period of Manufacture (approx.):
1933–1940

Period of Service (approx.):
1933–1945 (perhaps later in some countries)

Primary Service:
World War II Germany

Primary Tactical Use:
Individual infantry

The Steyr-Solothurn MPS1-100 was a prewar German gun of exceptional quality.

Steyr-Solothurn MPS1-100.

The S1-100 Steyr-Solothurn was commonly encountered in three 9mm loadings and somewhat less commonly in 7.63mm Mauser and 7.65mm Parabellum. It was extensively exported and saw at least nominal service in most every war during its manufacturing life. The gun was produced in Switzerland and Austria and copied elsewhere; though utterly conventional, it was superbly well made.

The impetus behind the design was German, and the gun saw wartime service in German hands though it was never made in prewar Germany. Somewhat confusingly, this weapon may also be called the "MP34," its Austrian designation.

ERMA MACHINE PISTOL

Name:
Erma Machine Pistol

Model:
EMP

Caliber:
9mm

Overall Length:
35.5 inches

Barrel Length:
9.9 inches

Weight:
9.1 pounds

Type of Fire:
Selective

System of Operation:
Blowback

Cyclic Rate (approx.):
500 RPM

Feed System/Ammunition Delivery:
20- or 32-round box magazine

Country of Manufacture:
Germany

Manufacturer:
Erma

Countries of Use:
Germany, Bolivia, Yugoslavia, Paraguay, and Spain

ERMA MACHINE PISTOL (continued)

Period of Manufacture (approx.):
1931–1940

Period of Service (approx.):
1932–1945

Primary Service:
Military sales prior to World War II

Primary Tactical Use:
Individual

This is yet another central European gun that may be correctly labeled "MP34," though such a marking is rare on Erma EMPs and is only Erma's factory designation. Exported extensively, these guns were also copied in Spain.

The gun utilizes Vollmer patents, later used in the MP38/40 series, meaning that a telescoping metal tubular housing encloses and controls the mainspring and enters the bolt during operation.

This weapon is made from very high quality seamless steel tubing, and the early models show excellent machining and finishing. There were long-barreled variations, silenced guns, and some that took bayonets.

MP38

Name:
Schmeisser

Model:
MP38

Caliber:
9mm

Overall Length:
Stock extended: 32.8 inches
Stock folded: 24.75 inches

Barrel Length:
10 inches

Weight:
8.9 pounds

Type of Fire:
Full auto

System of Operation:
Blowback

Cyclic Rate (approx.):
500 RPM

Feed System/Ammunition Delivery:
32-round box magazine

Country of Manufacture:
Germany

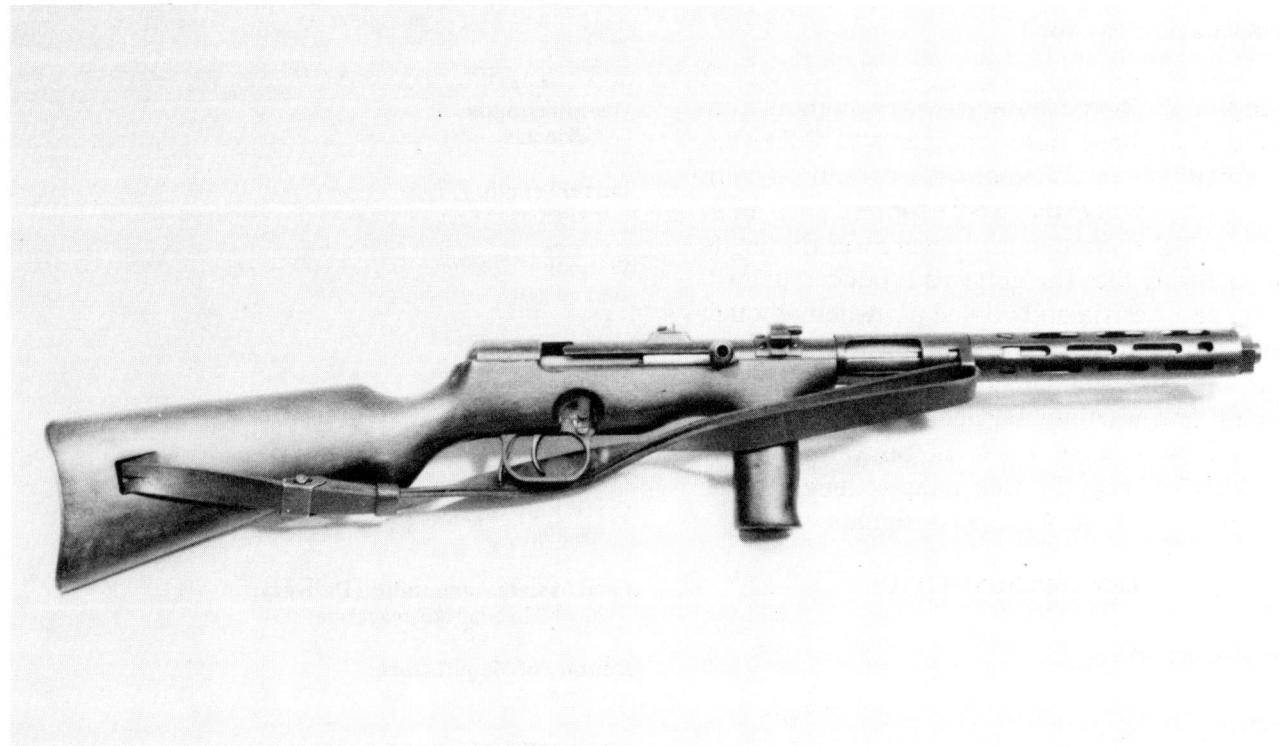

The Erma EMP was another finely made, expensive prewar German submachine gun. It was preferred by the SS.

Manufacturer:
Erma

Country of Use:
Germany

Period of Manufacture (approx.):
1937–1941

Period of Service (approx.):
1938–1945 (later in some countries)

Primary Service:
World War II Germany

Primary Tactical Use:
Individual infantryman

The MP38 was the first submachine gun ever constructed without any woodwork, and one of the first to use plastic extensively on noncritical parts, primarily the grip frame covering. Cheaper by far than its predecessors, the original MP38 was still more expensive than the Germans wished. They had envisioned the gun as a specialist's weapon for armored vehicle crews and paratroopers, but found out during the Spanish Civil War that small military units were much more effective when using such weapons.

The telescoping bolt/recoil spring assembly and quick field-stripping were important features of the design. Early models used a one-piece actuating handle; when dropped, it did not restrain the bolt. Apparently, there were some accidents with this gun since a two-piece handle that could lock the bolt assembly forward was adapted for subsequent versions and retrofitted to many MP38s. The folding stock was not entirely new, but was the first that was fitted to a major production gun.

Though the MP38 is commonly called a "Schmeisser," most scholars believe Hugo Schmeisser played little or no part in its development. His firm, however, by then called Haenel-Schmeisser, did manufacture a few MP38s and many of the later MP40s.

MP38/40

Name:
Schmeisser

Model:
MP38/40

Country of Manufacture:
Germany

Manufacturer:
Steyr

MP38.

This weapon, marked MP40, was the initial attempt to reduce the amount of time and money necessary to fabricate Germany's basic submachine gun during World War II. Spot welds, a higher proportion of stamped parts, and fewer fine finish points appear in this weapon. Its size and other characteristics are identical to those of the MP40.

Though Steyr simply marked them "MP," collectors usually call these guns MP38/40s because they use oddments of MP38 fittings and fixtures (usually the original bolt and actuating handle without the push safety). Haenel and Erma seem to have produced few, if any, of these mixed models. Parts, however, do have matching numbers.

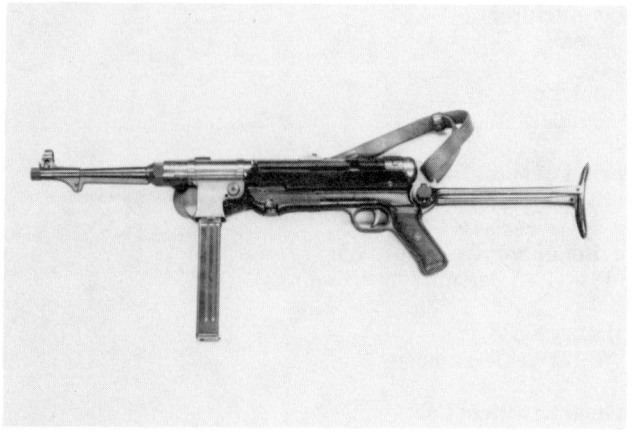

MP38/40.

MP40

Name:
Schmeisser

Model:
MP40

Manufacturer:
Steyr

Period of Manufacture (approx.):
1940–1945

For its period, the MP40 was the quintessential submachine gun. It was reasonably light and very compact. Very reliable, it was easily fixed, cleared, or cleaned if there was some malfunction. Heavily subcontracted by firms far away from the assembly points, the weapon offered true, 100 percent parts interchange without fitting. The magazines, though similar to those used in the Sten, gave no real difficulty. Such reliability and serviceability explain why this old veteran was still in first-line use in Austria and some Eastern European countries until

Firing the MP38/40.

Marty Mandall firing an MP40.

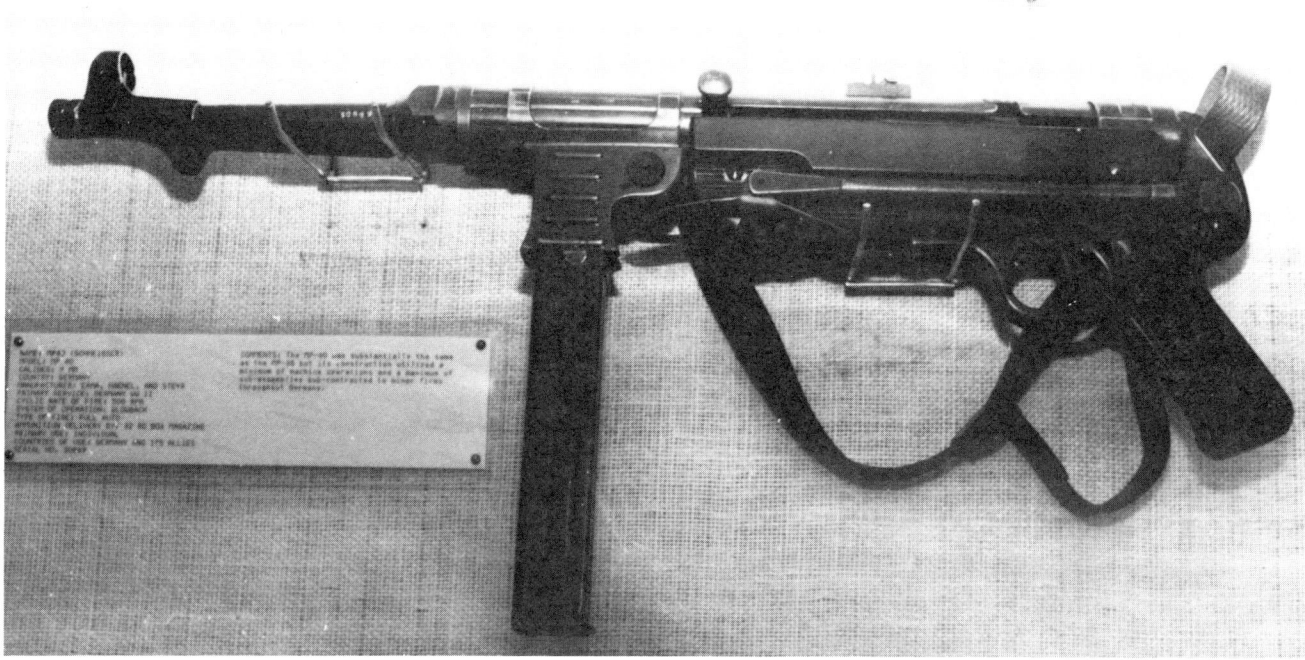

The MP40 was the original "cheapy" submachine gun, having many stamped or welded parts in its fabrication. It was, however, much more reliable than the later Sten.

very recently, and is still in reserve throughout much of Central Europe.

There were several minor variations in magazine housings, including one that allowed a spare magazine to actually be carried next to the one in use. There were several patterns of relief cuts/positive "corrugations," but the basic weapon remained the same. It was often used by Allied and Soviet troops in preference to their own weapons.

MP41

Name:
Schmeisser

Model:
MP41 (selective-fire, wooden-stocked derivative of the MP40)

Type of Fire:
Selective

Country of Manufacture:
Germany

Manufacturer:
Haenel-Schmeisser, Suhl

Period of Manufacture (approx.):
1941–1945

Period of Service (approx.):
1941–1945

Why Germany took the trouble and time to produce this splendid, commercial weapon in the middle of a war is anyone's guess. It is basically a reversion to the construction techniques of the pre–World War I period, complete with wooden stock. Every part shows detail finishing that is fully the equal of German custom gunsmiths of the 1920s. The weapon bears full, uncoded commercial markings, yet the basic workings are strictly MP40 style.

Alone among MP40/MP38 variants, this weapon may accurately be called a Schmeisser since it is so marked and was made by Haenel-Schmeisser. Some scholars believe that Hugo Schmeisser was behind Erma's MP40 prototypes, and cite these guns and their markings as evidence.

The wooden stock probably aided stability and therefore accuracy, but it also added twenty-four ounces to the weapon's weight. It also meant the gun could not be collapsed.

More rare than the MP41 are correctly marked magazines, one of which is in this specimen's magazine well.

Many stamped parts similar to and in some cases identical to MP40 units are employed. Great care was taken in polishing and finishing even these prosaic components. The wooden stock and fire-selector mechanism are similar to those used in the MP28/II.

The MP41 is the only German MP38/40 variant properly called a Schmeisser by even the most pedantic collector because it is marked as such. It is a mystery why the Germans waited so long to make this superb, commercial submachine gun. This one was found in Adolf Hitler's headquarters.

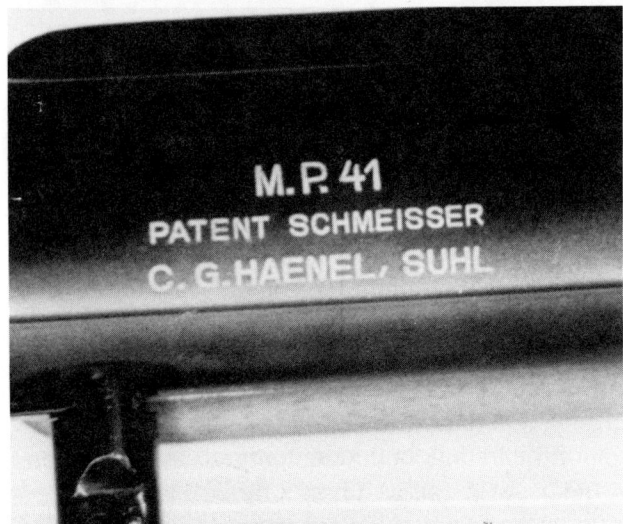

The Schmeisser marking on the MP41.

MG15

Name:
Ground-mount light machine gun

Model:
1944–1945 MG15

Caliber:
7.92x57JS

Overall Length:
54.7 inches

Barrel Length:
29.7 inches

Weight:
33.4 pounds

Type of Fire:
Full automatic

System of Operation:
Recoil/gas boosted

Cyclic Rate (approx.):
750+ RPM

Feed System/Ammunition Delivery:
75-round saddle drum magazine

Country of Manufacture:
Germany

Manufacturer:
Kreighoff

Countries of Use:
Germany

Period of Manufacture (approx.):
1944–1945 as ground gun (rebuilds)

Period of Service (approx.):
1944–1945

Primary Service:
Aircraft, primarily flexible mount/converted to ground applications

Primary Tactical Use:
Infantry personnel

When the Luftwaffe almost entirely disbanded its bomber command or changed remaining multiple-seat aircraft to heavier guns or the even-faster MG81, many available MG15s were without employment. Fitted with basic sights, a primitive buttstock, and a bipod, sometimes with a "new" cooling grille, these awkward weapons were provided to German ground personnel, primarily the *Volksturm Wehrmacht* ("People's Assault Army," actually

MG15.

Home Guard units). Though poorly balanced and very awkward to carry, they were reliable.

The original MG15 was developed from Solothurn prototypes designed by Louis Stange. Rheinmetall further developed the system as a specialized aircraft gun, which entered service between 1932 and 1934.

MG17

Name:
German aircraft machine gun

Model:
MG17

Caliber:
7.92mm

Overall Length:
48.2 inches

Barrel Length:
29.7 inches

Weight:
27.8 pounds

Type of Fire:
Full auto only

System of Operation:
Recoil

Cyclic Rate (approx.):
Synchronized: 1,000 RPM
Unsynchronized: 1,100 RPM

Feed System/Ammunition Delivery:
Continuous steel link belt

Country of Manufacture:
Nazi Germany

Manufacturer:
Kolbach & Company, Maschinen-fabrik, Leipzig W33

Countries of Use:
Germany

Primary Service:
Military aircraft

Primary Tactical Use:
Aircraft fixed mounting

The MG17 is basically a remote-controlled, rear-seared version of the MG15 intended for installation in fighters and attack aircraft. The gun deleted the open-bolt feature; in the interest of rapid operation, it fired from the closed bolt. Cook-off was not considered a problem in aircraft installations on the presumption that they were less dangerous and that airflow from forward speed would cool the bolt face, barrel, and ammunition. The gun was modified to remote charging and firing, which worked by compressed air in the case of charging. Triggering could be electrical solenoid or mechanical, though the latter was seldom used.

MG81

Name:
German aircraft machine gun

Model:
MG81

Caliber:
7.92mm

Overall Length:
39 inches

MG81 (continued)

Barrel Length:
25 inches

Weight:
13.75 pounds

Type of Fire:
Full auto

System of Operation:
Recoil

Cyclic Rate (approx.):
1,200–1,500 RPM

Feed System/Ammunition Delivery:
Disintegrating steel link belt

Country of Manufacture:
Nazi Germany

Manufacturer:
NordDeutsche Maschinenfabrik, Berlin

Countries of Use:
Germany

Period of Manufacture (approx.):
1939–1945

Period of Service (approx.):
1939–1945

Primary Service:
Military aircraft flexible machine gun

Primary Tactical Use:
Defensive aircraft armament

This extremely compact, handy gun was put into production at Mauser and elsewhere in 1939. Used in remote and manned mounts, its bolt mechanism was that of the MG34. A more efficient muzzle booster and abnormally strong buffer spring helped boost the rate. No flash hider was fitted, which is especially odd since the flash effect from firing this gun at night not only gives away the firer's position, but it tends to temporarily blind him. A disintegrating belt was used instead of the usual saddle drum or nondisintegrating MG34 belt.

While the gun was mounted in most German bombers until about 1942 in this form or the "Z" (twin) form, it was replaced by heavier caliber guns in most combat aircraft by 1942. It was then relegated to the rear pits of observation, air/sea rescue, and ancillary aircraft.

MG81Z

Name:
German dual aircraft machine gun

Model:
MG81Z

Caliber:
7.92mm

Overall Length:
39.2 inches

Barrel Length:
27.6 inches

MG17.

Weight:
31 pounds

Type of Fire:
Full auto only

System of Operation:
Recoil

Cyclic Rate (approx.):
2,400–3,000 RPM

Feed System/Ammunition Delivery:
Disintegrating steel belt

Country of Manufacture:
Nazi Germany

Manufacturer:
Mauser

Countries of Use:
Nazi Germany

Period of Service (approx.):
1939–1945

Primary Tactical Use:
Defensive antiaircraft, free or swivel machine gun

MG81Z.

MG81Z.

Known as the "MG81Z," this gun is the usual double mounting of the MG81, the suffix letter denoting *zwilling,* or "twin." These coupled guns are capable of delivering about the same firepower as the much-heavier 7.62mm electric, multiple-barreled mini-guns now in use in U.S. aircraft designed for strafing. Like the single gun, it retained the bolt mechanism and similar quick-change barrel capability it inherited from the ground MG34. These guns could all accept remote triggers for the rear-firing and other optically sighted remote turret and barbette installations the Germans used on their bombers and sometimes on their heavy fighters. However, the gun was still rifle caliber. By 1942, the Germans were using heavier defensive armament on their aircraft wherever possible.

MG34

Name:
MG34

Caliber:
7.92mm

Overall Length:
48 inches

Barrel Length:
24.75 inches

Gross Weight:
26.7 pounds

Weight:
42.5 pounds

Type of Fire:
Selective and full auto

System of Operation:
Short recoil

Cyclic Rate (approx.):
800–900 RPM

Feed System/Ammunition Delivery:
Metal-linked belt or saddle drum

Country of Manufacture:
Germany

Manufacturer:
Gustloff Werke (Suhl)

Countries of Use:
Germany

Period of Manufacture (approx.):
1933–1945 (Guns were refitted, refurbished, and perhaps built new in Czechoslovakia and Israel well into the 1950s.)

MG34 (continued)

Period of Service (approx.):
1934–1945 (First introduced in quantity in 1936, the guns are still in service in some areas outside Europe.)

Primary Service:
World War II Germany

Primary Tactical Use:
Multipurpose

Though the Germans retained some Maxims over and above what was technically allocated them by the Allied Truce Commission after World War I, it was their intention after 1919 to alter completely the whole business of war. The tank and dive bomber, essential elements in the blitzkriegs of 1939 to 1941, were only the most visible components of this radical change in approach. Everything had to be more mobile and more generic; there could be no logistic nightmares and, most of all, no war of attrition like the last war. The general-purpose machine gun was part of this evolving plan.

Based on a series of patents by Louis Stange, Scotti, and others and a huge body of prototypical and even some production work at Solothurn, Bofors, Rheinmetall, and other companies, Mauser developed the world's first general-purpose machine gun. Had the war gone the way the Germans wished, the MG34 would have been the only German machine gun encountered in the field. The war very decidedly did not go the way they planned, and so as early as 1940 the Germans were already experiencing some local shortages of machine guns. Part of the problem was the MG34's design, which was very good but was also very labor-intensive to produce.

The Germans put great effort into the MG34 because they considered the machine gun to be the core of every infantry unit. By contrast, the "new" rifle adopted between 1934 and 1935 was a shorten-

MG34.

Firing an MG34.

ed rehash of the World War I version. The Germans viewed the rifle as support and therefore a tactically subordinate weapon. When they finally realized a broader overall increase in firepower could be even more productive, it was far too late to reequip a by-then much larger army.

The partial combination of gas and recoil operation was nothing new. It was the application that was unique. Gas mechanism boosters were designed by Hiram Maxim as early as 1900 and were used in most Maxim and Vickers guns during World War I. The MG34's booster was more efficient. The muzzle cone tapped high-velocity gases in its cup and gave the barrel a healthy push on its way back. At the end of its very short stroke, the relatively light bolt rotated through 90 degrees to unlock. Continuing after the barrel stopped, the bolt was spring rebounded and returned, and it reinitiated action by picking up a new round from the belt.

The quick-change barrel, easy stripping, and sensible use of new polymers were other small, but significant, innovations. Upper pressure on the trigger yielded semiautomatic fire, the lower detent being fully automatic. The elaborate but extremely versatile tripod was devised to facilitate the gun's many roles. It is worth noting that the tripods are even more rare than the guns, selling for roughly the same price as the guns—sometimes even

more—on the collector's market.

As the war dragged on, the MG34 was changed and several variants were developed, some of which were not selective fire. The Czechs produced and/or refurbished and resold the guns after the war. They sold much of their equipment for manufacture and inventory of parts and guns to the Israelis, who either made or assembled considerable numbers of the MG34 as late as the 1950s. The MG34 was a lot of work to make and was in some ways an intricate design. It was also a tightly fitted gun, resulting in jams when the gun got fouled or foreign matter was introduced.

Regarded as a superb weapon, the MG34 tends to show up all over the world. Recently, quite a number were seized in Lebanon, and considerable numbers have found their way to Latin America.

MG34 VEHICULAR

Name:
Vehicular general purpose machine gun

Model:
MG34

Weight:
27 pounds

Manufacturer:
BSW (Berlin Shuler Waffen)

Vehicular version of the MG34.

A true general-purpose machine gun, the MG34 was produced in several vehicular versions, the one shown here being the closest to the base gun. A heavier, unventilated jacket was fitted; some authorities say a heavier barrel was also fitted since airflow was not good in tanks and the barrel had to serve as its own heat sink. There were also shorter versions of the MG34 for vehicles and some with different detail furniture.

Vehicular versions of the MG34 stayed in production in numbers long after the gun had been replaced by MG42 for other purposes. Using the MG42 in all vehicles would have demanded changing a lot of mountings around on tanks, assault guns, tank-hunting vehicles, and other weapons. Also, the

MG34's cross section is slightly narrower than that of the MG42, and every fraction of an inch is important in vehicles that are basically large, movable iron boxes.

MG34 ANTIAIRCRAFT

Name:
Antiaircraft general purpose machine gun

Model:
MG34

Manufacturer:
BSW (Waffen Berlin Shuler)

Whereas the Americans and the British used complete mounts with cradles and bearings and geared elevators for infantry antiaircraft use of conventional machine guns, the German mount was a simple tubing device by which a gun was secured with a single bolt. Sights were more specialized. Both approaches have virtue. For some other applications, the Germans used more complex mounts, even the *Dreifuss* 34/42, in the same role. Spare ammo boxes were often hung on the adjustment levers.

The MG34's high rate of fire made it handy in the antiaircraft role, more so than many Allied guns.

Antiaircraft version of the MG34.

MG42/MG1

Name:
MG42/MG1

Caliber:
7.62mm NATO

Overall Length:
48 inches

Barrel Length:
21 inches

Weight:
25.5 pounds

Type of Fire:
Full auto only

System of Operation:
Short recoil

Cyclic Rate (approx.):
750–1,350 RPM (depending on modifications)

Feed System/Ammunition Delivery:
Metal-linked belt

Country of Manufacture:
West Germany

Manufacturer:
Maget Maschinen und Geratebau, Berlin

Countries of Use:
West Germany

Period of Manufacture (approx.):
1941–present

Period of Service (approx.):
1942–present

Primary Service:
Germany's current machine gun

Primary Tactical Use:
Multipurpose

The MG42 contains much that is revolutionary and much that is evolutionary. It is truly unique in one way: its designer knew very little about guns in general and almost nothing about machine guns. Dr. Grunow was a well-known industrial designer and a true genius of mass production. With Mauser and Rheinmetall engineers at his elbow, he concocted the ingenious MG42 so that it could be produced rapidly, cheaply, and *well* at minimal cost in time and money. That the gun is still in production almost fifty years after its birth, is used by foreigners who have to pay for it in hard cash, and has been copied by other countries attests to the fact that

such a radical design technique not only can work, but can work splendidly. The gun embodies everything good in the MG34 in a package that uses metal stampings, rivets, spot welding, brazing, and, often, rough-looking parts.

Instead of the rotating bolt with interrupted head locked into the barrel extension, as on the MG34, Edward Stecke's locking system is used directly. The bolt head carries two small rollers that are held close to the bolt until ready to lock; they are then forced outward into the grooves of the barrel extension. The firing pin cannot move forward between their bases until they are fully in their grooves, thus assuring bolt locking at the instant of ignition. Upon initiation of recoil, the rollers ride in a cam path that forces them inward, out of their detents, unlocking the bolt and continuing the firing cycle. This system allows considerable clearance for fouling and dirt, even acting in a self-cleaning manner.

Close up, the MG42 may look like junk, but the wartime guns only looked crude (postwar commercial guns are somewhat better polished and cleaned up). No soldier who encountered this weapon could ever forget it; it sounded like tearing canvas. At about 1,000 rounds per minute, the brain can no longer distinguish individual rounds, and this gun typically delivers 1,200 rounds per minute. The gun remembered by World War II veterans as "Hitler's Saw" was intended to be terrifying, and gunners were taught to use long bursts even in the light role, even if accuracy suffered and the barrel deteriorated. The barrel change method was adapted from the Italian Breda light guns and was faster and more efficient than anything that has come along since.

The MG42 so impressed American troops that opposed it that a very serious effort was directed toward cloning the gun for immediate adoption by U.S. armed forces. This attitude was in sharp contrast to the public, sneering assessment of the gun by a successful American general, who said the gun's roughness showed "the desperation to which the Germans have sunk in producing weapons of such inferior quality." The Saginaw Steering Gear Division of General Motors started on the project in June 1943 once it had specimens from which to work and was test-firing guns by October. The project failed miserably, however, since the engineers assigned to the task failed to make sufficient adjustment in the machine gun's mechanism for the much longer (5 to 8mm) U.S. .30-06 cartridge. The copy was called the "Machine Gun Cal. .30 T24." Though

This World War II vintage MG42 was updated to handle the 7.62x51mm NATO cartridge, probably for German military use in the 1950s. The optical sight and Lafette 34 ground carriage are World War II items. The Germans and much of the rest of the world still use the MG42, and many consider it the finest general-purpose machine gun ever designed. In the background is a World War I vintage Maxim.

MG42/MG1.

it was the first effort to copy the gun, it would not be the last.

The Swiss copied the gun in several variants. Since they disliked the cheap look of the German original, they used expensive and elaborate solid forged parts in place of sheet metal and stampings. By so doing, they defeated the entire purpose of this general-purpose machine gun—to produce a gun that looks like the MG42, probably works just as well, but weighs about thirty-six pounds. Germany was making guns in Yugoslavia toward the end of the war, and the Yugoslavs "inherited" the machinery by killing the German supervisors and taking over the factory. They were making guns and killing Germans with them before the war was over, and the gun reentered production there in its original form in 1953 as the M53 SARAC, still available on the international military export market. The Italians use and produce a version of MG42, though many of their current guns are of German manufacture. Austria, Norway, Denmark, Iran, Pakistan, and several other countries have adopted the gun as standard. The U.S. M60 was inspired by the MG42.

As a footnote, it takes perhaps one minute to convert a World War II MG42 in 7.92mm to the current 7.62x51mm NATO round.

MG42 LIGHT

Name:
General purpose machine gun

Model:
MG42

Manufacturer:
Steyr

Though the MG42 could pump out more than twice the amount of bullets pumped from standard Allied heavy machine guns and almost three times the rounds dispensed from the light machine guns and automatic rifles of the Western Allies, it weighed only a little more than the Bren. It was therefore highly portable. The German rifle support, lacking the firepower and fluidity of the British infantry units, was far inferior to its American equivalent—though this was to change later with some units. Therefore, it was very important that the German automatic base of fire be mobile and shoot fast.

Shown is a bipod-mounted MG42 in its original World War II caliber and light machine gun configuration.

MG42.

Firing the MG42.

MG42/59

Name:
German general purpose machine gun

Model:
MG42/59

Manufacturer:
Rheinmetall

More than 200,000 postwar MG42s have been produced by Rheinmetall since World War II, and shown here is one of the very earliest ones. Produced in 1958, before export/commercial production officially began, it was made mostly of wartime parts. The MG42 never went out of use in the postwar period, as the *Bundesgrenzschutz* (border police) in Germany and many other European units continued to use the wartime guns, many of which are still in issue today.

The German-issue guns are called the MG1/MG3, depending on the fittings used, but they are basically the same as the wartime guns. Use of the heavy (V950) bolt and modified R or R2 buffer can greatly reduce the cyclic rate, and some nations (notably Italy) use this setup on light guns, retaining the regular setup for vehicular guns and some other infantry applications. Some other variations still in service are the MG1A1, a wartime gun converted to a chrome-lined 7.62mm NATO barrel and appropriate sight with modified trigger; MG1A2, which has a modified ejection port, slightly different receiver, heavy bolt/buffer kit, and a modified bearing and recoil booster to slow cyclic rate, standard for light gun uses in Italy; the MG1A3, set up to accept U.S. or German-style belts; and the MG3, a new gun that is similar to the MG1A3. There are also buttless vehicle guns, sightless guns for multiple mounts, and others.

The MG42 has even been copied in a miniaturized version in Spain as the *Ametalladora ligera Ameli,* from the same CETME research and production facility that produced the Spanish service rifle. The same firm also produces the full-size MG42 at Oviedo, for this forty-plus-year-old design is still the general-purpose machine gun against which all

MG42/59.

MG42/59.

Postwar MG42 guns, like this MG42/59, were made mostly from wartime parts.

others must be compared; it is the standard machine gun of the Spanish services. The little CETME-*Ameli* in 5.56mm (.223) may soon become the reduced-caliber squad automatic weapon for much of the Iberian peninsula.

WALTHER MPK

Name:
Walther MPK

Model:
1963

Caliber:
9mm

Overall Length:
Stock extended: 26 inches
Stock folded: 15.01 inches

Barrel Length:
6.78 inches

Weight:
6.25 pounds

Type of Fire:
Selective

System of Operation:
Blowback

Cyclic Rate (approx.):
550 RPM

Feed System/Ammunition Delivery:
32-round box magazine

Country of Manufacture:
West Germany

Manufacturer:
Walther

Countries of Use:
Germany, other countries

Period of Manufacture (approx.):
1965–present

Period of Service (approx.):
1965–present

Primary Tactical Use:
SWAT and antiterrorist units

The Walther MPK is a blowback weapon that uses steel stampings for most of its basic structure. The bolt is overhung, the bulk of which is above the axis of the barrel and overlaps the breech in its closed position.

There is also a longer version, sold in much of the world as a semiautomatic carbine.

These guns are used by many SWAT and antiterrorist units.

Walther MPK.

H&K G3

Name:
H&K *Gewehr* (rifle)

Model:
G3 (commercial versions sold as the H&K 91)

Caliber:
7.62mm NATO

Overall Length:
40.2 inches

Barrel Length:
17.7 inches

Weight:
With bipod, scope: 11 pounds (more with heavy bipod)
Without bipod: 9.9 pounds

Type of Fire:
Selective

System of Operation:
Blowback, roller-delayed

Cyclic Rate (approx.):
550 RPM

Feed System/Ammunition Delivery:
20-round box magazine

Country of Manufacture:
Germany

Manufacturer:
Heckler & Koch

Countries of Use:
Germany, many others

Period of Manufacture (approx.):
1958–present

Period of Service (approx.):
1959–present

Primary Service:
Used by 45 nations currently

Primary Tactical Use:
Assault rifle

H&K G3.

Shown here with its Hensholdt scope, the Heckler & Koch G3 replaced the FN FAL (G1) in German service starting around 1959. It has since been adopted by forty-five countries, becoming one of the most popular rifles in the Western world.

Its arrival in Germany and on world markets was via an unusual route. The Gerat 06, or StG45, a Mauser design, was transplanted to Spain, along with most of its designers. This piece was supposed to be a replacement for the MP44 series, but it worked via delayed blowback, using a unique delay system of locking rollers seated in a locking piece attached to the barrel. The prototypes were all in the German 7.92x33mm Kurz loading. A fluted chamber allowed gas wash to boost primary extraction, but it also etched a distinctive pattern onto the brass. This prototype evolved in Spain into a rifle named after the ordnance research and design establishment, the CETME (Centro de Estudios Tecnicos de Materiales Especiales). This was a 7.62mm weapon that could fire either the reduced-charge Spanish load or full-power NATO ammunition once a simple adjustment of the mechanism was made. This weapon, transplanted to Germany, the original home of the system, became the selective-fire G3.

The G3 is far cheaper than the G1 (FAL), but most shooters prefer the Belgian-designed rifle since the G3 is rather severe in full-automatic fire.

The G3 uses an actuating level—which does not cycle with the action—that is well forward on the barrel's left. Another new twist is the rotating drum sight; it is not terribly precise, but it is very rugged and fast to use.

Heckler & Koch has wisely expanded the G3/HK-91 system to include machine guns, submachine guns, .223 and 7.62x39mm weapons, and other specialized units, all of which have at least partial commonality of parts and similarity in layout to the original weapon. This simplifies training and logistics.

The rifle is quite accurate. However, recoil is rather disturbing to this accuracy. The HK21, a light machine-gun version, is belt-fed; substantially similar, it is, however, designed for a reduced caliber loading.

The United States Springfield Armory firm in Geneseo, Illinois, produces a copy of the original, and its Rock Island affiliate converts these to fully automatic applications for law enforcement.

H&Ks, designed around steel-cased ammo, are hard on brass.

HK-54/MP5

Name:
H&K submachine gun

Model:
HK-54 or MP5

Caliber:
9x19mm Parabellum (Some police guns in Europe are in 7.65mm Parabellum.)

Overall Length:
Fixed stock or retractable stock extended: 26 inches
Folded stock: 19.3 inches

Barrel Length:
8.85 inches

Weight:
5.5 pounds (approx.)

Type of Fire:
Selective fire

System of Operation:
Delayed blowback

Cyclic Rate (approx.):
600 RPM

Feed System/Ammunition Delivery:
30-, 32-, and 40-round magazines

Country of Manufacture:
West Germany

Manufacturer:
Heckler & Koch

Countries of Use:
Germany, small quantities elsewhere

Period of Manufacture (approx.):
1968–present

Period of Service (approx.):
1968–present

Primary Service:
Border guard and police

Primary Tactical Use:
Local and area defense, close-in fighting and police applications

This gun has been used by the West German *Bundesgrenzschutz* and by police all over Europe. It fires from the closed bolt and is quite accurate. Used with subsonic ammo, the AWC or H&K suppressors are quite effective, and the gun loses no accuracy.

Many parts of the KH-54/MP5 are common to the G3 service rifle.

HK-54.

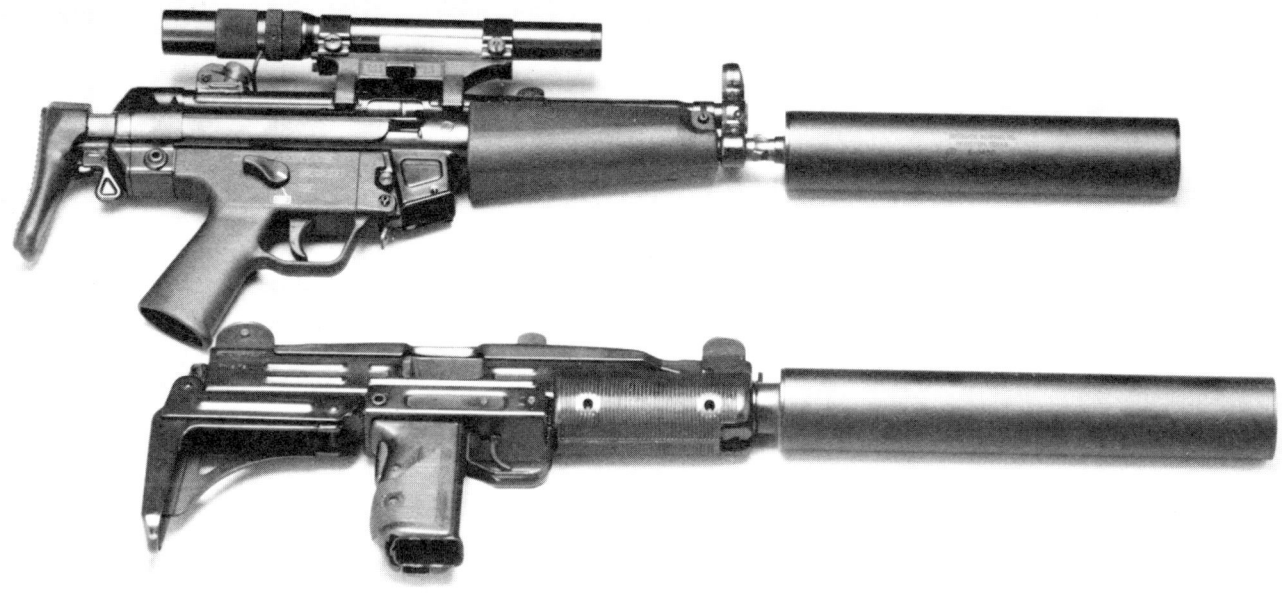

An HK-54 (top) with folding stock, suppressor, and scope, compared with a suppressed Uzi. (Photo courtesy of AWC Systems Technology.)

CHAPTER 13

Great Britain

The Vickers was designed by the world's largest armaments firm at the suggestion of the British Army, which wanted something lighter than the classic Maxims with which they were equipped. The toggle was inverted, careful use of materials and metallurgy mapped out with great attention to engineering detail, and the depth of the receiver trimmed. And thus a legend was born.

The Vickers was incredibly reliable. The .303 cartridge causes no particular problem with extraction or feed from the belt. There exists an intimidating list of stoppage causes, but most of them come down to headspace and ammunition problems.

Some stories about the Vickers are just plain hogwash. Writers who've never tried it tell us that tea was brewed in the jacket. Most Vickers guns used bronze or brass and sometimes aluminum tubing, and if you close the system to make tea, the "tea" would be toxic and taste terrible. I know. I tried it. There was so much metallic junk in the "tea" thus concocted that it stained the cup black on contact. We then cleaned the jacket out with lye, flushed and rinsed it repeatedly, and made a type of still dripping over filter paper off the condensate. This was palatable, though I didn't drink it. Don't try using urine to cool the gun either (another popular legend), as this can cause terrible corrosion in the gun.

VICKERS MARK I

Name:
Vickers

Model:
Mark I

Caliber:
.303

Other Chamberings:
7mm and .303 were by far the most common.

Overall Length:
45.6 inches

Barrel Length:
28.5 inches

Weight:
33 pounds (41 pounds with water)

Type of Fire:
Automatic

System of Operation:
Short recoil (gas boosted)

Cyclic Rate (approx.):
450+ RPM

Feed System/Ammunition Delivery:
Fabric belt (some were modified to use a link belt)

Country of Manufacture:
Great Britain

Manufacturer:
Vickers, Colt, Herstal, and some subcontractors

Countries of Use:
British Commonwealth, U.S., Belgium, and many others worldwide

Period of Manufacture (approx.):
1912–1945

Period of Service (approx.):
1912–1968 (still in service in some countries)

Primary Tactical Use:
Fixed fire base

Vickers Mark I.

Detail of the Vickers Mark I.

There were seven major models of Vickers, all of which used the same receiver, but the Mark I was the infantry gun. The guns were sometimes modified with feed mechanisms from other models so as to use different belts or for other, specialized applications, but such modifications are exceptionally rare today. British tank units, which employed the 8mm Besa, sometimes also had 8mm (7.92 × 57JS) Vickers guns, and the Long Range Desert Group owned quite a number of Belgian Vickers guns and ancient British Maxims in the same caliber. This also allowed the use of captured German ammo. No special designation was applied to these guns, though much distinguishing marking was applied to keep the overzealous soldier from trying to cram .303 into these units.

LEWIS LIGHT MACHINE GUN

Name:
  Lewis light machine gun

Model:
  1914

Caliber:
  .303 British

Other Chamberings:
  7mm, .30-06, and various others in limited quantities

Overall Length:
  50.5 inches

Barrel Length:
  26 inches

Weight:
  27 pounds

Type of Fire:
  Automatic

System of Operation:
  Gas

Cyclic Rate (approx.):
  450 to 550 RPM

Feed System/Ammunition Delivery:
  47-round drum (a 97-round unit was also available)

Country of Manufacture:
  Great Britain (the same gun was made in Belgium and the U.S.)

Manufacturer:
  BSA

Countries of Use:
  Belgium, Great Britain, France, and many others

Period of Manufacture (approx.):
  1914–1918

Period of Service (approx.):
  1912–1945

Primary Tactical Use:
  Individual infantry mobile light machine gun and antiaircraft

Though an American design, the Lewis saw very little U.S. use in World War I.

Produced and readily accepted in Great Britain and Belgium, the Lewis was controversial in the United States. Isaac N. Lewis derived the weapon from a design by Lissak and McClean, and basically simplified the hopelessly overdesigned original. The first prototypes were set up for both air and water cooling, and used complex mounts with arrays of attachments and adjustments. The first job Lewis was to undertake was to eliminate the extraneous. Along the way, Lewis, a former Ordnance Board member, apparently offended or embittered General William Crozier of the U.S. Army Ordnance Board; Crozier was determined to block the use of

British infantry in 1917 deploying a Lewis against a German attack.

Detail of the Lewis light machine gun.

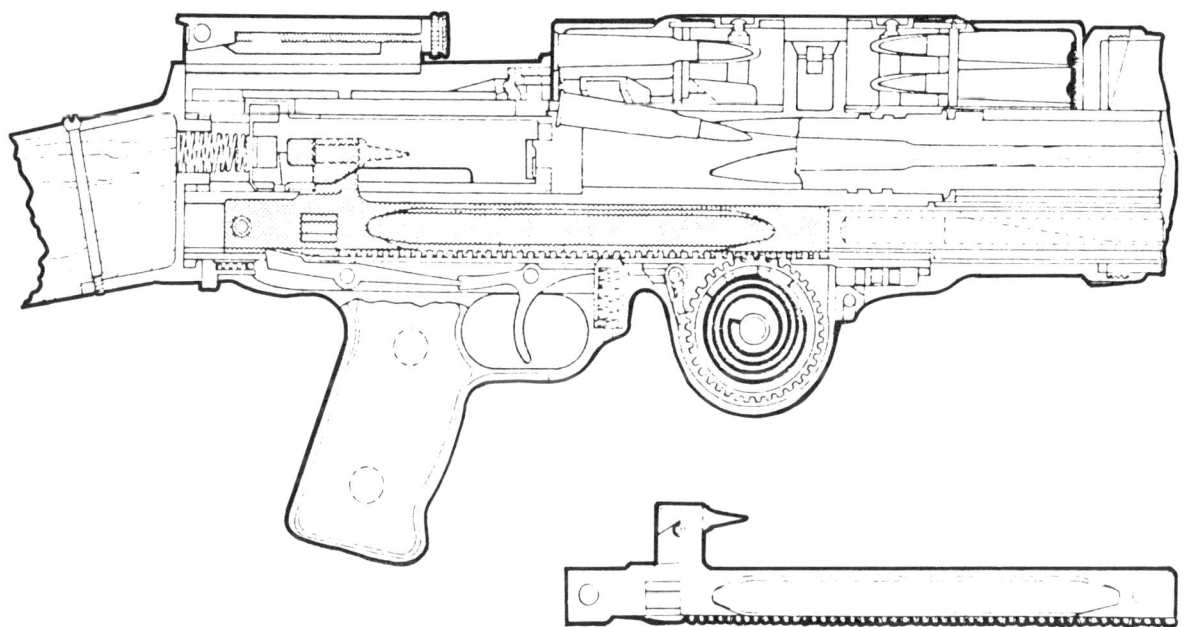

Internal mechanism of a typical Lewis light machine gun.

the Lewis by U.S. Army personnel.

Chinn suggests that, as late as 1917, the Ordnance Board was testing an old series Lewis with excessive rate of fire and insufficient "dwell"—the null point after gas tap before the bolt actually is activated. Others suggest that Savage, which made the U.S. Lewis, had some difficulty with converting it to the rimless .30-06 cartridge. This is unlikely, since the eldest Lewis guns, the Buffalo Automatic Arms guns, were made in that chambering as far back as the June 7, 1912, test in which the Lewis gun became the first machine gun discharged from an airplane. It probably didn't delight General Crozier, incidentally, that Lewis had not bothered to get authorization for such use of army aircraft and personnel.

Lewis was only a retired colonel, and his promotions probably angered army staff.

The Belgian license to produce the Lewis guns automatically became void, of course, when the Germans overran the country, but the plans and most jigs and tools were spirited to England. Savage also produced Lewis Guns for the British. The Germans liked the gun, used all they could capture, and were still copying features of the gun as late as 1942. The French firm, Darne, and the government factory system, especially at St. Etienne, produced Lewis guns, primarily aircraft models, for supply to all fronts.

Originally assigned at a rate of two guns per battalion, the Lewis was reallocated at four guns per battalion in 1915. The original view that the Lewis was somehow second-rate and a good substitute only for a few riflemen changed rather quickly when senior officers noted the mobility of the Machine Gun Corps personnel, who could be in position and suppressing enemy movement without the need for helpers and crew before the Vickers could even be readied for movement. Obviously, its air-cooling system of radial fins inside the tubular jacket could not maintain the rate of fire of the Vickers. However, two or three guns working together could disrupt an offensive or provide cover for one with far greater mobility than the Vickers. The gun also had much better concealment potential and nearly the same tactical command without the need for extensive crew or water.

Armchair historians have always viewed the drum magazine as suspect. However, when not terribly damaged, the magazines work quite well. These drums are quite unlike the clock-spring-wound devices used in submachine guns. They are, in fact, cut-out pans in layers, two in the usual infantry magazine, controlled by two stop pawls. Located on the gun, the pawls determine the exact spacing. A rack on the lower piston engages a pinion, winding a clock spring that initiated the drive, thus reversing the backward movement to a forward stroke and chambering and firing the round. The bolt is of a rotating type with lugs dovetailed into recesses in the barrel extension. The Lewis was and is an elegant device, and it never got below the $600 procurement price at a time when a car could be had for $500. The schematic here gives some idea of the detailed machining necessary on the internals and their intricate interaction.

The term *intricate,* however, does not imply that the gun was delicate. Hardening specifications for the bolt assembly alone required selective, local treatment, and the gear/pinion teeth had to be precise in their interface. Once the gun was built, there were fairly large numbers of technical reasons for malfunctions, mostly ammunition-related, nearly none of which were encountered in the field. Kept in good condition, properly lubricated, and used with quality ammunition, with only perhaps a couple of springs and a spare barrel or two, Lewis guns can last a very long time. Many have seen thirty years of nearly continuous use.

The Lewis is more accurate than most modern GP/light machine guns given a good barrel. Because the gun is inherently muzzle heavy, it is rather easy to handle and swing. The bipod designed for the

Lewis is the best of all those designed for World War I light guns.

LEWIS

Name:
 Lewis

Model:
 1914

Manufacturer:
 BSA

Exhibited at the Champlin Museum, this Lewis is a mint original, displayed complete in its original commercial packing with service kit.

Many such guns saw actual military service, having been privately purchased and sneaked into the inventory of frontline U.S. units. Others saw more interesting, if less productive, use in the hands of brigands, thieves, raiders, and border toughs all over the world.

As with many American designs, military establishments abroad and miscreants worldwide recognized the brilliance of the concept behind the Lewis. General Crozier of Army Ordnance, however, decided that, for World War I, the French Chauchat was a "superior" device. History has already judged

Lewis Model 1914.

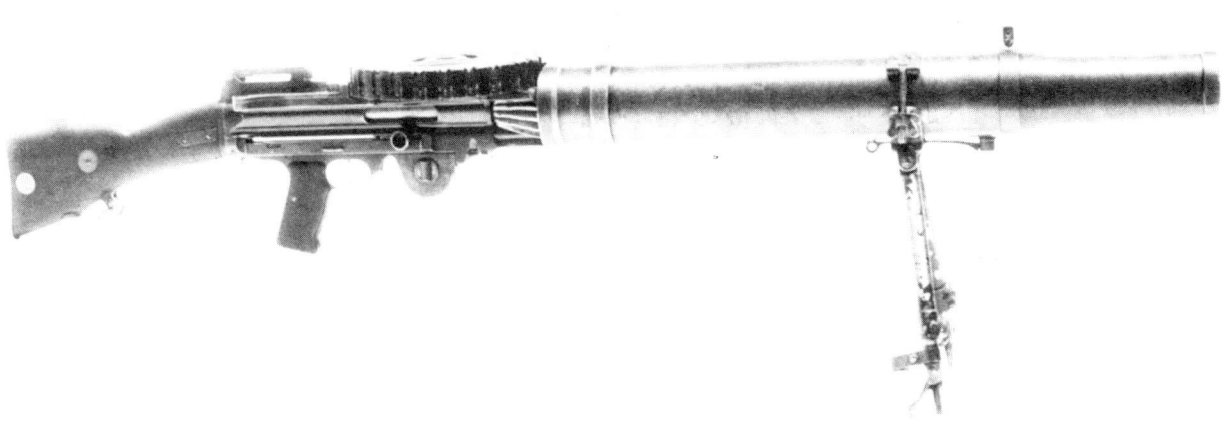

Lewis Model 1914.

that the Lewis is the better gun, and Crozier's criteria for his decision remains a mystery more than seventy years later. Shoot both—if you dare: the Chauchat is rather abusive and quite dangerous—and you'll know which is better within five rounds. Go downrange and study your target, and you'll realize the balance in favor of the Lewis is even greater than you thought.

For the private shooter or collector, the Lewis is quite a bargain today, since, when adjusted for inflation, it sells for less relative value today than at the height of its production and service. This is perhaps because the Lewis, though a splendid mechanism, looks larger than it really is and lacks some of the "sex appeal" of more publicized guns. It is a far better weapon, however, than others that are more expensive. Considering its fairly brisk rate of fire—typically around 550 RPM in ground versions—the Lewis is very comfortable to shoot. The very early and very late guns are perhaps the best-finished models, though there are no really rough Lewis guns. A rough or imprecise Lewis would likely not function at all.

VICKERS MARK I AC

Name:
Aircraft Vickers

Model:
Mark I AC

Caliber:
11mm

Other Chamberings:
.303 British, U.S. .30, and others for export

Overall Length:
44.19 inches

Barrel Length:
28.4 inches

Weight:
Early models: 38+ pounds
Later models: 25 pounds

Type of Fire:
Full auto

System of Operation:
Recoil (short)

Cyclic Rate (approx.):
Early models: 450-550 RPM
Later models: 750-900 RPM

Feed System/Ammunition Delivery:
Usually disintegrating metal-linked belt; sometimes cloth in other than 11mm

Country of Manufacture:
Great Britain

Manufacturer:
Vickers, Colt, BSA, and others under license and for export

Countries of Use:
Great Britain and its allies

Period of Manufacture (approx.):
1915–early 1920s

Period of Service (approx.):
1915–early 1920s (Many aircraft Vickers guns were exported in many calibers, especially after World War I. Many were

VICKERS MARK I AC (continued)

also converted to air cooling, and new guns were modeled after the old breech design. Such guns served until the end of World War II.)

Primary Tactical Use:
Pursuit aircraft; primarily fixed

Air-cooled Vickers guns were exported in many calibers, especially after World War I. Many were also converted to air cooling, and new guns were modeled after the old design breech. Such guns served until the very end of World War II.

Both the Vickers and the German MG08/15 were lightened Maxims, though with slightly different layouts and characteristics. The further lightened aircraft versions of this American design were used by English, German, Italian, and Russian forces, as well as others during World War I. The Vickers aircraft gun continuously went through a bewildering series of developments and small improvements.

Since the remaining guns were culled, rebuilt, and stored or sold after World War I, the guns that are to be found today tend to be of one or two patterns.

Since many of the early aircraft guns were actually converted ground guns, many of the ground guns around today are converted aircraft guns, either executed by the British in the early days of World War II or by collectors who found parts kits but found out quickly that 11mm ammunition was nonexistent. The few rounds here are those of J. Curtis Earl, and those fifteen or so constitute all I have ever seen. The metal links are probably as rare as the ammunition, though some authorities claim the cloth belts would function.

The 11mm cartridge had a rather poor trajectory, and its penetration was not particularly good. Its big bullet could carry useful amounts of incendiary material, however, and was handy with wood and fabric aircraft but terminal to hydrogen-filled observation balloons and zeppelins. There seem to have been two 11mm cartridges—one based upon a French case, the other an elongated 7.62 × 54R Russian case. The French round could be fired in

An Aircraft Vickers Mark I mounted on a Sopwith Pup.

A Sopwith Camel with twin Vickers aircraft machine guns.

either chamber, but the longer round became standard before the end of the war; even the French used it.

The synchronizers that seared out the action when the propeller mechanisms was in the way are perhaps more interesting and more intricate than the guns. George Chinn referred to their setup as "excruciating, exacting . . . a cross between fine art and hard science." The slightest maladjustment of their hydraulic, electrical, or mechanical parts—the Allies used at least three models—and a five-cent bullet interacting with a seventy-five-dollar propeller would shoot down the five-thousand-dollar airplane. Physical damage could also cause synchronizers to malfunction.

Since the controls of the gun itself were the same as those of the ground gun and the barrel shank was identical, these guns tied into an already well-established system. The very first guns were probably produced in .303, and many of the postwar guns were apparently converted back to the standard rifle round as supplies of the 11mm cartridge disappeared.

All Allied air forces used this gun, some even building clones. The gun was built in Belgium both before and after the war. Even the Germans used any ground and aircraft models of the gun that they captured. As a matter of fact, they printed a manual in German and actually produced barrels for the gun.

LEWIS MODEL 1914

Name:
Aircraft Lewis

Model:
1914

Manufacturer:
BSA

Special Note:
See U.S. aircraft Lewis for other tabular data.

This BSA-built British Lewis is mounted on a French Nieuport, the aircraft bearing British markings of the period. Such teamwork was typical of the cooperative nature of the effort by the Western Allies to combat the Central Powers during World War I. The gun is chambered for the British cartridge, and likely would have been so had the aircraft been in Belgian, French, Italian, Russian, or U.S. service regardless of where the gun and/or aircraft had been manufactured. All these allies used the gun and the airplane.

The Lewis was difficult to synchronize, and the drum magazine obscured the pilot's forward vision. Many pilots didn't trust synchronizers anyway, so this topside mounting above the propeller arc became more or less the standard way to mount the Lewis. Later, some units mounted the guns on the wings.

Lewis Model 1914.

The Lewis underwent continual improvement and modification during the war in an international effort, and the gun evolved from simple conversions of ground guns into a fast-firing, handy weapon for flexible and fixed installations. The ammunition also considerably improved by war's end.

MARK 2

Name:
British aircraft machine gun

Model:
Mark 2

Caliber:
.303 British

Type of Fire:
Full auto

System of Operation:
Recoil

Cyclic Rate (approx.):
1,000 RPM

Feed System/Ammunition Delivery:
Disintegrating steel-link belts

Country of Manufacture:
Great Britain

Manufacturer:
BSA

Countries of Use:
Great Britain

Period of Manufacture (approx.):
Early 1930s–1945

Period of Service (approx.):
Early 1930s–late 1940s

Primary Service:
British aircraft

Primary Tactical Use:
Aircraft mounted machine gun

Except for bits of trim like a flash hider, this gun is an exact copy of the U.S. AN-M2 .30-caliber gun. Great Britain manufactured this gun during World War II, with rights purchased in the 1930s, and the British used the gun in more installations than the Americans well after the war (some turrets used four of these guns). However, the British also used great numbers of the AN-M2 and Colt MG40, including many for the American .30 cartridge. The British had some difficulty with the guns in early high-altitude applications, but the use of special lubricants solved that problem.

British Browning Mark 2.

BREN MARK 1

Name:
Bren

Model:
Mark 1

Caliber:
.303

Overall Length:
45.5 inches

Barrel Length:
25 inches

Weight:
22.5 pounds

Type of Fire:
Full auto or single shots

System of Operation:
Gas

Cyclic Rate (approx.):
500 RPM

Feed System/Ammunition Delivery:
30-round box magazine

Country of Manufacture:
Great Britain

Manufacturer:
Royal Small Arms Factory at Enfield

Countries of Use:
Great Britain, countries of the British Empire (e.g., Burma, India, South Africa), modern Commonwealth countries, and British allies

Period of Manufacture (approx.):
1937–1941

Period of Service (approx.):
1938–late 1950s (in original form)

Primary Tactical Use:
Infantry and small vehicles

A modification of the superb Ceskoslovenská Zbrojovka, Brno Model 26 with some features of the Model 30, the ZGB Vz-33 prototypes resulted from the collaboration between the Royal Arsenal at Enfield and the Brno firm (hence the name, Bren, taking the *en* from Enfield and the *br* from Brno). Vaclav Holek, who for over twenty years was the primary designer of most of the excellent Czech weapons, can also therefore take credit for this splendid British weapon, which many authorities consider the finest light machine gun ever designed.

Considerable work was required to alter the Czech gun to accept the bottle-shaped, heavily rimmed .303 British cartridge, and the curved magazine was the most visible result.

The design was accepted and ready in 1933. Quantity production began in 1938, and the gun was just beginning to reach units in major quantities when World War II broke out.

The quick-change barrel and sturdy receiver made servicing the gun in the field relatively easy. By no means an easy gun to produce, the Bren was nonetheless cheaper than the Lewis gun it replaced.

The specimen shown has its tripod in an antiaircraft configuration. The pinkish color to be found on the gun is the precise result of paints mixed according to King's Regulations. Many tanks and aircraft bore the same color. The Bren was the most common armament of an entire family of carrier vehicles developed by the British.

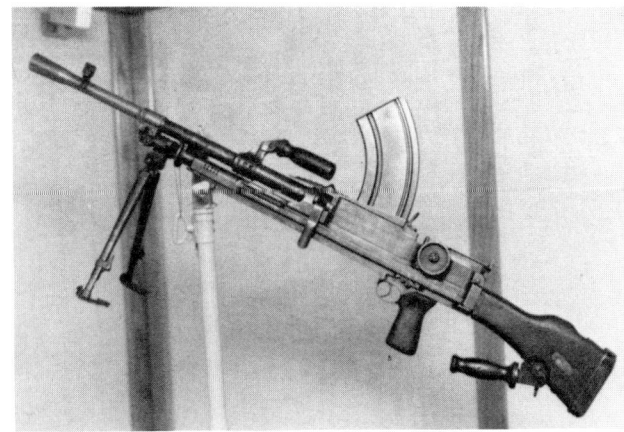

Bren Mark 1.

BREN MARK 2

Name:
Bren

Model:
Mark 2

Manufacturer:
Inglis (Canada)

Period of Manufacture (approx.):
1941–1945

Period of Service (approx.):
1941–present (in modified form)

By 1944, over half of the Brens entering the British Empire came from Canada. The Inglis guns, simplified Brens, were all Mark 2s. The rear sight was amplified, and some of the "trimmy" hardware of the original was eliminated.

Updated and modified for the 7.62 × 51mm NATO cartridge and looking rather like its ZB-26/30 Czech forebears, the Bren is still in service in Commonwealth countries and the United Kingdom, where it is known as the L4A1 to L4A6 series. It is the standard light machine gun of all noninfantry units. The guns also show up in their original form from time to time in former British colonies.

BREN MARK 2 LIGHT MACHINE GUN

Name:
Bren light machine gun

Model:
Mark 2

Caliber:
7.92x57mm

Type of Fire:
Semiauto or full auto

Country of Manufacture:
Canada (for China)

Manufacturer:
Inglis (Canada)

Period of Manufacture (approx.):
1941–1945

Period of Service (approx.):
1941–unknown

Primary Service:
China

Inglis, a Canadian firm, was so efficient in producing Bren guns that the weapon was redesigned so that it more closely resembled its Czech roots; it was then exported to China.

Bren Mark 2.

Bren Mark 2 light machine gun.

Called the Mark 2 by Inglis, the Chinese refer to both this gun and a .30-06 derivative they later built as the "Type 41." Using as many standard Mark 2 components as possible, thousands of these light machine guns were delivered before the end of World War II.

The research, tools, and jigs developed by Inglis were later applied at Enfield to the 7.62×51 mm NATO L4 family of weapons that still serve the British Army.

LANCHESTER MARK 1

Name:
Lanchester

Model:
Mark 1

Caliber:
9mm

Overall Length:
33.5 inches

Barrel Length:
7.9 inches

Weight:
9.65 pounds

Type of Fire:
Selective fire

System of Operation:
Blowback

Cyclic Rate (approx.):
600 RPM

Feed System/Ammunition Delivery:
50-round magazine

Country of Manufacture:
Great Britain

Manufacturer:
Sterling Armament Co.

Countries of Use:
Great Britain

Period of Manufacture (approx.):
1940–1945

Period of Service (approx.):
1941–1960s

Primary Service:
Royal Navy

Primary Tactical Use:
Individual

Except for the bayonet lug and the Enfield-style sharp-edged pistol grip on the stock, this weapon is a British-built MP28-II.

In 1940, the British procrastination about submachine guns caught up with them. They had tested just about everything available, written ridiculous specifications around their odd cartridges, then backed off and done more tests. There was a prejudicial attitude that the submachine gun

Lanchester Mark 1.

was a "gangster" weapon (true enough, but a meaningless statement, for hosing down one's opponent was just as effective at short range in Flanders as it was on a Chicago street).

They eventually opted to select a reliable enemy design and copy it with minimal modification. Known for its reliability, the MP28 was selected for testing, and George Lanchester did the detail design for Sterling Armament. There were still some wrinkles to be worked out, however, and though the weapon was intended for RAF (Royal Air Force) and Royal Navy service, the Navy and Royal Marines seemed to get all of the MK1s.

Exuding a look and feel of quality, this attractive weapon was a favorite of marine units, which would acquire them via official and unofficial means. A few Mark 1s even showed up with the Long Range Desert Group in Libya and Egypt. Mostly, though, they sailed around the waters in the arms lockers of Royal Navy ships until long after the war. Most of those surplused in the United States show the marks of steel rifle racks and very little actual use. A later version was automatic only.

STEN MARK 2

Name:
Sten

Model:
Mark 2

Caliber:
9mm

Overall Length:
30 inches

Barrel Length:
7.75 inches

Weight:
6.65 pounds

Type of Fire:
Selective fire

System of Operation:
Blowback

Cyclic Rate (approx.):
550 RPM

Feed System/Ammunition Delivery:
32-round box magazine

Country of Manufacture:
Great Britain

Manufacturer:
BSA and other Royal Ordnance factories

Countries of Use:
Great Britain

Period of Manufacture (approx.):
1941–1945

Period of Service (approx.):
1941–1954 in Great Britain; much later elsewhere

Primary Service:
British Empire, Allied forces, and guerrillas and partisans in occupied Europe during World War II.

Primary Tactical Use:
Individual

The British dilemma over submachine guns was deep and persistent. The Lanchester was too labor-intensive and therefore slow to produce and too expensive. The Americans could not supply Thompsons fast enough, which were in an odd loading for European service and entirely too expensive. The Sten was developed at Enfield by R.V. Shepperd and H.J. Turpin, whose last initials supply the *st* in the gun's name.

Troops in the field had many other names for the Sten Mark 2: "plumber's delight," "Woolworth special," and "Stench gun," among them. None were very complimentary. Subcontractors, who were formerly in the fields of costume jewelry, lawn mowers, scooters, and trash cans, made parts for the gun. While the gun actually worked very well, several early magazine manufacturers were the cause of problems in the early guns.

The most famous jam in history involved a Mark 2. During the assassination of Reinhard Heydrich, SS Governor/*ReichsProtektor* of Slovakia and Moravia, in Prague, May 17, 1942, one of the Czechs sent to do him in walked in front of his Mercedes at a stop sign. Though it was the perfect opportunity to shoot Heydrich, the assailant's gun jammed, and Heydrich was given attention with a #36 Mills

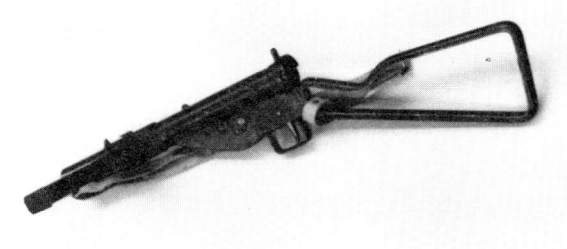

Sten Mark 2.

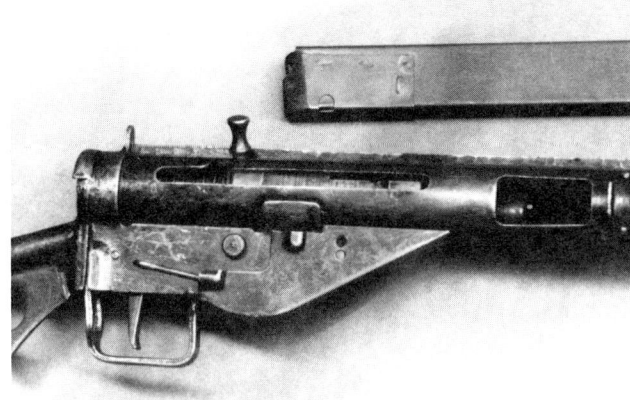

The Sten Mark 2 is ugly and crude, but it is a reliable gun despite its shaky reputation.

Bomb grenade, expiring from the effects of same on June 4. The Gestapo recovered the Sten, and the secret report to *Reichsfuhrer* Heinrich Himmler noted that its magazine feed lips were "compressed."

However, the Sten always worked much better than it looked. The Mark 2 was probably the worst looking of the lot, often finished with a haphazard coat of black or dark green paint. No effort was made to excise weld slag. The Mark 2 could rotate its magazine housing to use it as a dust cover.

A silenced version, the Mark 2S, was available for clandestine operations.

Thousands of Sten guns were air-dropped to resistance fighters from Norway to Yugoslavia.

One of the Sten's greatest assets was its compact size. With the buttstock removed, the gun could be carried under a coat. For some clandestine operations, the Sten was used to build a bicycle; the receiver tube formed the seat crossmember and the buttstock became the pump handle. This "bicycle" was supposedly ridden right past German guards.

STEN MARK 3

Name:
Sten

Model:
Mark 3

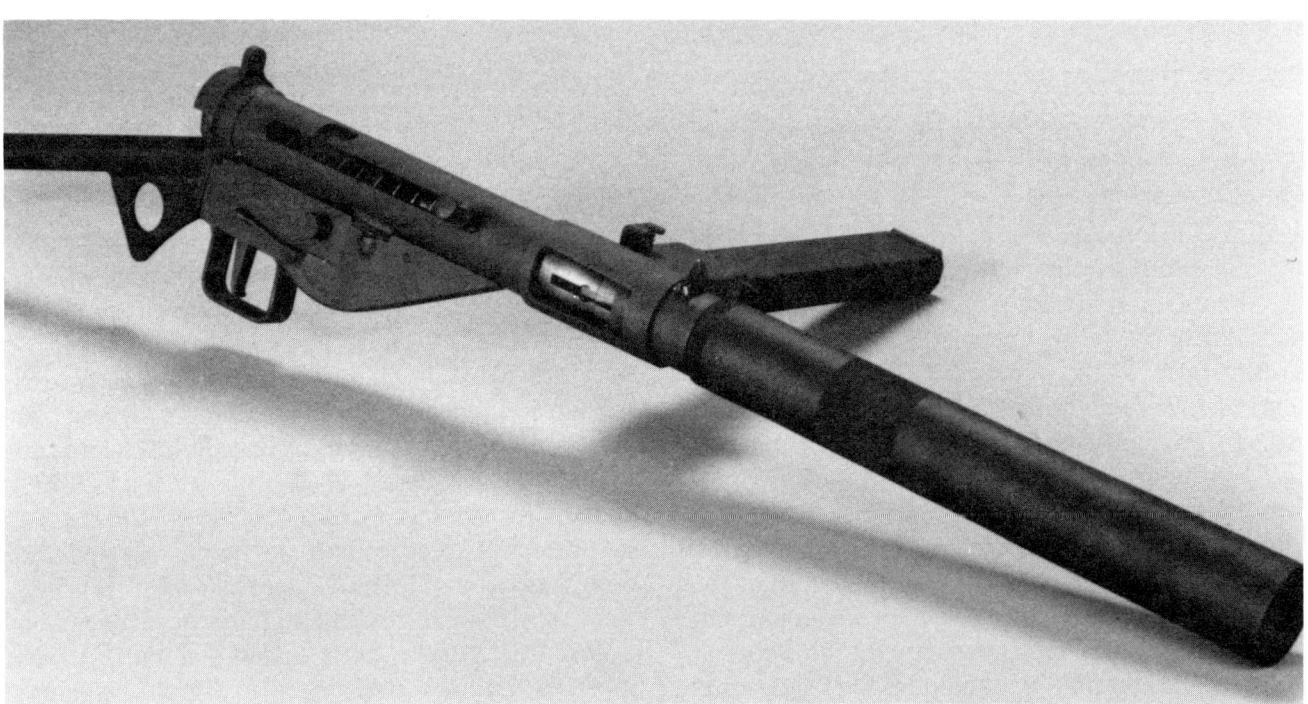

AWCs SG9 Suppressor utilizes ports to reduce most standard 9mm ammunition to subsonic velocity and includes a port locking collar to increase bore pressure. The unit is shown here on a Sten Mark 2. It can also be fitted to the S&W Model 76 and similar weapons. (Photo courtesy of AWC Systems Technology.)

STEN MARK 3 (continued)

Overall Length:
  30 inches

Barrel Length:
  7.75 inches

Weight:
  7 pounds

Type of Fire:
  Selective fire

Sten Mark 3.

In a continuing effort to make the Sten look and feel better, designers of the Mark 3 took a leaf from a Soviet manual and produced the Mark 3 receiver and barrel jacket from one welded steel tube, partly in order to give the barrel more support and stability. The magazine housing was welded to the receiver. The Mark 3 is probably the cheapest of all the Stens; one British source quotes the fabrication cost at £2—about $9.50 U.S. in wartime currency.

The barrel is not detachable as it is on the Mark 2.

This variant followed the silenced 2s into service, but it did not replace the Mark 2 in production. In fact, the Mark 3 was produced simultaneously with the Mark 2 for most of its life. Its introduction signaled the entrance of a new batch of contractors and subcontractors into the enormous small arms program, some of whom had previously made metal toys, automobile radiators, cigarette lighters, and lawn furniture.

Sten guns were slapdash war-emergency jobs, yet they worked well enough if good magazines were to be had. Most of the early problems were with the magazines themselves or were magazine-related. One former Tommy told of a 1942 order stating that some manufacturers had misunderstood specifications and made many defective magazines, further ordering that such magazines were to be destroyed by smashing or gutting them the instant they were identified. The Tommy had several of them, and began to smash them with the butt of his Sten when, on about the fourth stroke, the entire butt assembly parted company with the receiver, whose contents were then dumped all over the desert. Concerned—for he had seen men rather severely disciplined for damaging their weapons—he sheepishly reported the damage to the nearest NCO, who threw the weapon under the tracks of a passing Bren Carrier. He immediately had the Sten replaced without even requesting any paperwork or further explanation. "Tenth one this bloody week," the sergeant remarked. In a few days, a new written order was posted: "Persons locating defective Sten-type gun magazines are not—repeat *not*—to destroy same by striking with the butts of their weapons, but are to do so by other convenient means."

Some authorities claim that more than four million Stens were produced, though that figure may be low. Not only was the weapon made in England and Canada, it was also copied—with or without legal authority—in Belgium, Argentina, China, France, Indonesia, and Israel. Even the Germans produced two distinct families of clones, the *Gerät Potsdam,* an exact Mark 2 copy down to the proofs intended for clandestine operations, and the MP3008, which was intended for service in the Volksturm Wehrmacht. The initial German reaction to the Sten guns that were seized was expressed by one general in North Africa who, upon examining the piece, said, "Surely our victory cannot be far off!"

As a point of interest, the Canadians were willing to sell Mark 3 Sten guns after the war to major buyers for $10.99. They must have made some profit, for a 1944 Canadian soldier who lost his on maneuvers was docked $9.63. By comparison, M1 rifles were procured in the same period for $92.30 and relatively stripped '28 Thompsons for $176.72.

The Sten started a trend. Killing machines need not be elegant, attractive, or expensive. And the Sten was none of these. It merely worked. It is still fair to say, however, that though the Sten's bad reputation was greatly exaggerated—in fact, it was mostly fictional—troops who could procure another weapon generally did so, which is one reason the gun was so rapidly replaced by the Sterling.

STERLING L2A3

Name:
Sterling

Model:
L2A3 or Mark 4

Caliber:
9x19mm

Other Chamberings:
7.65 (.30) "Luger" Parabellum (for police duty)

Overall Length:
Stock folded: 26 inches
Stock extended: 34 inches

Barrel Length:
7.8 inches

Weight:
Unloaded, without bayonet: 6 pounds
Loaded, with bayonet: 8.25 pounds

Type of Fire:
Selective

System of Operation:
Blowback

Cyclic Rate (approx.):
550 RPM

Feed System/Ammunition Delivery:
34-round staggered row, curved-box magazine

Country of Manufacture:
Great Britain

Manufacturer:
Sterling Armaments, Dagenham

Countries of Use:
Many British allies; small units worldwide

Period of Manufacture (approx.):
1945–present

Period of Service (approx.):
1945–present (it was officially adopted by the United Kingdom to replace the Sten in 1953)

Primary Tactical Use:
Infantry and police

Sterling L2A3 (Mark 4) with stock extended and bayonet fixed.

The L2A3 is the current version of the Patchett, a weapon that debuted with British troops in combat during World War II. Its development was a matter of fairly high priority, not because there was actually anything seriously wrong with the Sten, but because the earlier gun was never really accepted by British troops, even after the magazine problems were solved. The gun combines classic features with ultramodern ones, using a folding stock more stable than most, a polymerized finish combined with high-quality bluing, plating and machining on many internal parts, and plastics in certain noncritical areas. The fixed firing pin is tilted out of alignment with the primer except when the trigger is back, a thoughtful safety feature.

The L34A1 variant uses a silencer and special barrel that is almost identical to the unit used on the 2S and Mark 6 silenced Sten guns. It therefore probably inherits the best true silencer system in service.

The standard British service bayonet can be fitted.

Like many FN products, the bolt has been cut with clearance slots to keep fouling away from vital moving parts and to act in a self-cleaning manner.

The gun is quite accurate, and has a good record for durability and reliability. Cassi, Incorporated, currently imports the weapon for law enforcement, and there are civilian semiautomatic carbine and pistol variants.

VICKERS MARK I

Name:
Vickers Aircraft

Model:
"K" Mark I (V.G.O.)

Caliber:
.303

Other Chamberings:
Possibly 8mm (7.92x57mm JS)

Overall Length:
44.8 inches

Barrel Length:
27 inches

Weight:
Gun: 23.5 pounds
Double mount, pans, accoutrements: 63 pounds

Type of Fire:
Full auto

System of Operation:
Gas

Cyclic Rate (approx.):
800–1,000 RPM

Feed System/Ammunition Delivery:
96-round nonrotating drum

Country of Manufacture:
Great Britain

Manufacturer:
Vickers

Countries of Use:
Great Britain, some allies

Period of Manufacture (approx.):
Early 1930s–1943

Period of Service (approx.):
1933–1945

Primary Tactical Use:
Aircraft and vehicles

This weapon was meant to replace the Lewis gun, once and for all, in aircraft and vehicular mounts. It never did. The guns were not as elaborate or as expensive to produce as the Lewis, but the Lewis guns were already made. Still, these guns served aboard many early World War II British aircraft and were carried on many SAS (Special Air Service) and LRDG (Long Range Desert Group) vehicles, almost always in the twin swivel mount.

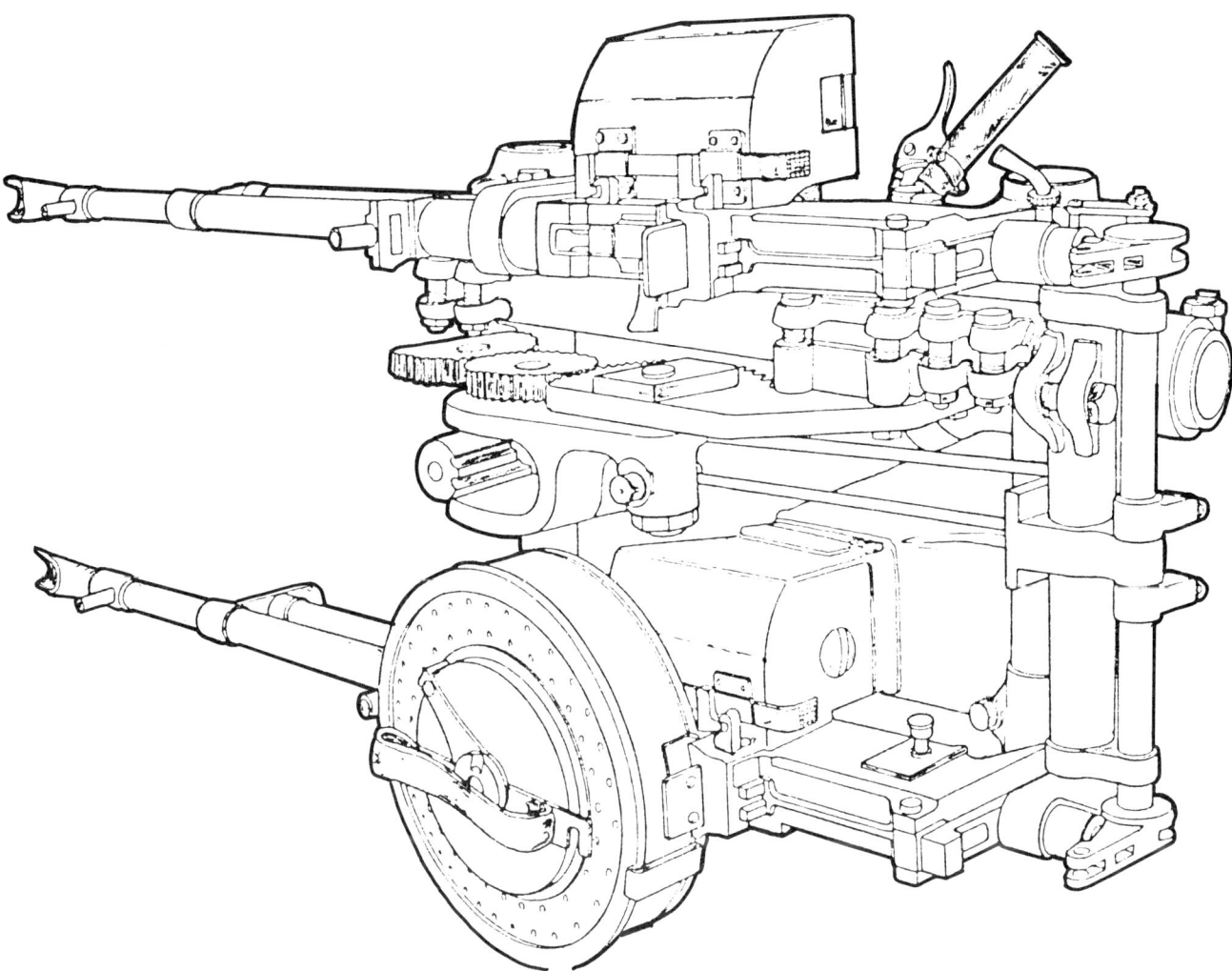

Vickers "K" Mark I.

CHAPTER 14

Hungary

The ultimate "machine carbine," this submachine gun will outshoot M1 carbines every time, shooting more accurately than many modern assault rifles. It is also more controllable. It fires the very potent 25mm Long 9mm Mauser Export cartridge, standard in Hungarian service, and propels the 132-grain service load downrange at about 1,500 fps (feet per second). The long barrel contributes to velocity, stability, and recoil recovery. The fixed wooden stock, consisting of two pieces in most models, helps steady aim. With its fixed stock, the later 43M is probably not as accurate.

I have fired only the 39M, and though it's been many years, I recall thinking the gun was worthy of even better sights than the Mauser-style units with which it was fitted; as I recall, it was calibrated to 600 meters. The cartridge approximates .357 Magnum, and the gun is quite liberal about feeding the more tapered Hornady and Speer hollow points. Fiocchi 7.62/7.63 (.30) Mauser brass may be reformed for use in this gun; some shooters are trimming .223/5.56mm for this gun. RWS and Fiocchi both load the round (or at least it's shown in their European catalogs that they do so), but getting the round factory-loaded in the United States could be arduous and pointless. Though I have never tried it, I have been told that .38 ACP or brisk Bergmann-Bayard loads may be used.

M39

Name:
Kiraly Gepisztoly

Model:
M39 or 39M

Caliber:
9mm Mauser Export

Overall Length:
39M: 41 inches
43M fully extended: 37.5 inches

Barrel Length:
M39: 19.6 inches
M43: 15.9 inches

Weight:
M39: 9 pounds
M43: 8 pounds

Type of Fire:
Selective

System of Operation:
Delayed blowback

Cyclic Rate (approx.):
700–750 RPM

Feed System/Ammunition Delivery:
Round box

Country of Manufacture:
Hungary

Manufacturer:
Danuvia (Budapest)

Countries of Use:
Hungary, Rumania, Slovakia, and other Nazi allies

Period of Manufacture (approx.):
1939–1943 (the more common 1943 variant was made between 1943 and 1945)

Period of Service (approx.):
1939–1950s

Primary Tactical Use:
Individual infantry

129

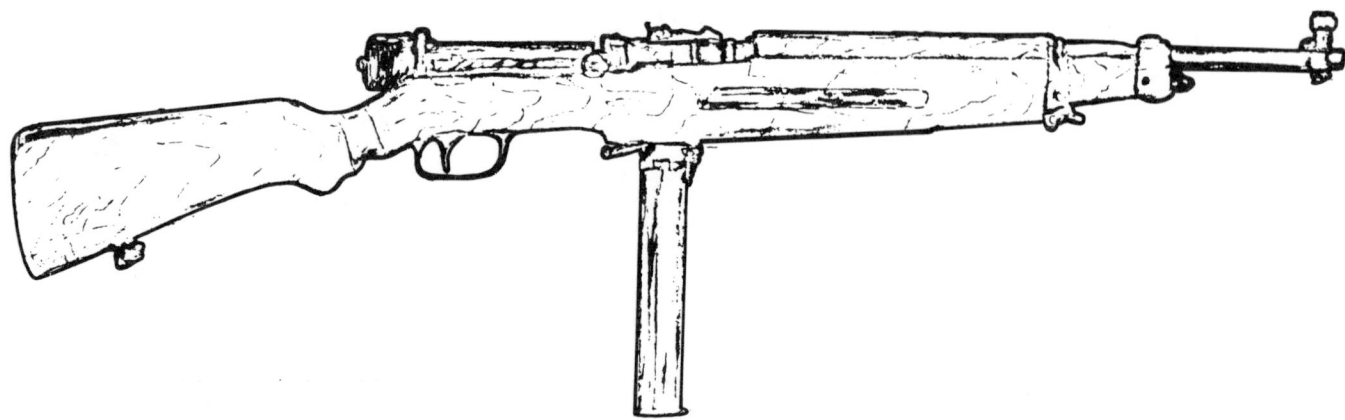

This M39 is the more rare version of the gun. The 1943 model was made in far greater quantity, almost always with a folding-stock, and uses a different, forward-sloped magazine that still folds inward. All the guns seem to have used bayonet lugs.

The two-part bolt provides delay by mechanical disadvantage, whereby the smaller portion encounters the larger one and must move it at the "dwell" position. This mechanism necessitates—and is indeed designed for safety with—brisk powerful ammunition. Therefore, weak loads often won't propel the entire breech innards.

At one point in 1939, the British Army made a 39M derivative, for which Kiraly had supplied drawings, and was on the verge of adopting it. This situation appears to have caused Kiraly much difficulty, since Hungary was a Fascist country and a Nazi ally. It was already fairly obvious that Great Britain and the Axis powers would soon be crossing swords.

The later 43M was produced in far greater numbers, but it operated on the same basic system. The folding-stock version of the 43M was probably initially intended for paratroopers and vehicle crews, but it wound up in general issue (the fixed-stock versions seem to have been prototypes only or may be postwar cobble jobs). These later 43Ms were as well made as their predecessors, but probably not quite as stable. They are excellent, well-made guns, though parts for them are a little hard to find. Ammo can be formed and, of course, 9mm bullets abound now more than ever.

CHAPTER 15

Israel

UZI

Name:
Uzi

Caliber:
9mm

Overall Length:
Stock folded: 17 inches
Stock extended: 25.2 inches

Barrel Length:
10.25 inches

Weight:
7.8 pounds

Type of Fire:
Full auto

System of Operation:
Blowback

Cyclic Rate (approx.):
600 RPM

Feed System/Ammunition Delivery:
25-, 32- or 40-round box magazine

Country of Manufacture:
Israel

Manufacturer:
Israeli Military Industries and Fabrique Nationale (Belgium) under license

Countries of Use:
Israel, Netherlands, West Germany, and many South American countries

Period of Manufacture (approx.):
1950–present

Period of Service (approx.):
1953–present

Primary Service:
Israeli, Dutch, and West German armed forces

Primary Tactical Use:
Individual

Using Czech research and some Italian ergonomics, Uziel Gal, a major in the Israeli Army, devised this handy submachine gun by 1950. Its short overall receiver/barrel assembly comes from the bolt surrounding the barrel, with the greater part of its mass forward of the chamber. The magazine goes into the pistol grip to allow the "hand can find hand" principle to work in its simplest form. A pistol grip is also provided.

The weapon is carried by the U.S. Secret Service and is used by many countries in vehicle applications.

Stripping for cleaning or repair is very straightforward.

Uzi.

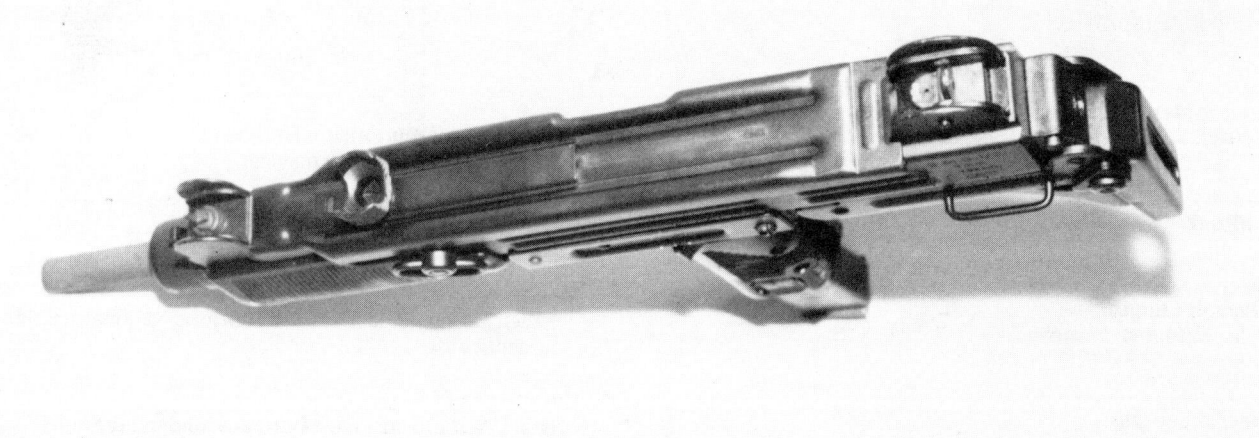

Top view of the Uzi.

Fixed-stock Uzi.

MINI-UZI

Name:
Uzi

Model:
Mini-Uzi

Caliber:
9mm

Overall Length:
9.45 inches

Barrel Length:
4.5 inches

Weight:
3.8 pounds

Type of Fire:
Full auto

System of Operation:
Blowback

Cyclic Rate (approx.):
950 RPM

Feed System/Ammunition Delivery:
20-, 25- or 32-round box magazine

Country of Manufacture:
Israel

Manufacturer:
Israeli Military Industries

Countries of Use:
Israel and many Western Bloc nations

Period of Manufacture:
1984–present

Period of Service (approx.):
1984–present

Primary Service:
Personal security agencies in many countries

Primary Tactical Use:
Individual and vehicle crews

Another of Uziel Gal's designs that has a very good reputation, the Mini-Uzi was designed to fill the same niche as the MAC-10. Many accessories are marketed for this family of compact weapons, including noise-suppression devices, flash hiders, special carrying cases, and holsters.

Mini-Uzi.

Clockwise from top: Uzi, Mini-Uzi, and MAC-10.

GALIL

Name:
Assault Rifle

Model:
Galil

Caliber:
.223/5.56mm

Other Chamberings:
Export versions are available in 7.62x39mm M43 and 7.62x51mm NATO. The Israelis have used small numbers of 7.62mm units in NATO caliber as light machine guns, but this is not a regular practice.

Overall Length:
Stock extended, short model: 32.3 inches
Stock extended, long model: 38.2 inches

Barrel Length:
Short model: 13 inches
Long model: 18.1 inches

Weight:
7.7–9 pounds

Type of Fire:
Selective fire

GALIL (continued)

System of Operation:
Kalashnikov gas

Cyclic Rate (approx.):
650 RPM

Feed System/Ammunition Delivery:
35- and 50-shot curved box magazine

Country of Manufacture:
Israel

Manufacturer:
Israeli Military Industries

Countries of Use:
Israel, South Africa, and others in small numbers

Period of Manufacture (approx.):
1973–present

Period of Service (approx.):
1973–present

Primary Tactical Use:
General purpose infantry

The Galil has already replaced the FAL in almost all applications except for border-patrol duties on the frontiers where range is very important. It should soon replace the M15 and M16A1, even on remote kibbutz duty.

The gun is a very straightforward Kalashnikov in direct-impingement gas-system copy, apparently built with the direct cooperation of the Finnish Valmet concern. Since its introduction in 1973, the gun has established a superb record of reliability.

Galil Assault Rifle.

Galil Assault Rifle with bipod.

CHAPTER 16

Italy

Many refer to the Villar Perosa, designed by Revelli, as the first submachine gun. This may have been the case, but it was not intended to be so. Really two guns stuck together, it was first intended to be a light machine gun, then tried as an aircraft gun, and later, primarily after the war, was split, stocked, and made into an acceptable submachine gun. Some specimens were encountered in sub-machine-gun form during World War II in North Africa.

At a combined rate of fire of 3,000 rounds per minute and a magazine capacity of only 25 rounds per side, one's ammo supply was good for one second of fire. Obviously, fast hands and a liberal supply of magazines were necessary. In addition, the 9mm Glisenti cartridge—physically identical to the 9mm Parabellum (Luger) but loaded more like the .380 pocket pistol round—was underpowered for the light machine gun or aircraft roles. It was very short on range and penetration.

The absence of sights on the original double units is the rule, not the exception. Had the gun been fitted with some more viable feed system, this hose-pipe method of shooting might have been very successful, despite the very limited range of the Glisenti load. However, in a real fight and with many weapons firing, it can be extremely difficult to observe whose hits are whose, especially when the gunner has only a second to make his corrections.

VILLAR PEROSA MODEL 1915

Name:
Villar Perosa

Model:
1915

Caliber:
9mm Glisent

Overall Length:
21 inches

Barrel Length:
12.5 inches

Weight:
15 pounds

Type of Fire:
Full auto

System of Operation:
Delayed blowback

Cyclic Rate (approx.):
1,500 RPM per side

Feed System/Ammunition Delivery:
25-round box magazine

Country of Manufacture:
Italy

Manufacturer:
Fiat S.p.A., Canadian General Electric Co. Ltd., and others

Countries of Use:
Italy

Period of Manufacture (approx.):
1915–1920s

Period of Service (approx.):
1915–1918 (as double unit)
1918–1940s (as submachine gun)

Primary Service:
Italy during World War I

Primary Tactical Use:
Aircraft and infantry

Machine Guns: A Pictorial, Tactical, and Practical History

Villar Perosa Model 1915. This pair was made by two different manufacturers (not uncommon among Villar Perosa pairs): General Electric and Fiat. Any Villar Perosa is extremely rare today.

Detail of the breech of the Villar Perosa Model 1915.

REVELLI MODEL 1914

Name:
Lewis aircraft machine gun (French)

Model:
Model 1914

Caliber:
6.5x52mm Italian

Overall Length:
46.5 inches

Barrel Length:
25.8 inches

Weight:
Gun: 37.5 pounds
Tripod: 49.5 pounds

Type of Fire:
Full auto

System of Operation:
Delayed blowback

Cyclic Rate (approx.):
400 RPM

Feed System/Ammunition Delivery:
50-round "mousetrap" box

Country of Manufacture:
Italy

Manufacturer:
Fiat S.p.A.

Countries of Use:
Italy

Period of Manufacture (approx.):
1914–1920s

Period of Service (approx.):
1914–early 1940s

Primary Service:
Italy during World War I

Primary Tactical Use:
Crew served

Revelli Model 1914.

A Revelli Model 1914 being used in action in Ethiopia.

A Fiat-Revelli M35 in antiaircraft application.

Italy had adopted two Maxims, the 1906 and 1911, but wanted to replace these with a weapon of Italian design, the Revelli Model 14. Italian designers generally distrusted belt feed, which was a common sentiment around the turn of the twentieth century. This distrust was particularly common in countries with tropical colonies since it was feared that heat and sun rot would damage the fabric belts.

Instead of the belt feed, a truly unique feed device was substituted. Designed to be handy and compact without the need for threading, it was a 50-

round mousetrap box of near square dimensions, containing ten compartments of five rounds each. Though it was intended to facilitate feed from rifle strippers, such was rarely the case.

Initial extraction was sluggish, so an oiler was provided to lubricate the cases. While this assembly is generally thought to be a source of problems on the machine guns, that is seldom the case. The Revelli is said by Italian sources to be extremely reliable, and it performed well on the Alpine front. It was unpopular twenty years later in Ethiopia, however, possibly because of the magazine setup and the fact that the guns were old by then.

On the other hand, the Fiat-Revelli, an air-cooled gun with the same basic receiver as the Model 1914, worked out rather well. Most texts claim that Fiat-Revellis were all belt-fed, but the manuals for the gun suggest that either feed system could be fitted as necessary. Most Fiat-Revellis replaced the oiler with a new barrel, using a fluted chamber, and some veterans complain that it caused more problems with sand than the oiler did.

Both versions fired from a closed bolt, yet there seem to have been few cook-offs.

Somewhat ironically, most troops during World War II that could locate the water-cooled guns actually preferred them, and many M1935 Fiat-Revellis were converted back to resemble the original configuration.

BREDA M37

Name:
Breda

Model:
M37

Caliber:
7.92x57mm (JS) German Service

Overall Length:
51 inches

Barrel Length:
26 inches

Weight:
43.5 pounds

Type of Fire:
Full auto

System of Operation:
Gas

Cyclic Rate (approx.):
450+ RPM

Feed System/Ammunition Delivery:
20-round strip magazine

Country of Manufacture:
Italy

Manufacturer:
Arsenal Roma (Rome)

Period of Manufacture (approx.):
1935–1945

Period of Service (approx.):
1937–1950s

Primary Service:
Primary Italian machine gun of World War II

Primary Tactical Use:
Crew-served infantry and antiaircraft

The Breda M37 was a scaled-down version of a 13.2mm heavy machine gun. Also produced in the standard Italian 8×59mm M35 loading and a 7.7mm variant (identical to the .303 British), this specimen is in the German service chambering and bears British proofs. The gun was much liked by the British, who used all the M37s they could capture since the gun was well known for its accuracy at great range.

The M37s used a cartridge oiler, potentially a cause for unreliability, yet they had a reputation for reliability that was better than that of many Allied guns, even in the Western Desert where sand was a problem. The 20-round feed trays reloaded with empties as they passed through the gun. Many latter-day "experts" question this, but the Italian manuals of the period make it quite clear that the trays were intended for reuse and that the cases kept them from malforming or bending during casual handling. Modern-day reloaders who shoot automatic weapons appreciate not having to gather up scattered, ejected brass and not losing cases, and the M37 treats cases very gently. Indeed, the tight headspace limits case expansion, the reason for the case oiler's installation.

The gun was retained in service for some time after the war, especially for vehicle use, where spent cartridge casings scattered all over the floor can become a genuine hazard.

The M37 was sold to Portugal, Spain, and some other countries. Belt-fed aircraft versions and an M1938 tank version with a top-mounted box magazine were also produced. A Spanish version is called the Alfa M1944, and still serves alongside converted Breda M1937s as the Alfa M55, now in the 7.62mm CETME or NATO loadings.

This gun was from a prewar Portuguese order. The British proofs were applied during its stay in

The Breda M37, shown here on an antiaircraft mount, is often maligned by writers, but in fact had an excellent reputation for reliability and accuracy. It was copied in Spain, supplied to many countries, and scavenged by the British SAS and LRDG for vehicle mountings.

The British used all the M37s they could capture. This one accompanies an ancient Lewis on a Long Range Desert Group Chevrolet truck.

Great Britain, probably in the late forties or fifties.

Champlin acquired this gun from Gary del Signore. The spare barrel and feed strips are correct, matched accessories. Del Signore reports putting many thousands of rounds through the gun with very rare stoppages, which were due to the intermittent weak round of ancient surplus ammunition. "An A-1, fun piece," he calls it.

Many who criticize Italian weapons are unaware of the changes ordnance personnel were attempting to institute. The M35 8×59mm cartridge for which this weapon was originally intended, for example, was a very powerful, long-range load that punched a 190-grain bullet downrange at a muzzle velocity of 800 meters per second. Its calculated range was 5,400 meters, maximum, and shooting at a mile with this very stable bullet was not especially difficult if the sights were properly adjusted. The round is considerably more powerful than the standard German, U.S., or British rifle-caliber rounds.

BERETTA 38A

Name:
Beretta

Model:
38A

Caliber:
9mm

Overall Length:
37.25 inches

Barrel Length:
12.4 inches

Weight:
9.25 pounds

Type of Fire:
Select, semiauto or full auto

System of Operation:
Blowback

Cyclic Rate (approx.):
600 RPM

Feed System/Ammunition Delivery:
10-, 20-, 30- or 40-round box magazine

Country of Manufacture:
Italy

Manufacturer:
Pietro Beretta S.p.A.

Countries of Use:
Italy, Germany, Rumania, Argentina and others

Period of Manufacture (approx.):
1938–1950

Period of Service (approx.):
1938–present

Primary Service:
Axis forces during World War II

Primary Tactical Use:
Individual

Beretta's long reputation for innovative design and quality manufacture was reinforced when Tullio Marengoni devised this submachine gun at the Gardone Val Trompia factory. Many regard the Modello 38A as the finest submachine gun ever made, and the original weapons are still popular with Italian police units. The original 1934–1935 design was for a simple, accurate semiautomatic carbine; by 1938, though, it had developed into a submachine gun that became very popular immediately. Made by traditional techniques from the very finest mate-

Beretta 38A.

Beretta 38A.

rials, the gun was expensive and attractive, particularly the prewar and postwar models.

The forward trigger is for single shots, the rear one for fully automatic bursts. The very first guns used elongated slots in the barrel jacket and a single hole compensator with a bar across the opening. These first guns also used a folding bayonet. By late 1939, however, the gun was standardized (a copy of which is shown here). By 1943, a pressed, welded jacket was standard.

The gun used a separate firing pin and rather high-quality hardwood for stocks. The long barrel, moderately heavy weight, and stability over the length of the action and barrel are usually cited as reasons for the Beretta's accuracy.

Many countries bought the weapon in small quantities after World War II, and there were copies

made in several countries. The Germans and Rumanians used the gun extensively during the war, and captured specimens were popular with the Allies.

BERETTA 38/42

Name:
Beretta

Model:
38/42

Caliber:
9mm

Overall Length:
31.5 inches

Barrel Length:
8.4 inches

Weight:
  7.2 pounds

Type of Fire:
  Select, semiauto or full auto

System of Operation:
  Blowback

Cyclic Rate (approx.):
  550 RPM

Feed System/Ammunition Delivery:
  20- or 40-round box magazine

Country of Manufacture:
  Italy

Manufacturer:
  Pietro Beretta S.p.A.

Countries of Use:
  Italy, Germany, and Rumania

Period of Manufacture (approx.):
  1942–late 1950s

Period of Service (approx.):
  1942–present

Primary Service:
  Axis forces during World War II

Primary Tactical Use:
  Individual

Though Beretta continued to produce the original Modello 38, a cheaper, lighter, and more compact version was introduced about a year after Italy entered World War II. Tullio Marengoni drew upon another of his prototypes (the Modello 1) as a weapon for airborne forces, and added the beefier but unjacketed barrel of that gun to a simplified receiver. The compensator became two simpler, tapered cuts. Deep parallel fluting ran along the barrel's length to dissipate heat and reduce weight.

The simplified bolt carried an integral firing pin, and the two-trigger system was retained. Some later guns did not use fluted barrels.

Just when production of this model ended is unknown. New guns were still available, however, well into the 1960s. Most authorities believe they were stocks from an earlier production run. An even more simplified version, the 38/44, was produced primarily after the war.

BREDA M30

Name:
  Breda

Model:
  M30

Caliber:
  7x57mm Mauser

Overall Length:
  48.5 inches

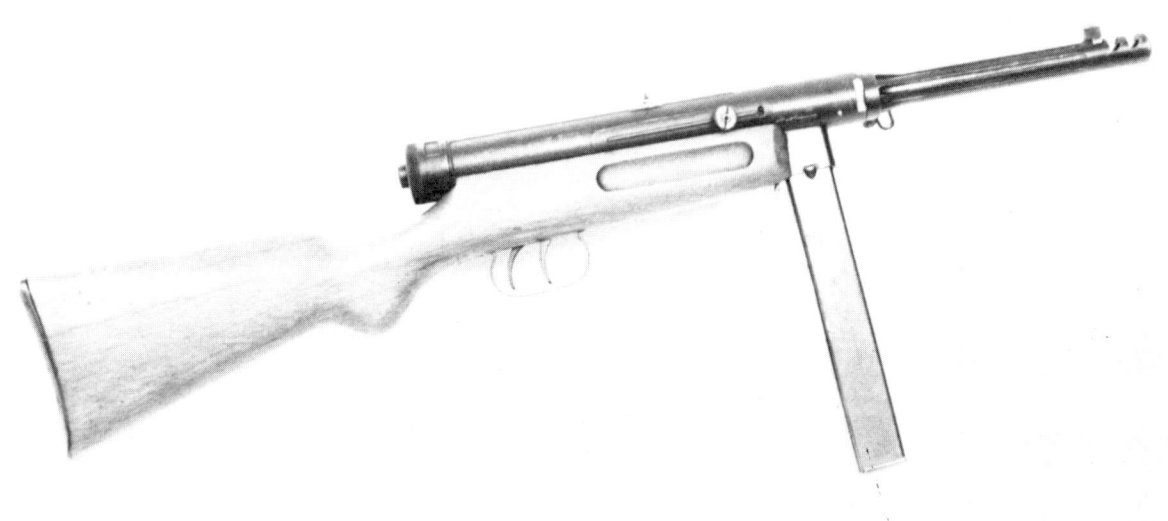

Beretta 38/42.

BREDA M30 (continued)

Barrel Length:
21 inches

Weight:
22.75 pounds

Type of Fire:
Full auto

System of Operation:
Delayed blowback, recoiling barrel

Cyclic Rate (approx.):
375+ RPM

Feed System/Ammunition Delivery:
20-round box

Country of Manufacture:
Italy (Costa Rican contract)

Manufacturer:
Breda

Countries of Use:
Italy, Costa Rica, and others

Period of Manufacture (approx.):
1928–1944

Period of Service (approx.):
1930–1945

Primary Service:
1930–1940 in Costa Rica

Primary Tactical Use:
Crew-served infantry

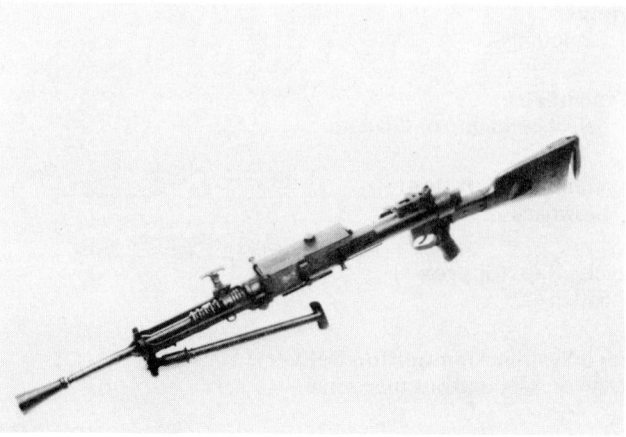

Breda M30.

BREDA 30 LIGHT MACHINE GUN

Name:
Breda light machine gun

Model:
30

Caliber:
6.5x52mm Carcano M95

Special Note:
See Breda M30 (Costa Rican model) for other tabular data.

The Breda 30 introduced some new features and omitted other simple ones that could have made it a much better weapon. Its considerable length and weight and nearly tubular profile made it rather awkward, yet a simple carrying handle was omitted. Felt recoil was quite low.

The magazine was a permanent, hinged fixture on the right side, loading from 20-round clips. This meant a quality precision-feed setup could be used more or less permanently; once damaged, however, the gun was out of action until the magazine could be replaced.

The barrel was a very handy, quick-change unit, perhaps the best in the world at that time and for many years to come.

The Breda was fairly successful and reasonably reliable. Exported to several countries, it was also sold to Italy's allies in some quantity. A few simple changes, though, could have made it a much better gun without the need for spending much more money.

Italy got through World War II without a real light machine gun, unless one counts the Villar Perosa. By 1928, the Model 30 had evolved at Fiat, where it was designed, but the Breda firm produced most of them, and actually sold the gun to the Italian government. Unusual in its blowback operation with recoil propelling to unlock point (where bolt and barrel begin to part company), the guns can treat brass rather brutally or be quite gentle due to the ejector's edge and the chamber gross diameter specification, rather than the usual headspace glitches. The ejector can be smoothed with a stone, but a chamber that's .004 inches or more over minimum (well within military specifications) can cause brass stretching and slight overexpansion. This in turn leads to dings and dents, and only a more tightly chambered barrel will solve the problem.

With these guns, it is important to assure the condition of the front barrel bearing surface. Though this may sound ridiculous, one should apply touches of automotive Molygraph bearing high temp/pressure grease to assure seal and stability.

Because the only reliable source of ammunition for these guns in their Italian loading is new Norma ammo, it is *vital* for a shooter to do everything possible to get maximum mileage from this expensive fodder. New barrels are hard to get. I had a local

Breda 30 light machine gun.

Breda 30 light machine gun.

BERETTA MG42/59

Name:
General Purpose Machine Gun

Model:
MG42/59

Cyclic Rate (approx.):
750–950 RPM

Manufacturer:
Beretta (Gardone, Italy)

Special Note:
See German MG42/59 for other tabular data, except for differences noted below.

There's no question that the MG42 is a far better and more field-serviceable weapon in any form than, say, the M60. It's also cheaper and easier to handle, especially when it's time to change the barrel. Not to indict the M60, it should be said that it's overpriced, not as good as the MAG or MG42, and requires too much expensive care in handling and manufacture. The MG42 is the standard gun in at least nine countries and is common in fifteen or twenty more. In contrast, the entire list of countries

machinist turn a unit from an oversized E.R. Shaw blank, then ultra-precision chamber the unit. This is a lot of trouble, but such a barrel brought this ugly and awkward gun from an unacceptable level of accuracy and brass condition (which can only be described as brutal) to well above average accuracy and brass which, save for the dented primers, looked unused.

This gun is sighted to 2,000 meters, and the sights are superb.

The Costa Rican contract guns are probably a smarter shooting proposition, since 7mm Mauser ammo is much easier to get. I felt obliged to test the gun at least once precisely as the Italians used it, however, before commenting on the gun.

Unlike the M37, the M30 gives the general impression of being a slightly unfinished product, rough, awkward, and very ugly. However, a gun whose every feature is bad-mouthed by those who've obviously never fired it and who often simultaneously praise guns nowhere near as efficacious, the M30 is a fairly pleasant surprise.

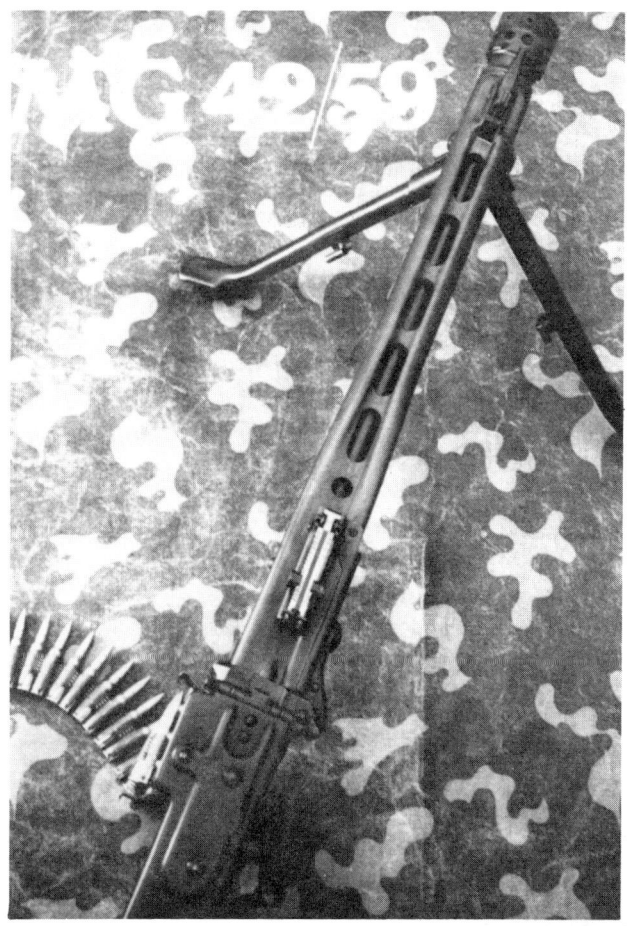

Beretta 42/59.

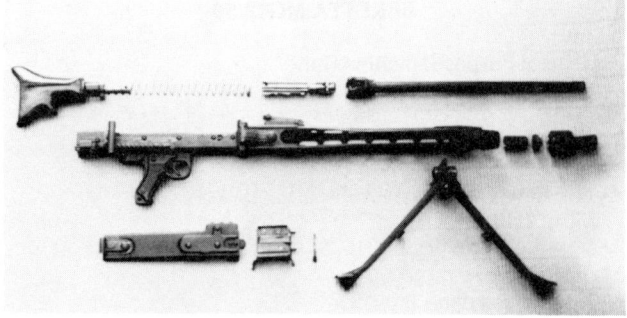

A Beretta 42/59. These guns look much better than war-time German guns, evincing Beretta's usual exceptionally high standard for fit and finish.

using the M60 is comprised of folks who get them free under the ANZUS Treaty (Australia/New Zealand/United States) or MAP (Military Aid Program).

Beretta licenses its guns from Rheinmetall and uses the "universal" feed group to handle both U.S. and original belt styles (Beretta supplied the graphics shown here). The gun is essentially the same as the German export 42/59, but a 990-gram bolt and R/R2 buffer kit is employed to moderate the rate of fire. Naturally, these guns are used in the 7.62 × 51mm T65 NATO caliber. Some guns in the original high-speed configuration are used in armored and fixed mounts, but my spies in Europe tell me that they are mostly German leftovers from the war, still going strong, and will gradually be modified to the new standard.

BERETTA BM59

Name:
Beretta Assault Rifle

Model:
BM59

Caliber:
7.62x51mm NATO

Overall Length:
42.5 inches

Barrel Length:
21 inches

Weight:
10.4–12 pounds

Type of Fire:
Selective fire (most variants)

System of Operation:
Gas

Cyclic Rate (approx.):
750 RPM

Feed System/Ammunition Delivery:
20-round detachable box (shorter and longer magazines are available)

Country of Manufacture:
Italy

Manufacturer:
Beretta, Breda, and Indonesian and Moroccan national arsenals

Countries of Use:
Italy, Nigeria, Indonesia, Morocco, and others

Period of Manufacture (approx.):
1959–1980s

Period of Service (approx.):
1960–present

Primary Tactical Use:
Individual

With much less dollar layout, hoopla, balderdash, and boondoggle, the Italian Beretta firm produced a rifle that was functionally much like the U.S. M14. Domenico Salza and Vittorio Valle executed a modified M1 Garand setup into a MB59 and had the rifle in production and issue while the U.S. rifle was still the subject of much controversy. The BM59 handles much like the M14, though with its sturdy barrel and more robust M1 clone receiver, it is less fragile and recoils somewhat less sharply. The barrel is shorter, so muzzle blast is quite profound. The fire-select switch is at the receiver's left front.

The rifle is a little heavier than the M14 in most versions, but there are eight major (and many other minor) versions, including folding stock, sniper, grenade-launching, and non-grenade-launching rifles. The grenade launcher's location is just far enough forward to have some beneficial effects in holding the muzzle down, but by no means enough to make the BM59 vastly superior to the M14. It is still a selective-fire weapon whose best work is done in very short bursts or in semiautomatic mode. Some versions, in fact, employ burst-control devices.

The standard Italian rifle looks very much like a sporty M1 with modified feed for a 20-round magazine, which is a fairly exact description of the rifle. The BM59 magazine is far more expensive on the U.S. market than the M14 magazine, one reason the BM59 is not as popular as it might be otherwise.

FRANCHI LF57

Name:
Franchi

Model:
LF57

Caliber:
9mm

Overall Length:
Stock extended: 27 inches
Stock folded: 16.5 inches

Barrel Length:
8 inches

Weight:
7 pounds

Type of Fire:
Full auto

System of Operation:
Blowback

Cyclic Rate (approx.):
500 RPM

Feed System/Ammunition Delivery:
20- or 40-round box magazine

Country of Manufacture:
Italy

Manufacturer:
Franchi S.p.A.

Countries of Use:
Italy

Period of Manufacture (approx.):
1956–late 1960s

Period of Service (approx.):
1957–present

Primary Service:
Post-World War II Italian Navy

Primary Tactical Use:
Individual

The Brescia-based Franchi firm is best known for an excellent series of gas-operated combat shotguns and sporting firearms. The LF57 uses a recessed bolt head to compress the weapon, carrying the mass of the bolt above the barrel.

A well-designed weapon of compact size and nearly an ideal combination of stampings, pressings, and precision-forged parts, the LF57 also is well made and shoots well. Competition in this size and cartridge parameter was fierce at a time when

Franchi LF57.

military establishments and police authorities were beginning to question the efficacy of the submachine gun.

BERETTA PM12S

Name:
Beretta submachine gun

Model:
PM12S

Overall Length:
26 inches (31.5 inches with butt unfolded)

Barrel Length:
8.4 inches

Weight:
6.6 pounds

Type of Fire:
Selective fire

System of Operation:
Blowback

Cyclic Rate (approx.):
550 RPM

Feed System/Ammunition Delivery:
32-round box magazine

Country of Manufacture:
Italy

Manufacturer:
Beretta

Countries of Use:
Italy and some other Western countries

Period of Manufacture (approx.):
Late 1960s–present

Period of Service (approx.):
Late 1960s–present

BERETTA PM12S (continued)

Primary Service:
Armored vehicle crews, military and civilian police, paratrooper units

Primary Tactical Use:
Short-range defensive fire

This handy little weapon proves a point about the submachine gun: for a weapon that's supposedly in its tactical death throes, it's proliferating like fleas on a dog.

This is another gun that's fitted with "self-cleaning" grooves in the receiver ferrule.

A wooden-stocked version was available until recently.

BERETTA 93R

Name:
Beretta Machine Pistol

Model:
93R

Caliber:
9x19mm

Overall Length:
Stock extended: 14.5 inches
Stock folded: 9.45 inches

Barrel Length:
6.15 inches (with flash hider and muzzle break)

Weight:
47 ounces

Type of Fire:
Selective fire

System of Operation:
Walther sliding block (hinged) recoil

Cyclic Rate (approx.):
3-round burst control at 110 RPM

Feed System/Ammunition Delivery:
20-round staggered box magazine

Country of Manufacture:
Italy

Manufacturer:
Beretta

Countries of Use:
Italy, some Latin American countries, and others

Period of Manufacture (approx.):
Mid 1970s–present

Period of Service (approx.):
Mid 1970s–present

Primary Service:
Civil and military police

Primary Tactical Use:
Local defense and suppression

This is perhaps the most intelligently thought-out machine pistol on the market. Based on the excellent 92-series service pistols, the 93R's 3-round burst capability makes it exceptionally handy since it forestalls the heavy trigger fingers of eager shooters. The folding grip is convenient for burst firing, and the shoulder stock avoids the temptation to shoot one-handed. The gun employs a loaded chamber indicator.

Beretta 93R. (Photo courtesy of Beretta.)

MODELLO 70/90

Name:
Assault Rifle/Weapons System

Model:
Modello 70/90

Caliber:
.223/5.56mm

Overall Length:
AR: 39.3 inches
SC: 38.8 inches
SCS: 34.5 inches
AS: 39.4 inches

Weight:
AR: 8.8 pounds
SC: 8.8 pounds
SCS: 8.4 pounds
AS: 11.8 pounds
(these figures are without bipod or magazine)

Type of Fire:
Selective fire on most models

System of Operation:
Indirect gas

Cyclic Rate (approx.):
670–800 RPM

Feed System/Ammunition Delivery:
30-round box magazine

Country of Manufacture:
Italy

Manufacturer:
Beretta

Countries of Use:
May soon be adopted by Italy and others

Period of Manufacture (approx.):
Mid-1970s (in small lots) to present

Period Service (approx.):
Mid 1970s to present in very limited numbers

Primary Service:
Infantry, airborne, general military units, and police

Primary Tactical Use:
Military assault

This family of weapons is intended to appeal to the countries that like the intermediate .223/5.56mm round but dislike the M16A1 HB. That category includes almost everyone, for this gun sells at a price far lower than the M16, and has performed better in tests. Some research has been done on a version in the Soviet 7.62 × 39mm round, a better idea for much of the Third World and probably a better bet for countries in the West.

Like the various Stoner systems, the Modello 70/90 has been modularized so that a common receiver can be used to produce several guns quickly. The AR is the assault rifle, the SCS a compact carbine, the SC a folding-stock full-sized unit, and the AS a light machine gun. Burst-control units are available, as are heavy bipods and optics.

Beretta Modello 70/90. The gun on top is the assault rifle (AR 70/90), and the bottom gun is the light machine gun (AS 70/90). (Photo courtesy of Beretta.)

CHAPTER 17

Japan

Japanese policy regarding submachine guns was vague and indecisive. It is unlikely that Japan produced more than 25,000 submachine guns of all types for service in World War II. Many historians believe that the Japanese Navy alone ordered and employed far more foreign guns—especially Suomis, Bergmanns, and Ermas—than the total number of submachine guns produced in Japan. Since the submachine gun is a close-to-ideal weapon for short-range shooting in jungle warfare, the details of this indecisive behavior remain obscure. It is known that Japanese soldiers in the field coveted submachine guns and used captured specimens—but production decisions were made in Tokyo.

Probably less than half a dozen Type 100 second model (sometimes called Model of 1944) guns exist. Though it is an extremely crude weapon, reflecting deteriorating conditions in Japan, it had a good reputation for reliability. Virtually all Japanese sub-

machine guns were fitted for bayonets, as is the Type 100 shown here.

The first model Type 100 is almost as rare, particularly in the folding stock, or paratrooper version. This model is better finished, but is no more reliable and no more accurate than the second model.

Original ammo for this weapon is unreliable and often unsafe. Several hundred thousand rounds of original format ammunition are supposedly available in China, loaded after the war for pistols to higher specification; so far, though, they have not been imported stateside. Nonte has suggested turning the round from .41 LC or .38 Special, but this requires turning down the rim, an unpleasant task at best. Forming the round from .223 may be possible. However, it is probably not smart to shoot a Type 100 anyway since it is a nonreplaceable gun, as are most of its parts.

TYPE 100

Name:
Japanese submachine gun

Model:
Type 100 (second pattern)

Caliber:
8mm Nambu pistol

Overall Length:
36 inches

Barrel Length:
9.2 inches

Weight:
8.5 pounds

Type of Fire:
Full auto only

System of Operation:
Blowback

Cyclic Rate (approx.):
800 RPM

Feed System/Ammunition Delivery:
30-round staggered box, curved

Country of Manufacture:
Japan

Manufacturer:
Kokura Arsenal

Countries of Use:
Japan

Period of Manufacture (approx.):
1940–1945

Period of Service (approx.):
1940–1945

Primary Service:
Military

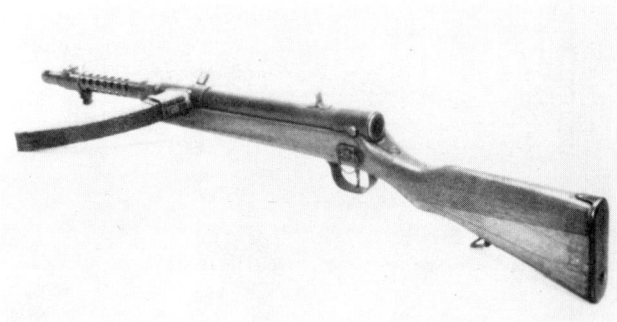

Type 100 (second pattern).

TYPE 97

Name:
Japanese tank machine gun

Model:
Type 97

Caliber:
7.7x58mm semirimmed Japanese

Overall Length:
34.5 inches

Barrel Length:
28 inches

Weight:
24 pounds

Type of Fire:
Full auto only

System of Operation:
Gas

Cyclic Rate (approx.):
500 RPM

Feed System/Ammunition Delivery:
Staggered cartridge box magazine

Country of Manufacture:
Japan

Manufacturer:
State arsenals

Countries of Use:
Japan

Period of Manufacture (approx.):
1937–1945

Period of Service (approx.):
1937–1945

Primary Service:
Military Tank Corps

Primary Tactical Use:
Armored tank machine gun

Type 97 was intended to replace the earlier Type 91 tank machine gun, though it never quite did so. It is a beefed-up, heavy-barreled copy of the Czech ZB26/30 series, with the breech internals close to identical. The buttstock is a fold-around unit, which

Type 97.

could be shoved out of the way to save space in crowded interiors of armored vehicles. These guns usually had telescopic sights coupled with periscopes or episcopes, though some were used with no integral sights at all.

TYPE 92

Name:
Japanese heavy machine gun

Model:
Type 92

Caliber:
7.7mm

Overall Length:
45.5 inches

Barrel Length:
28.8 inches

Weight:
Gun, unloaded: 62 pounds
Tripod: 60 pounds

Type of Fire:
Full auto only

System of Operation:
Gas

Cyclic Rate (approx.):
450 RPM

Feed System/Ammunition Delivery:
30-round feed-strips

Country of Manufacture:
Japan

Manufacturer:
Tokyo Arsenal and others

Countries of Use:
Japan

Period of Manufacture (approx.):
1932–1945

Period of Service (approx.):
1933–1945

Primary Service:
Military

Primary Tactical Use:
Crew-served machine gun

Type 92.

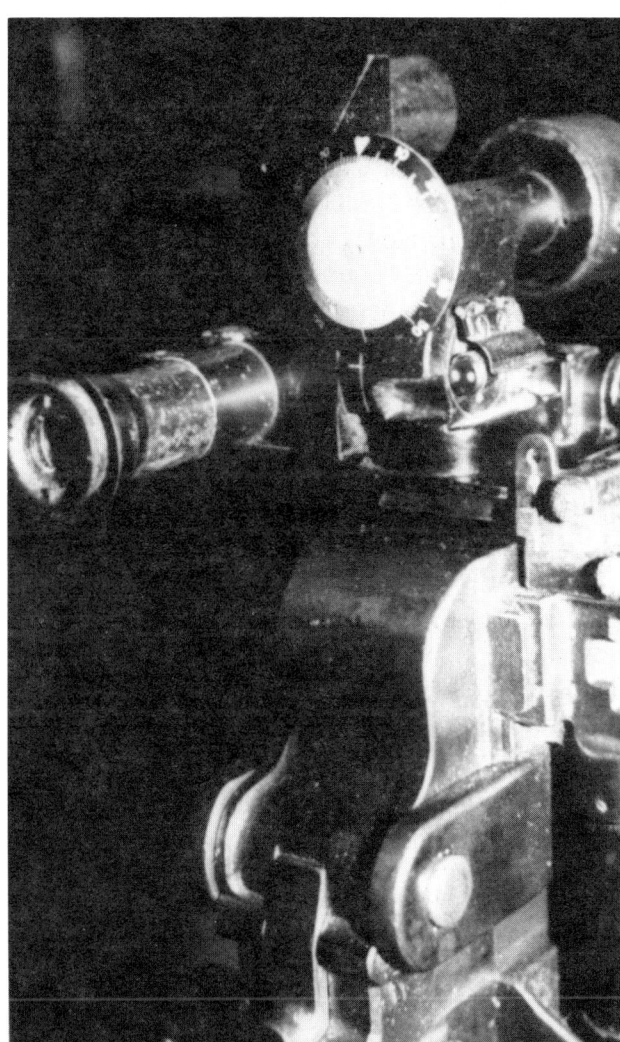

Detail of the Type 92 optics system.

With an excellent system of support accessories, the Type 92 was a much-improved Hotchkiss design, capable of a considerable degree of sustained fire. With this gun, the Japanese intentionally designed a special, semirimmed, very powerful version of their 7.7x58mm cartridge so that it could not be used in contemporary rifles. This gun could, however, handle 7.7mm rifle ammunition.

Used to carry the intact gun from place to place, the poles affixed to the mount were standard.

While most of the mechanism was Hotchkiss, the bolt head drew heavily on the Lewis gun, which had been manufactured in Japan. The mount design was durable and stable, and the Japanese were innovative in their use of optics. The periscopic effect, achieved with tubes and prisms, kept the line of sight away from the muzzle blast, thus assuring visibility during bursts.

Norma manufactures this round in rifle loadings; with its 180-grain load, excellent results were achieved. Old Chinese ammo on correct feeder strips shot reliably when the boxes were not water-stained; though this ammunition is corrosive, it shot quite cleanly. It was not as accurate as the Norma but, of course, it also cost nowhere near as much and the hard-brass feeder strips were included. The Type 92s are big, heavy machine guns with sturdy barrels; accuracy and stability are excellent. Despite their present value, there is no reason not to shoot a gun whose headspace has been checked. The 7.7x58mm round is quite powerful, full the equivalent of .30-06 or 7.92x57mm on which it is based. Federal may soon introduce a Norma-brass, full-metal jacketed version of this load into its American Eagle line.

These guns were derived directly from the Taiaho 3 (Type 14). Except for the Type 14's more conventional pistol grip, the Type 92 is almost identical externally to the Type 14. The earlier version was in the 6.5x51mm loading. These guns are fairly gentle on brass, though I am told there are exceptions.

The Type 92 may be regarded as the ultimate development of the Hotchkiss and is a genuine improvement of the French original. The cartridge oiler, so thoroughly tongue-lashed by many writers, causes no difficulties whatsoever and seems to be extraneous with good brass. Rate of fire tends to vary during the cycle: slow on the initial pickup of the feed strip, but accelerating rapidly. To some, the sound of fire resembles the noise a woodpecker makes while starting on a log, hence the gun's nickname, the woodpecker.

TAISHO 11

Name:
Japanese light machine gun

Model:
Taisho 11

Caliber:
6.5x50mm

Overall Length:
43.5 inches

Barrel Length:
19 inches

Weight:
22.5 pounds

Type of Fire:
Full auto only

System of Operation:
Gas

Cyclic Rate (approx.):
500 RPM

Feed System/Ammunition Delivery:
30-round hopper

Country of Manufacture:
Japan

Manufacturer:
Kokura Arsenal and others

Countries of Use:
Japan

Period of Manufacture (approx.):
1922–late 1930s

Period of Service (approx.):
1922–1945

Primary Service:
Military

Primary Tactical Use:
Individual weapon or crew served

Following the *3 Nen Shiki Kikanju* 1914 gun, a 1900 Hotchkiss copy, the Japanese made this copy of the light Hotchkiss, in which the feed strips were replaced by a hopper intended to take five-round batches of cartridges from the Type 38 rifle stripper clips. The idea seemed wise since any infantryman could feed the machine gun. However, under fire in China from the early 1930s on, the system proved to be a fairly serious problem since preloaded box magazines or belts could be introduced far more rapidly.

The hopper itself is far less complex than one might imagine. It works quite well, though rounds inserted backwards can cause difficulty, as can foreign objects of any size. Sights are offset to the right to clear the hopper.

Like most light Hotchkiss designs, the Taisho 11 feels very clumsy except for when it is actually being fired. Its forward center of gravity then becomes an advantage. The cartridge oiling system

Taisho 11.

Detail of the Taisho 11 hopper.

was well applied and appeared not to cause any problems, though a lower-powered cartridge was devised due to the swollen cases and extraction problems encountered with some early guns.

The hopper feed was tried with this gun primarily because it wouldn't snag, which the old feed strips did when the gun was loaded. Though it proved to be a good idea, it did not meet expectations. I fired a Taisho 11 with handloads only, using Winchester ball powder, downloaded to about minimum, since most texts claim the guns required a weak load for protection against excessive wear. Speer's 140-grain #1441 Spitzer fed well and delivered solid accuracy, better than the similar Hotchkiss .303 generally does. Hornady's #2633 boat-tail hollow-point 140-grain unit, also a brilliant performer in rifles and the Type 96 Light, put the gun into the excellent accuracy category. The gun shot superbly with carefully developed loads employing fast-burning 680 and almost as well with 748. However, I lacked time to do more experimentation since I was not doing my own handloading on this project. This weapon in particular has always been bad-mouthed as clumsy (which it is) and unreliable and inaccurate (which it most definitely isn't). I just wanted to test that proposition.

The Taisho 11 is more fragile than most, and the hopper feed is an idea whose time never really came. But a bad gun? No, just an attempt to do too much.

TYPE 96

Name:
Japanese light machine gun

TYPE 96 (continued)

Model:
Type 96

Caliber:
6.5mm (1936 model)

Overall Length:
41.5 inches

Barrel Length:
21.75 inches

Weight:
20 pounds

Type of Fire:
Full auto only

System of Operation:
Gas

Cyclic Rate (approx.):
550 RPM

Feed System/Ammunition Delivery:
30-round box magazine

Country of Manufacture:
Japan

Manufacturer:
Tokyo Arsenal and others

Countries of Use:
Japan

Period of Manufacture (approx.):
1936–1945

Period of Service (approx.):
1936–1945 (used afterward by some secondary armies and the Chinese)

Primary Service:
Military

Primary Tactical Use:
Individual weapon or squad machine gun

Type 96.

Though often described as a Hotchkiss variant, the Type 96 is really a modification of the Czech ZB series, primarily intended for the Japanese Navy, which retained the 6.5mm cartridge somewhat later than the army. There are persistent and apparently accurate reports that the eldest model of these guns was actually produced in China under Japanese supervision. The gun's loader retains cartridge oiling.

The Type 96 was a satisfactory light machine gun, and the 2.5-power telescopic sight was a standard-issue item. These guns retain a bayonet mounting lug, which was awkward to use on a machine gun.

The Japanese used machine guns with great boldness and cunning, and their light gun designs were solid and gave excellent service in humid and tropical climates. The bores were chromium-plated.

The Type 96 approximates the Bren and uses the excellent and accurate 6.5x50SR Japanese load. It also performs much like the Bren, though it is not quite as stable and, therefore, not quite as accurate. Still, downrange, if the gun is scoped, actual accuracy is often better than that of the Bren because the sight picture is more specific. Exceptional ammo like the handloads I tried with Hornady's #2633 bullet further improve the gun's performance.

The Type 96 was fired in an intense Arizona dust storm, and the blowing sand (which I could feel on my face) caused no problems whatsoever despite the much-maligned cartridge oiler. In fact, one quickly becomes unaware of the mechanism; if anything, it appears to minimize the sand's capability to adhere to chamber internals.

Despite admonitions that the action is weak and uses a special low-powered round, the gun works best with fairly brisk reloads and Norma factory ammo. Some ancient 1916 Kynoch and Chinese postwar ammo do fire, but they unfortunately deliver erratic accuracy.

The oiler employed with the gun is usually activated at the loader, and I didn't use it much of the time. There were no malfunctions. A trough on the bolt bottom may have once held a pad oiler.

People who claim this gun is inaccurate have either never fired one or have never fired one with quality ammunition. The gun is not as well-made as the Type 92 (heavy, ground) or Type 99 (light), and headspace and chamber finish could cause difficulties with a barrel mismatch.

The chrome-lined bore, a genuine time-saver when it comes to cleaning the gun, makes the use of corrosive ammo less of a headache.

The Japanese used light machine guns much as the allies used submachine guns, often in sniper teams, allowing a party to pass to a point in front of a well-sited gun. Riflemen behind the target party used the machine gun's distinctive fire to cover their sniping, and it took some time for ambushed troops to realize the actual killing was usually being done by rifles from high ground. On the offensive, the guns were used to make up for the almost total lack of submachine guns among Japanese infantry units.

Many writers dismiss the Japanese cartridge as underpowered and inaccurate. Oddly, many of them hail the new "assault rifle" cartridges as some kind of positive revolution. Even during the war, some U.S. soldiers believed (and were apparently told by "experts" in training) that the "Jap .25" was a weak round, "not much worse than a pinprick." Apparently, some fool had confused the 6.5x50mm with the .25 ACP.

Federal's new American Eagle round, a 139-grain hardball type on Norma brass, is very accurate, and the handloads used were as good or better. Basing accuracy conclusions on "tests" with incorrect or ancient ammunition that's been stored under horrible conditions can give some very strange and negative results. I could have as easily come to the conclusion that a brilliant custom match or benchrest rifle was grossly inaccurate if I intentionally located sufficiently horrible ammo. That is almost what such "tests" do.

TYPE 99

Name:
Japanese light machine gun

Model:
Type 99

Caliber:
7.7x58mm semirimmed

Overall Length:
46.75 inches

Barrel Length:
21.6 inches

Weight:
23 pounds

Type of Fire:
Full auto only

System of Operation:
Gas

Cyclic Rate (approx.):
850 RPM

Feed System/Ammunition Delivery:
30-round box magazine

Country of Manufacture:
Japan

Manufacturer:
Tokyo Arsenal

Countries of Use:
Japan

Period of Manufacture (approx.):
1939–1945

Period of Service (approx.):
1939–1945

Primary Service:
Military

Primary Tactical Use:
Individual weapon or crew served

The Type 99 was a very straightforward, reliable copy of the Czech ZB. It was found to be far more reliable than the Type 96, partly because the more powerful 7.7mm round boosted initial extraction. Coming along as it did only three years after the Type 96 and looking very much like it, confusion over ammunition and magazines inevitably resulted. The Type 99 could use either the rimless or semirimmed round, but it was primarily intended that rimless rifle ammunition be used. The barrel change method was improved over that of the Type 96.

The Japanese never had enough machine guns to go around, and the Type 99 was in especially great demand. This was a very well-made gun. This particular specimen bears several bullet dings, one of which inhibits the scope from seating fully.

The Japanese paid special attention to detailed barrel fit and headspace adjustment on these guns, and they incorporated a headspace adjustment nut on the barrel lock. The support at the buttstock's rear, inherited directly from the gun's Czech forebears, is handy for setting up fixed lines of fire.

It has been some years since I fired a Type 99. However, the 180-grain bulleted Norma round functioned splendidly in the gun, and both Hornady and Speer bullets of similar weight and pointed configuration worked well in reloads. Most of the old scopes are fogged by now, but enterprising shoot-

A Type 99 light machine gun with an extremely rare scope.

Type 99 with bayonet.

ers sometimes machine-mount for standard one-inch Weaver rings, copying the slide on the Japanese scope base but terminating the substitute units in a standard slotted rail setup. Similar work-ups are often done by hobbyists for Maxims, .50 Brownings, and other guns with convenient mount areas that are capable of sufficient accuracy to make use of the improved sight picture. Thus equipped with optics, the Type 99 is a Bren or ZB clone in function; in fact, some of the bullets we used during tests were pulloffs from .303 "Special Issue" (sniper) ammo.

As with the Type 96, the 99 was used much like a submachine gun. Originally intended for army issue only, the Type 99 later came into naval garrison service, with those units often erroneously called marines. There were also specialized paratrooper versions of the Type 99.

TYPE 87

Name:
Japanese aircraft machine gun

Model:
Type 87

Caliber:
7.7mm

Overall Length:
39 inches

Barrel Length:
26.8 inches

Weight:
22.8 pounds

Type of Fire:
Full auto only

System of Operation:
Gas

Cyclic Rate (approx.):
600 RPM

Feed System/Ammunition Delivery:
A flat, circular drum magazine holding 47 rounds

Country of Manufaccture:
Japan

Countries of Use:
Japan

Period of Manufacture (approx.):
1927–1930

Period of Service (approx.):
1927–late 1930s

Primary Tactical Use:
Aircraft free machine gun

This rare aircraft gun, which saw service in some bombers of the late twenties and early thirties, is a combination of the basic Czech VZ26/30 action, rotated ninety degrees, and a feed system and drum adapted form the Degtyarev. These guns were never common since better designs were being developed.

The sights are self-adjusting for speed and elevation via a system of vanes, the idea being to track smoothly without adjustment on a consistent azimuth.

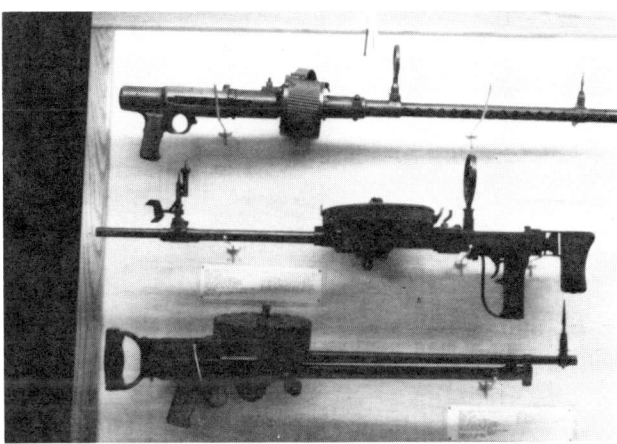

Type 87 (center).

TYPE 89

Name:
Japanese aircraft machine gun

Model:
Type 89

Caliber:
7.7mm

Overall Length:
41.4 inches

Barrel Length:
27 inches

Weight:
37 pounds

Type of Fire:
Full auto only

System of Operation:
Recoil

Cyclic Rate (approx.):
600+ RPM

TYPE 89 (continued)

Feed System/Ammunition Delivery:
Fabric web belt

Country of Manufacture:
Japan

Manufacturer:
State arsenal (Tokyo)

Countries of Use:
Japan

Period of Manufacture (approx.):
1928–1945

Period of Service (approx.):
1928–1945

Primary Service:
Japanese military air force

Primary Tactical Use:
Aircraft

This Vickers copy is almost indistinguishable from the World War II English gun, though the cooling jacket is somewhat more slender.

The standard cowl gun of some early Japanese Navy fighters like the A5M4 "Claude" and used throughout the war in army fighters, including the Ki-61 *Hien* ("Tony"), the Type 89 was used mainly as a ranging machine gun. Using his larger stock of 7.7mm ammunition, the pilot would open fire. Once the range was found, he would then switch to his 12.7, 13.2, 20mm, or heavier guns.

Generally used in pairs with a liberal ammunition supply, the guns were quite effective all by themselves, particularly in strafing ground targets.

The barrel and jacket of these Japanese copies are very sturdy, obviously intended to handle long bursts. The Japanese also copied the Browning .30. The Type 97, a naval gun, is similar to the Type 89 and was used in some of the early type 00 (Zero) A6M fighters.

The Type 89 shown here came to the United States with a serviceman who removed it from a downed Japanese fighter.

Type 89.

Detail of a Type 89.

Aircraft 92 light machine gun (center).

AIRCRAFT 92 LIGHT MACHINE GUN
Name:
Japanese Lewis aircraft machine gun

Model:
Aircraft 92 (1932)

A precise clone of the British model Lewis of similar configuration, the gun shown here was used in similar applications. This jacketed version was sometimes used as an infantry gun, though it was more often used in semi-open or blister mounts on aircraft.

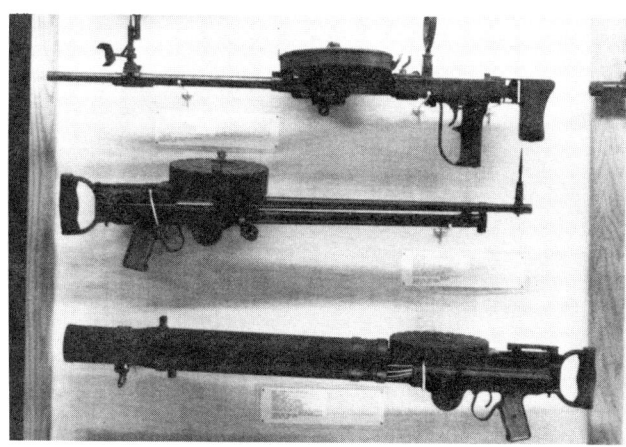

Type 92 (center).

AIRCRAFT LEWIS MACHINE GUN
Name:
Japanese aircraft Lewis machine gun

Model:
92

Caliber:
7.7mm (.303 British)

Type of Fire:
Full auto only

System of Operation:
Gas

Cyclic Rate (approx.):
550–600 RPM

Feed System/Ammunition Delivery:
47- or 96-round drum magazine

Country of Manufacture:
Japan

Manufacturer:
Tokyo Arsenal

Countries of Use:
Japan

Primary Service:
Aircraft

The Japanese adopted this part-for-part Lewis copy in 1932, using it as a flexible gun on several dive-bombers and scout aircraft.

The specifications are exactly the same as those of a similar British Lewis, including the caliber, which is odd since the Lewis was fully adaptable to cartridges similar to the 7.7 Japanese and was loaded in the 7mm and .30-06 calibers early in its career. However, the Japanese introduced still another cartridge into their system with this gun.

TYPE 98
Name:
Japanese aircraft machine gun

Model:
Type 98

Caliber:
7.7mm

Type of Fire:
Full auto only

System of Operation:
Recoil

Cyclic Rate (approx.):
950 RPM

Feed System/Ammunition Delivery:
Dual-feeding 75-round drum

Country of Manufacture:
Japan

Manufacturer:
Tokyo Arsenal

Countries of Use:
Japan

Primary Service:
Aircraft

Primary Tactical Use:
Swivel-mounted aircraft machine gun

The Japanese copied many guns during World War II and afterward. The Type 98 pictured here is an exact license-built copy of the German MG15, and was used on many medium bombers, patrol aircraft, and flying boats form 1938 until the end of the war.

Type 98.

TYPE 1941

Name:
Japanese aircraft machine gun

Model:
Type 1941 (01)

Caliber:
12.7mm

Overall Length:
55.8 inches

Barrel Length:
35.8 inches

Weight:
60 pounds

Type of Fire:
Full auto only

System of Operation:
Recoil

Cyclic Rate (approx.):
800 RPM

Feed System/Ammunition Delivery:
Steel-link belt

Country of Manufacture:
Japan

Manufacturer:
Nagoya Arsenal (state arsenal, southern branch)

Countries of Use:
Japan

Period of Manufacture (approx.):
1941–1945

Period of Service (approx.):
1941–1945

Primary Service:
Aircraft

Primary Tactical Use:
Offensive aircraft machine gun

One of the standard aircraft guns used by the Japanese Army, this specimen of the Type 1941, now extremely rare, comes from a downed Japanese fighter.

The Japanese produced many variants of M2 Browning copies, and the "01" was the standard gun of the Ki-43 "Oscar" and many other army fighters. Other Browning clones were flexible guns in army and navy bombers. One version of the vaunted Zero —A6M5b Model 52B (470 of which were built)— used a similar Browning design as one of its two cowl guns (see page 55 of *Famous Fighters of the Second World War,* by W. H. Green). Since the Japanese armed forces operated with almost total autonomy and disdained to use each other's equipment, it is not surprising that this increase in firepower originated with the aircraft manufacturer instead of the navy.

The Japanese 12.7mm cartridge is virtually indistinguishable from the U.S. original.

Type 1941 (center).

CHAPTER 18

Russia/Soviet Union

Intended at one time to replace the submachine gun and conventional pistols like the Tokarev, the Stechkin APS was very short-lived. The Soviets withdrew the pistol from service virtually before it was well-known in the West. It may have been introduced in prototypical lots in the fifties, but is very rare among active Soviet troops, though it may live on elsewhere in the Soviet bloc.

Ammunition for this weapon is hard to come by. While a trimmed 9mm Parabellum round will function, reloading data for the round is also hard to get. European military authorities claim the 9mm Ultra round will function in the Stechkin APS, and others suggest reworking 9mm Bergmann-Bayard or using .38 Super/ACP brass as a good alternative for this weapon and the newer Makarov.

These guns appear well made. From all reports, the metallurgy is good, but actually firing a fairly light pistol as a full auto can cause fairly subtle heat damage and cracking. The gun I examined looked as if enough damage or breakage in the aft slide rails could cause the slide to depart the frame if the front bearing separated, which apparently happened sometimes in service.

Most authorities suggest that the Stechkin was originally intended for vehicle crews or specialist troops carrying bulk equipment, and not for regular use.

STECHKIN APS

Name:
Stechkin

Model:
APS

Caliber:
9x18mm

Overall Length:
Pistol: 8.85 inches
Pistol and stock: 21.25 inches

Barrel Length:
5 inches

Weight:
Pistol: 1.7 pounds
Pistol and stock: 3.92 pounds

Type of Fire:
Selective fire

System of Operation:
Blowback

Cyclic Rate (approx.):
700–725 RPM

Feed System/Ammunition Delivery:
20-round box, staggered

Country of Manufacture:
Soviet Union

Manufacturer:
Soviet state arsenals

Countries of Use:
Warsaw Pact, East Bloc, and limited use by patron states

Period of Manufacture (approx.):
Early 1960s–late 1960s

Period of Service (approx.):
Early 1960s perhaps to present (though no longer used much in the Soviet Union)

Primary Tactical Use:
Individual infantry and police

161

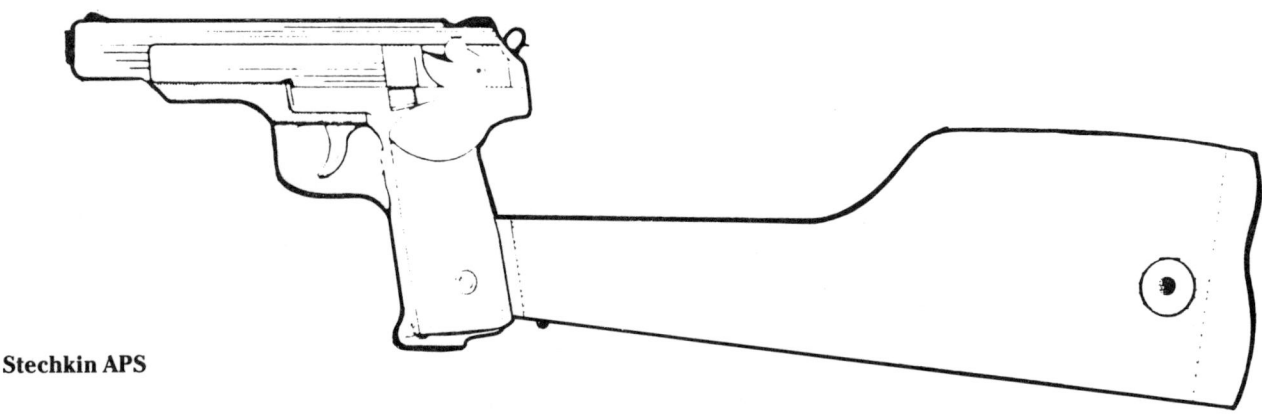

Stechkin APS

MAXIM 1910

Name:
Maxim

Model:
1910 (SPM)

Caliber:
7.62x54mm Soviet rimmed

Overall Length:
43.6 inches

Barrel Length:
28.4 inches

Weight:
Gun: 52.5 pounds
Wheeled mount (with shield): 100 pounds

Type of Fire:
Full auto

System of Operation:
Recoil

Cyclic Rate (approx.):
500 + RPM

Feed System/Ammunition Delivery:
Fabric-belt fed, 250 rounds

Country of Manufacture:
Russia/Soviet Union

Manufacturer:
Tula Arsenal and others

Countries of Use:
Russia/Soviet Union, all Soviet Bloc countries, and China

Period of Manufacture (approx.):
1910–1945

Period of Service (approx.):
1910–1970s

Primary Service:
From Czarist Russia to present Soviet-backed satellite countries

Primary Tactical Use:
Crew-served machine gun

Imperial Russia used Maxim guns virtually as soon as they were available, first on warships, then with infantry and cavalry units. In 1905, Tula Arsenal began production of an elaborate copy of the German commercial Maxims then entering world weapons markets, improving and simplifying it in 1910 with a version whose main distinguishing feature was a huge water entry port. Some had pleated jackets, while others were smooth. All were chambered for the effective but heavily rimmed Soviet M1891 Nagant cartridge. Steel was substituted for much of the bronze in the M1905.

The wheeled carriage was an item of great importance to the Russians, who continue to place many heavy and medium guns on similar mounts.

M1910s are still found from time to time in the hands of irregulars. Like all Maxims, they are very reliable and easily serviced. They are, however, very rare in U.S. collections.

The specimen shown in the close-up is especially unusual, for it was captured from the Japanese in 1944 in the Philippines, where its former owners were somewhat reluctant to surrender. That explains the eleven bullet holes and a layer of rust indicative of its demise by flamethrower. It bears several Japanese property marks. Presumably, the Japanese captured this Maxim variant either from the Chinese or the Soviets, with whom they fought a series of border wars on the Asian mainland between 1931 and 1939. This particular specimen is on display in the J. Curtis Earl collection of the Champlin Fighter Museum.

This Maxim variant proves, as does the Vickers, that rimmed cartridges are at no particular disadvantage when used in a well-designed gun, especially in a belt-fed unit with a massive extractor. These guns still show up once in a while since the Soviets made them until 1945 (this means that there were plenty of them around after postwar demobilization and modernization). The guns were regarded

Maxim 1910 (SPM).

Troops deploying a Maxim 1910 in World War I.

fensives, regardless of technology.

Several 2,000- to 3,000-meter-deep zones were planned so that every point of ground or cover was under fire from no less than three high-velocity antitank guns and five machine guns. Since mines generally slow advances, the preferred gun of the day, the SPM, was worked as if it were a range day. Even in sharp local actions where the Germans enjoyed technical and numerical advantages, movement was slowed to a frustrating pace, and the Soviets won the greatest armored battle of World War II, completely eliminating some of Nazi Germany's finest divisions.

as extremely reliable, and the Soviets learned to use them with great effect on the defensive.

At Kursk in 1943, the first time the Nazis were defeated in a straightforward manner by superior Russian planning, M1910s were used with great intelligence, overlooking deep mine fields and carefully mapped artillery ranges complete with range flags. The overconfident Germans and their "secret weapons" were swallowed up in a battle that proved that World War I defensive tactics, given adequate preparation, can work even against the best-prepared of-

GORYUNOV SG43

Name:
 Goryunov

Model:
 SG43, SG43M, SGM, and others

Caliber:
 7.62x54mmR Soviet

Overall Length:
 44.1 inches

GORYUNOV SG43 (continued)

Barrel Length:
28.3 inches

Weight:
Gun: 29–32 pounds (various versions)
Mount (without shield): 60 pounds

Type of Fire:
Automatic only

System of Operation:
Gas

Cyclic Rate (approx.):
600–700 RPM

Feed System/Ammunition Delivery:
250-round metal-linked belt (some versions can be or have been modified to accept the old Maxim belt)

Country of Manufacture:
Soviet Union

Manufacturer:
Soviet state arsenals

Countries of Use:
Warsaw Pact, other Soviet client states, and China

Period of Manufacture (approx.):
1943–mid 1950s

Period of Service (approx.):
1943–present (used mainly in its modified form in Warsaw Pact countries; now being replaced by the PK)

Primary Tactical Use:
Heavy machine gun; usually controlled by company headquarters

The Goryunov is extremely rare in the United States. The one specimen I have seen was a deactivated Vietnam capture piece with no mount at all.

Like most Soviet weapons, the Goryunov has been manufactured in several communist countries, and is straightforward and very rugged. There seems to have been something wrong with the system, for the Soviets kept modifying it, trying constantly to replace the gun since its introduction. This may reflect its weight, since the gun and mount weigh nearly one hundred pounds. The Soviets issue the old-fashioned front plates for all their tripod guns, and still persist with wheeled mounts. Such a setup concedes that the gun is heavy, yet allows one man to drag it without taking it out of action for the removal of crosspins, pintles, or bolts. Presuming the ammo can is left in place, the gun is never out of action. The wheeled mount means a low firing position requires either a lot of sandbags or digging in the gun, which is not handy on the offensive.

DShK 38 and DShK 38/46

Name:
Degtyarev heavy machine gun

Model:
DShK 38 and DShK 38/46

Caliber:
12.7mm Soviet M38

Overall Length:
62.5 inches

Barrel Length:
42.1 inches

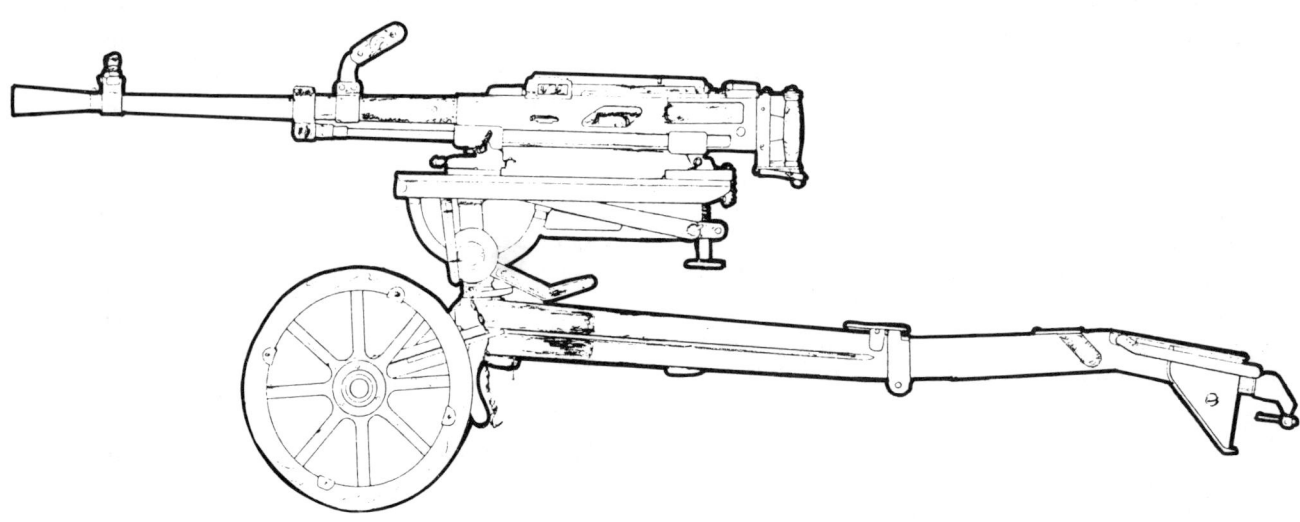

Goryunov SG43.

Weight:
Gun: approx. 80 pounds
Mount: 259+ pounds

Type of Fire:
Automatic only

System of Operation:
Gas

Cyclic Rate (approx.):
540–600 RPM

Feed System/Ammunition Delivery:
Extendable 50-round metallic linked belts

Country of Manufacture:
Soviet Union and others

Manufacturer:
Soviet, Chinese, and other state arsenals

Countries of Use:
Warsaw Pact, Soviet and Chinese patron states, and some neutral countries

Period of Manufacture (approx.):
1938 to at least the 1960s in the Soviet Union; later elsewhere

Period of Service (approx.):
1938–present

Primary Tactical Use:
Heavy support, antiaircraft, long-range defensive fire, sustained cover fire, etc.

DShK 38.

Tank version of the DShK 38 being used in Berlin, 1945.

Using a cartridge very similar to the U.S. .50 caliber, the Soviet equivalent boasts slightly better performance, flinging its 760- to 790-grain bullets downrange at about the same 2,800 to 2,950 fps (feet per second) velocity as the U.S. 670- to 710-grain slugs. It is an even sturdier case, but one which is almost impossible to find in the United States. It is quite likely (in fact, more or less certain) that a DShK barrel could be fabricated to handle the U.S. round. You'd have to build a new one, though, since the Soviet round is longer and requires a deeper chamber. To approximate Soviet ballistics, you'd have to load fairly briskly or the mechanism might not function properly. Most automatic conversions are a problem with longer-than-designed rounds or radically different case shapes; this case involves neither.

While this gun is often described as the equivalent of the U.S. .50 BMG M2HB (Heavy Barrel), that is not the case. The mount for ground use adds about the weight of an NFL tackle to the package, though the gun itself is actually a few pounds lighter. The comparison is valid on tanks and other vehicles, but in infantry units, these guns are tightly controlled at battalion level.

Like the Goryunov series, these guns are seen in many subvariants, though there are only two major variants, the original 1938 model and the 1946 revision, the latter using a conventional feed pawl system instead of the rotating block feed setup.

Most of these guns sport chromium-plated bores.

The designator letters pay tribute to Degtyarev and Shpagin, the gun's primary designers.

The ZPU and other weapons are supposedly replacing the DShK series in most roles, but the DShK was still in use in Afghanistan as late as 1988. The Goryunov was, in fact, developed because of the DShK's awkward weight and bulk. However, the DShK is a very steady, reliable, and secure weapon. It is almost always fitted with a shield and capable of superb accuracy at a mile or more. Whatever weapon finally does replace it will have to be very good indeed.

Even new Soviet T-72 and derivative tanks mount this weapon as coaxial and local defense for the same reason the United States has removed the so-called "replacements" for the M2 from production and reinstated the old, reliable Browning. The DShK has not only outlived its replacements, but it has reduced them to expensive footnotes. Its cyclic rate (as with the M2) is low for antiaircraft use, but most such employments involve several guns.

I have spoken with soldiers who have used this gun extensively, some against the Germans in World War II, one in realistic maneuvers in the Yugoslavian army, and others who've used issued or captured specimens more recently. The Yugoslavs, who use the DShK much as we use the M2HB, often mount it on modified U.S. mounts, using a step-up collar because the gun requires more clearance over the mount. Others praise the gun and strongly dislike moving the mount, which is supposedly a two-man job but is often performed in combat by one man.

I have never been fortunate enough to get the gun and ammunition together to test the DShK. I have, however, examined the excellent, rugged, simple, and uncluttered optics the Soviets employ with many of these guns. These sights are probably not very expensive, but they effectively raise or lower the line of sight, pass up muzzle gases, and change visual focus. The sights are one of those handy innovations that could easily be copied by Western armies. The guns do not employ gimmicky drop systems or range finders or anything else that complicates controls or clutters up viewfinders and causes malfunctions. A simple cross hair occupies the center, with range markings for reference and other details in the periphery. On a gun of this power, accuracy, and range, such sights are very handy and convenient.

DP LIGHT MACHINE GUN

Name:
Degtyarev light machine gun

Model:
DP

Caliber:
7.62x54mmR

Overall Length:
51 inches

Barrel Length:
23.8 inches

Weight:
20.5 pounds

Type of Fire:
Full auto only

System of Operation:
Gas

Cyclic Rate (approx.):
500-600 RPM

Feed System/Ammunition Delivery:
47-round drum magazine

Country of Manufacture:
Soviet Union

Manufacturer:
Soviet state arsenals

Countries of Use:
All Soviet Bloc countries

Period of Manufacture (approx.):
1928–1950

Period of Service (approx.):
1928–1960s (with irregular service well into the 1980s)

Primary Tactical Use:
Individual

The secret of *Degtyaryova Pakhotnyi* was its simple locking system, based upon the Frijberg-Kjellman patents, using flaps on the bolt that are pushed out by the firing pin. This ancient system proved highly resistant to dirt and fouling, but the bottleneck-shaped, heavily rimmed Soviet cartridge M1891 proved awkward to handle, necessitating the use of the pan magazine and considerable redesign of the extraction/ejection setup.

All Degtyarev guns were altered and new production redesigned to move the spring aft and/or beef it up since heat attacked its temper, riding as it did just below and in close proximity to the hot barrel.

Designer Vasily Degtyarev worked on the odd Federov automatic rifle, a 6.5mm Japanese weapon of the immediate post-Revolutionary period, and came to understand the needs of the field infantry unit.

This was the standard Communist bloc light machine gun of World War II and Korea, and was used till the 1960s.

RPD LIGHT MACHINE GUN

Name:
Degtyarev light machine gun *(Ruchnoi Pulemet Degtyareva)*

Model:
RPD

Caliber:
7.62x39mm (M43)

Overall Length:
40.8 inches

Barrel Length:
20.5 inches

Weight:
15.6 pounds

Type of Fire:
Full auto

System of Operation:
Gas

Cyclic Rate (approx.):
700 RPM

Feed System/Ammunition Delivery:
Belt-fed from drum

Country of Manufacture:
Soviet Union and China

Manufacturer:
Soviet state arsenals

Countries of Use:
Soviet Union, China, and various Soviet- and Chinese-supplied guerrilla forces and satellite countries

Period of Manufacture (approx.):
1946–1960s

Period of Service (approx.):
1950s–present

Primary Service:
Soviet and Chinese squad weapon

Primary Tactical Use:
Individual

Now technically obsolete among Warsaw Pact countries, the Degtyarev squad light machine gun is still common in Asia, as are its Chinese and various other copies.

The RPD is an excellent compromise between the demands for a powerful fire base with a high rate of sustained fire and the need to keep the M43 cartridge common to small unit infantry weapons. The Degtyarev action was modified and shrunk to accept the shorter cartridge. Feed is normally via 100-round belts contained in drums, though the drum—mostly just a convenient canister to keep the belts from snagging—may be dispensed with.

Normal length of the belts is 50 rounds, two of which are customarily linked together in the drum. The Chinese use 25-round belts, loading four belts in each drum.

DT MACHINE GUN

Name:
Russian tank machine gun

Model:
DT

Caliber:
7.62mm

Overall Length:
With stock: 46.46 inches
Without stock or with stock retracted: 39.76 inches

Barrel Length:
23.5 inches

Weight:
28 pounds

Type of Fire:
Full auto only

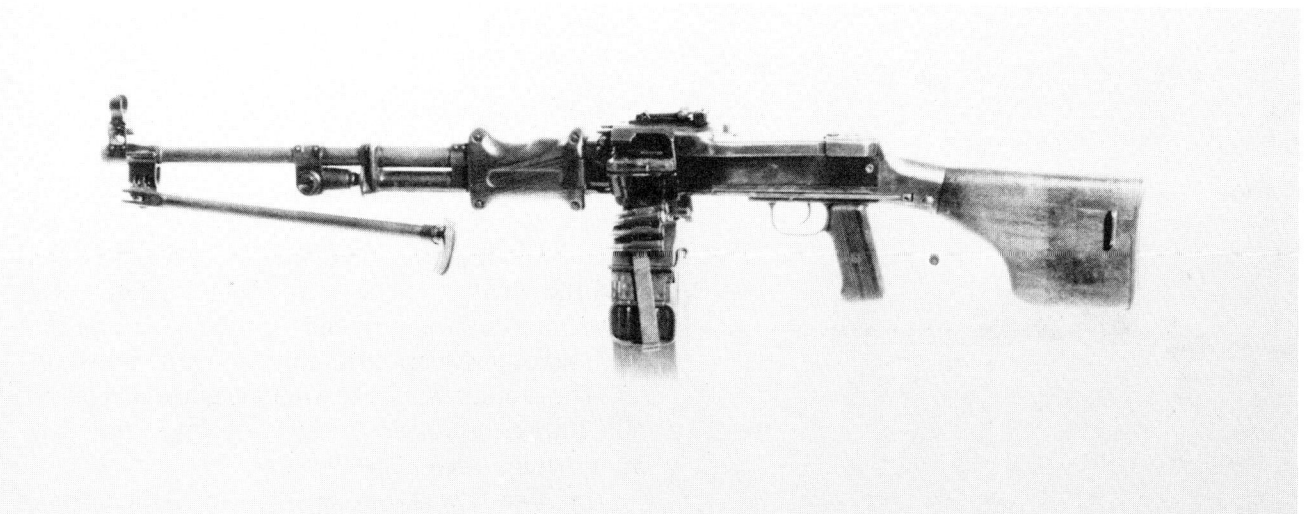

Degtyarev RPD light machine gun.

DT MACHINE GUN (continued)

System of Operation:
Gas

Cyclic Rate (approx.):
600 RPM

Feed System/Ammunition Delivery:
60-round drum

Country of Manufacture:
Soviet Union

Manufacturer:
Soviet state arsenals

Countries of Use:
Soviet Bloc countries

Period of Manufacture (approx.):
1928–1940s

Period of Service (approx.):
1928–present

Primary Service:
Military tank corps

Primary Tactical Use:
Crew-served tank weapon

The DT and DTM were the basic armored vehicle guns of the Soviet Army from the early thirties until well after World War II.

A Degtyarev design, the operating rod spring rides the piston rod that's seated in the gas tube under the barrel. When in service, accumulated heat attacked the temper of these springs, causing distortion and malfunctions (tank crews tend to fire very long bursts). During the war, existing guns were modified to beef up the spring and move it rearward. After that, the guns established an excellent reputation for reliability.

These guns are still in place on World War II vintage tanks still in service, such as the T-34 and JS-3, and on the Su-100 assault guns.

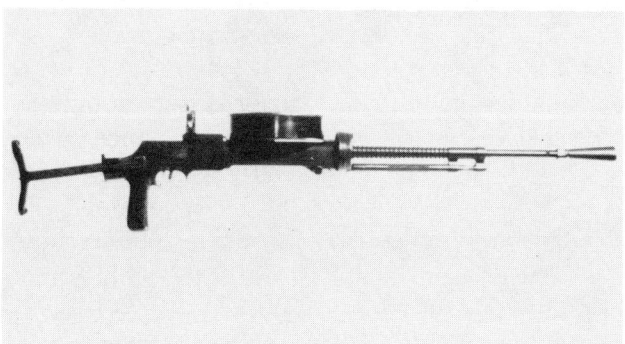

Russian DT tank machine gun.

PPSh41

Name:
Russian submachine gun

Model:
PPSh41

Caliber:
7.62x25mm Soviet (same as .30 Mauser)

Overall Length:
33.1 inches

Barrel Length:
10.6 inches

Weight:
8 pounds

Type of Fire:
Select, semiauto or full auto

System of Operation:
Blowback

Cyclic Rate (approx.):
900 RPM

Feed System/Ammunition Delivery:
71-round drum or 31-round box magazine

Country of Manufacture:
Soviet Union

Manufacturer:
Soviet state arsenals

Countries of Use:
Soviet Bloc countries

Period of Manufacture (approx.):
1941–1950s

Period of Service (approx.):
1941–1970s (still in service in Asia and with irregular personnel)

Primary Service:
Military

Primary Tactical Use:
Individual

Scholars may argue as to which was the first submachine gun, which was best, and which is the handiest, but there can be no question as to which had the greatest impact: the Soviet PPSh41. Entire battalions (some say whole regiments) were armed with no other weapon. Its Russian name translates to "The Automatics," and what the gun did in places like Kursk and Kharkov was to destroy whole German armies in great swallows.

The PPSh41 was developed close on the heels of two Suomi-inspired, traditionally built weapons of the PPD series. Georgi Shpagin intended this piece

PPSh41.

Firing a PPSh41.

to be built in huge quantities from the original 1939–1940 prototypes, and by the late 1940s, more then five million had been produced in the Soviet Union. China has probably produced several million more.

As far as possible, the piece is made from sheet metal stampings, with welding and riveting being used where possible. It looks old-fashioned because of the wooden stock, but the one-piece barrel jacket and receiver are of the most modern type for the period. Bores and chambers were chromed to reduce wear and facilitate cleaning, though this coating tended to tear and flake if a user chronically fired long bursts. There was a 35-round stick magazine, though it seems to have seldom been used during World War II. A typical tank rider rig consisted of six 71-round drums and one in the gun. It seems that few of the men who used this gun lived long enough to require more than seven drums.

The PPSh was inspired by the Finnish Suomi during the 1939 Winter War, as were the numbers in which it was issued and the tactics used in its employment. Perhaps the prettiest PPSh guns are the East bloc and Chinese copies made during peacetime, but the ugliest of them sport chrome-lined bores and shoot splendidly.

Fiochhi ammo in 7.63 Mauser is only nominally interchangeable with the Soviet round since power level is lower, neck specification is different, and some Soviet guns (especially Tokarev pistols) will not chamber the round. The Soviet submachine guns use a looser chamber, and eat Fiochhi ammo just fine, though they fire slower. Muzzle blast is also reduced. The 7.63 Mauser/7.62 Soviet case may be made (as may the 9mm Mauser round) from military format .223 brass, suitably trimmed and formed. However, the Fiocchi is exceptional brass. As this book goes to press, there is a rumor of non-corrosive, Boxer-primed Yugoslavian ammo about to be imported. If so, this would change the ammunition picture dramatically.

This cartridge *should* be loaded by some U.S. manufacturer, not because of demand from PPS and PPSh, but because of the number of Broomhandle Mausers in the country from China. These Broomhandles, incidentally, should *not* be fired with the Czech P&S rounds now in the U.S., as they are marginal with Soviet ammo. Tokarevs should use this ammo only with fresh, firm recoil springs. Submachine guns do just fine with it, though muzzle blast is impressive with the Czech rounds.

While German/Italian format ammo is an "iffy" fit with Soviet guns, the East bloc ammo will fit Western guns with ease—but that doesn't make it correct. The Czech ammo is designed for the CZ52 and a whole series of heavily built guns, mostly roller-delayed, and is more powerful than necessary for other firearms.

PPS43

Name:
Soviet submachine gun

Model:
PPs43

Caliber:
7.62x25mm

Overall Length:
Stock extended: 37.72 inches
Stock folded: 24.25 inches

Barrel Length:
8 inches

Weight:
8 pounds

Type of Fire:
Full auto

System of Operation:
Blowback

Cyclic Rate (approx.):
700 + RPM

Feed System/Ammunition Delivery:
32- to 35-round box magazine

Country of Manufacture:
Soviet Union

Manufacturer:
Kotlin/Leningrad Naval Arsenal

Countries of Use:
Soviet Union and allies

Period of Manufacture (approx.):
1942–1945 in Soviet Union; to 1960s elsewhere

Period of Service (approx.):
1942–1950s

Primary Service:
Soviet Union during World War II, especially in Leningrad

Primary Tactical Use:
Individual infantry

It is rare that a gun becomes identified not with a particular military unit, battle, or theater, but with a city. Such is the case with the PPS43, the formalized, standardized version of a weapon designed for simple production in the besieged city of Leningrad. In many units in the Soviet Northern Theater, the PPS42 (the even more primitive, early version of the gun) was the *only* available weapon. The manufacture of magazine springs and followers was so crude on some units that magazines might take 32, 33, 34, or 35 rounds, or sometimes, 36, of which the last three were brutally difficult to insert. Nonetheless, the weapon worked. Rough and ugly, it was quite reliable and cheap enough so that it was expendable. A. Sudarev intended that the submachine gun he designed should liberate the city, and it almost did.

The gun was copied by many Soviet allies. Interestingly, during the purges of the Leningrad Communist Party in the late forties, the gun could not be used or displayed by guards at any of the many Soviet World War II memorials. Wherever the guns were stored, they have reappeared since 1985.

The PPS43 has also been copied in China and elsewhere within the Communist bloc, both directly and as derivatives. The gun was also copied in Finland and Spain, and saw some service, in clone form, with the German *Bundesgrenzschutz* as the DUX 53 and 59. These latter copies were all in 9mm Parabellum. Cheap to make like the Sten and cruder still in some ways, the longevity of the gun designed to save a city is surprising. They are still found in the hands of irregulars from time to time.

Like the PPSh41, this gun opens like a single-shot shotgun, hinged at the receiver-stock point, for access to barrel and bolt. Almost all originals and all peacetime copies used chrome-lined barrels.

The Czechs, Germans, Finns, and others made 9mm barrels for these guns, which drop in and work

PPS43.

The PPS43 experienced slight difficulty with some of the new Fiocchi ammunition, but Yugoslavian ammo from Century and Sarco worked fine. (Fiocchi ammo worked fine with other Soviet guns.) We were able to use Hornady and Speer .308 o.d. "plinker" bullets in the cartridge, but seating and crimping were shaky and tended to depend on a particular weapon's eccentricities.

with alacrity. If you own both types of barrels, however, make sure you know which one is in the gun before loading. Surprisingly, no special provisions are necessary for the shorter 9mm round.

AK-47

Name:
Russian Assault Rifle *(Automat Kalashnikova)*

Model:
AK-47

Caliber:
7.62x39mm (M43 Soviet)

Overall Length:
34.65 inches

Barrel Length:
16.34 inches

Weight:
9.45 pounds

Type of Fire:
Selective fire

System of Operation:
Gas

Cyclic Rate (approx.):
600 RPM

Feed System/Ammunition Delivery:
30-round curved box magazine

Country of Manufacture:
Soviet Union

Manufacturer:
Soviet state arsenals

Countries of Use:
Soviet Bloc countries

Period of Manufacture (approx.):
1947–1950s

Period of Service (approx.):
Late 1940s–present

Primary Service:
Military

Primary Tactical Use:
Individual

While the Germans can take credit for inventing the reduced-power assault rifle, it was the Soviet Union that made it the standard of entire armies. Modernized between 1953 and 1957 to become a somewhat lighter (1½ pounds) and cheaper weapon with a stamped receiver, the original forged receiver version, similar to the specimen shown, remains in use all over the world. It is copied and cloned in the Israeli Galil and the Finnish Valmet, as well as in numerous variants throughout the Communist bloc. Commercial semiautomatic versions of the Kalashnikov made in China and Yugoslavia are now on the U.S. domestic market.

Interarms president Sam Cummings discussed the AK series on CBS's "NightWatch," noting that approved military sales of the piece with its accessories put the price at around $150, with a choice of several countries of manufacture. The U.S. M16 sells in the same market for about $600. As a result, Cummings explained, the gun has become the hardware darling of the arms marketplace, losing any essence of politics along the way. It appears about as often in the hands of right-wingers as left-wingers. The gun has required a superb reputation for reliability in all its forms, though the sights are in some ways a throwback to a far more primitive era.

The AK series of rifles began to be noticed in the West about 1951. Though almost none were seen in the 1949–1953 Korean action, by Vietnam AKs were everywhere.

The original cartridge was inspired by the German 7.92x33mm Kurz round from Polte, captured rifles for and specimens of which fell into Soviet hands by late 1942 to early 1943. The first weapon for the cartridge, the SKS, was a credible, reliable, but uninspired rifle, semiautomatic only. M.T. Kalashnikov was on convalescent leave when he came up with the idea of combining the firepower of the submachine gun with the stability and some of the range of a rifle. Though his first designs proved fragile (what we in the West call the "original" AK-47 is probably the third version of the rifle, though Soviet nomenclature doesn't recognize these small variants), it was obvious by 1951 that the basic design was capable of tremendous development.

The AK-74, an almost visually identical variant, uses a small-bore 4.85mm projectile and has been encountered in Afghanistan. Some authorities claim these are special conversions for special uses, while others say that the entire Soviet military is going to adopt the new version. More likely, the new variant is a field experiment.

Many permutations of wood, top cover, fittings, and furniture are to be found on AKs, reflecting their long period of manufacture in many countries, as well as specialized applications for different units. There are more than fifteen known variants

AK-47.

AK-47.

and there are probably many more. Yet most receiver parts, barrels, and magazines will interchange, greatly simplifying logistics.

Folding stock variants were probably originally intended for paratroopers and vehicle crews, where the eleven-inch (approximately) shorter gross length was handy. There is no weight reduction, since the steel rods and butt are very sturdy and heavy. There is a slight reduction in accuracy due to induced wobble.

An AKM, imported by Steyr/Gun South.

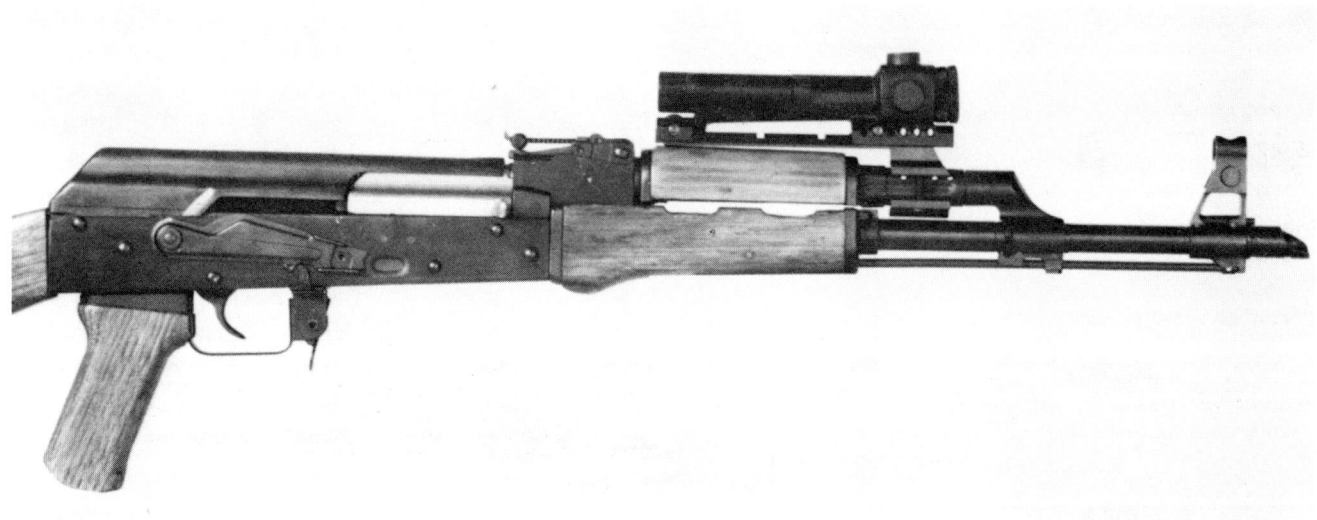

An AK-47 with a B-Square LER scope mount.

PK/PKM MACHINE GUN

Name:
General purpose machine gun

Model:
PK/PKM

Caliber:
7.62x54mmR (Soviet M91)

Other Chamberings:
Finnish, Czech, Hungarian, and Yugoslavian versions rumored in 7.62x51mm NATO

Overall Length:
47.2 inches

Barrel Length:
25.9 inches

Gross Weight:
Lightest version: 16.5 pounds
Support version: 21 pounds
(Mounts range from a new lightweight of 17 pounds to a large, heavy wheeled adaption of the old Sokolov/SPM carriage)

Type of Fire:
Automatic only

System of Operation:
Kalashnikov direct gas

Cyclic Rate (approx.):
650–700 RPM

Feed System/Ammunition Delivery:
100-, 200- and 250-round metallic-link belts and internally reeled drum

Country of Manufacture:
Soviet Union

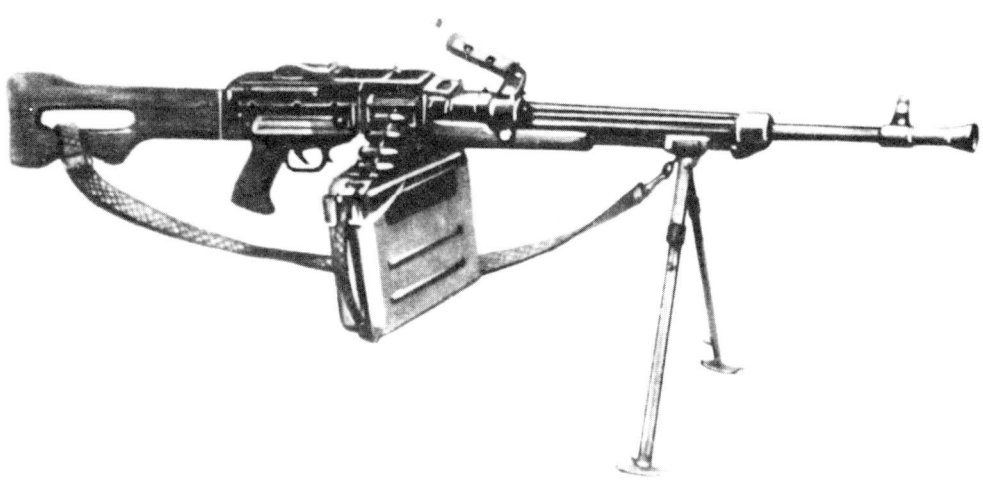

PK/PKM.

Manufacturer:
Soviet state arsenals

Countries of Use:
Warsaw Pact (the PK is a relatively new weapon seldom seen outside the Communist Bloc)

Period of Manufacture (approx.):
1968 or 1969 to present

Period of Service (approx.):
1969–present

Primary Tactical Use:
General-purpose squad weapon

If the PK looks like the FN MAG, it is not coincidental, for just as the MAG is a beefed-up BAR with an MG42 feed system, the PK is an inverted, enlarged AK design with a new feed system derived from (but not identical to) the RP46. The gun is an admission that the M43 cartridge is not ideal for all purposes since it uses the ancient, heavily rimmed M91 Nagant cartridge.

While the PK uses a fluted barrel, the PKM (M-modified) uses a smooth barrel. The PKS is tripod-mounted. The PKT is the tank gun, and uses the same breech as all PKs but heavier feed components and trigger/grip setup. The PKB is the same basic gun as the PK or PKM, but it has a spade grip and no buttstock and is designed for flexible vehicle mounts, especially on armored personnel carriers. Any PK can be converted to any configuration.

This gun sports an especially interesting feed system, for much aiming is necessary with the old cartridge since it must be withdrawn rearward from any belt (the rim would otherwise act as a very positive stop) and then moved forward again. This requires considerable vertical space since the cartridge must then clear the belt again on the way forward, accounting for the hump over the beltway.

In addition to known variants, several styles of buttstock and flash hider have been observed. The guns are seen in photographs (which may have been reversed) with the box hung on the left side, perhaps suggesting some models have reversible feed groups. The only specimen I have ever seen did not seem to have such a feed group.

CHAPTER 19

Spain

The Z-62 is the official submachine gun of Spain's Army and *Guardia Civil* police organizations in the potent 9mm Largo (Bergmann-Bayard) loading. The Z-70 is the commercial export version of the gun. Very rare in the United States, the Star Zs are part of the new generation of handy and light compact guns that border on being true machine pistols.

With the bolt forward—dangerous with most submachine guns if dropped hard—the Z-62/70 series employs a positive lock that prevents movement from that position. The spring-loaded cocking handle does not reciprocate with the bolt, and the automatic folding of the cocking handle makes for ease of handling during firing. When folded, the normal shoulder piece may be used as a foregrip.

This weapon is replacing the Z-45, an MP40 copy. It has been purchased on the international market by several countries, primarily in the 9mm Parabellum form, for use in armored vehicles.

These guns are handy and fun to shoot. Along with the Steyr, they are among the most accurate modern "subcompact" SMGs.

STAR Z70

Name:
Star

Model:
Z70 (Z62)

Caliber:
9x19mm Parabellum

Overall Length:
27.6 inches

Barrel Length:
7.9 inches

Weight:
6.3 pounds

Type of Fire:
Selective, semiauto or full auto

System of Operation:
Blowback

Cyclic Rate (approx.):
550 RPM

Feed System/Ammunition Delivery:
20-, 30- or 40-round box magazine

Country of Manufacture:
Spain

Manufacturer:
Bonafacio Echeverria y
Compania SA Espaná

Countries of Use:
Spain

Period of Manufacture (approx.):
1962–present

Period of Service (approx.):
1961–present

Primary Service:
Spanish military

Primary Tactical Use:
Individual

177

Star Z70 with stock folded.

Star Z70 with stock extended.

CHAPTER 20

Sweden

As a replacement for the Suomis the Swedes purchased and fabricated during the war, the Kulspruta (K) Model 45 was designed for economical but precise manufacture using modern methods. The original version, still in service, uses a special magazine housing setup to allow the use of old Suomi magazines or the new units designed especially for this series.

The gun is inexpensive and simple, but it has an exceptional reputation for reliability. Many special units worldwide use small quantities of these weapons. Egypt manufactures the gun as the "Port Said."

As do most countries, Sweden issues a special, light high-velocity 9mm round for submachine guns.

CARL GUSTAV M45

Name:
Carl Gustav

Model:
M45B "K"

Caliber:
9mm

Overall Length:
Stock extended: 31.75 inches
Stock folded: 21.75 inches

Barrel Length:
8 inches

Weight:
7.6 pounds

Type of Fire:
Full auto

System of Operation:
Blowback

Cyclic Rate (approx.):
600 RPM

Feed System/Ammunition Delivery:
36- or 50-round box magazine

Country of Manufacture:
Sweden

Manufacturer:
Carl Gustav

Countries of Use:
Sweden, Egypt, Indonesia, and others

Period of Manufacture (approx.):
1946–present

Period of Service (approx.):
1946–present

Primary Service:
Military sales to Indonesia and built under license in Egypt. Large numbers in service with Swedish forces.

Primary Tactical Use:
Individual

179

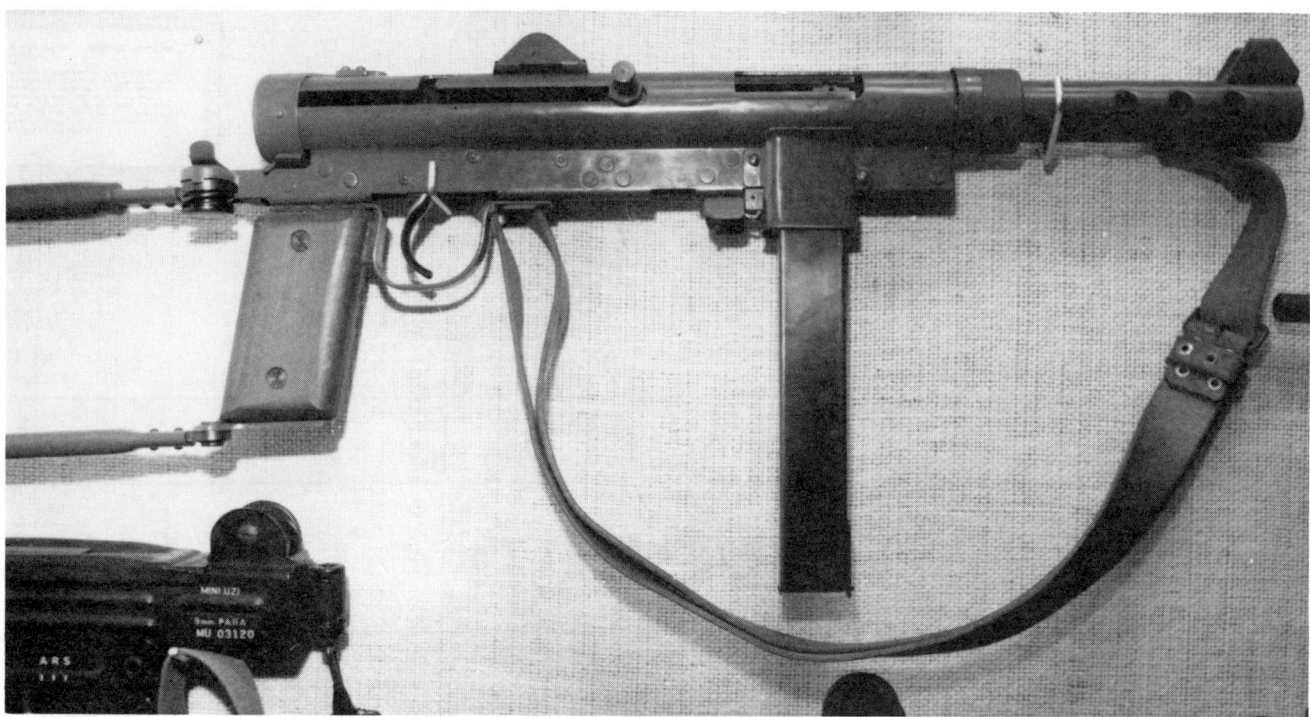

The Swedish "K" combines elements of the Finnish Suomi with modern manufacturing techniques. It is officially known as the Model 45. It is a popular gun and has an exceptional record for reliability.

Firing an M45B.

Carl Gustav M45B "K".

CHAPTER 21

Switzerland

This excellent and accurate Swiss rifle derives its operating system from the CETME/H&K rifles and suffers from the same strengths and weaknesses. However, it is more accurate than most other blowback rifles owing to an exceptionally high standard of manufacture.

The similar 510 series of rifles is in service in Chile and Bolivia in 7.62mm NATO.

A gas-powered, reduced-power derivative, the SIG530 in 5.56mm, is now under trial in several countries around the world.

The Swiss—fanatics about precision, serious shooters, and ardent reloaders—machine chamber these guns to extremely tight specifications and carefully work the extractors and ejectors, thus minimizing the sort of case damage common to other guns using similar lock work.

These guns look like finished-up gas pipes in order to reduce their bulk in tight armored fighting vehicles. Fit and finish, however, are superb.

StG57

Name:
Assault Rifle

Model:
StG57

Caliber:
7.5mm Swiss M11

Other Chamberings:
Some variants in 7.62 NATO

Overall Length:
43.4 inches

Barrel Length:
23 inches

Weight:
12.32 pounds

Type of Fire:
Selective

System of Operation:
Delayed blowback

Cyclic Rate (approx.):
450–550 RPM

Feed System/Ammunition Delivery:
24-round detachable box

Country of Manufacture:
Switzerland

Manufacturer:
SIG

Countries of Use:
Switzerland and several other countries

Period of Manufacture (approx.):
1957–present

Period of Service (approx.):
1957–early 1980s or later

Primary Tactical Use:
Individual infantry and general purpose

183

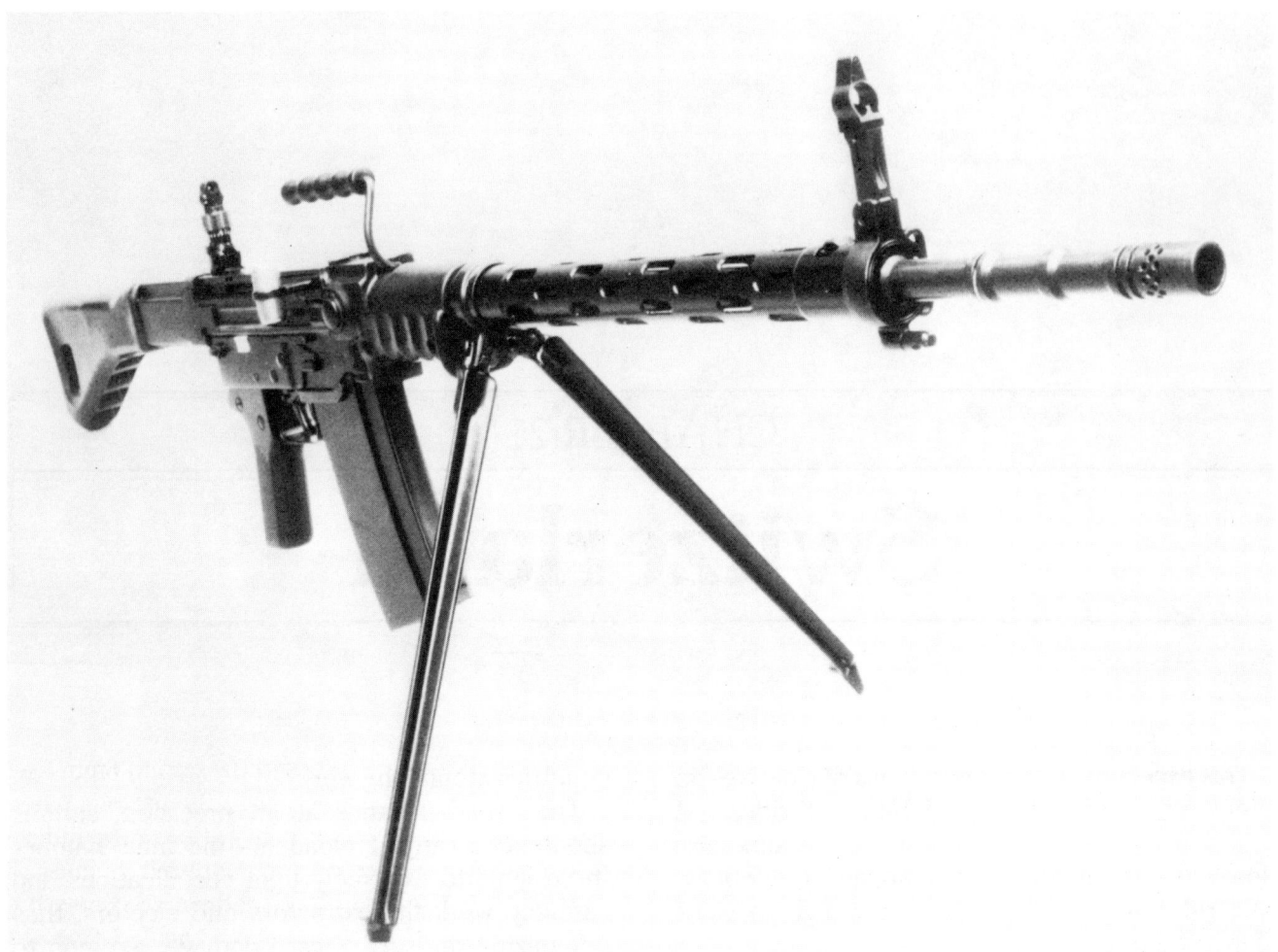

StG57 assault rifle.

CHAPTER 22

United States

The Colt-Browning was John Browning's first attempt to utilize the casual observations of his youth to make a true, fully automatic weapon. While shooting, he'd noticed the disruption caused in grass and reeds ahead of his muzzle, and felt that this was a wonderful source of energy, arriving at just the right time to operate the gun's action. Using a small vent close to the muzzle, the M1895 action employed an articulated rod to operate its mechanism and extract, eject, and feed ammunition. That rod hinged downward and made low-to-the-ground uses of the gun impossible. However, the device also accounted for the gun's exceptionally smooth extraction cycle and reliable operation.

The U.S. Navy first adopted the gun in 6mm Lee, and the army purchased a few in .30-40 Krag. When the services were ordered to ration ammunition use and supply, the navy rechambered its guns to match the chambering used by the army. Later, the .30 rimless was adopted, first in the 1903 variant and then in the popular .30-06 incarnation. Thus, Colt-Brownings in naval service became the first automatic weapons to undergo three, and possibly four, rechamberings/rebarrelings while in active service. The gun was also made in a considerable variety of Mauser-type and rimmed chamberings for export.

Colt-Brownings reentered manufacture during

COLT-BROWNING M1895

Name:
Colt-Browning

Model:
M1895

Caliber:
7x57mm

Other Chamberings:
6mm, U.S. Navy Lee, .30/40 Krag, .30-06 U.S., 7.65x54mm

Overall Length:
40.75 inches

Barrel Length:
28 inches

Weight:
Gun: 35 pounds
Mount: 61.25 pounds

Type of Fire:
Full auto only

System of Operation:
Gas

Cyclic Rate (approx.):
450 RPM

Feed System/Ammunition Delivery:
Fabric web belt, 250-round capacity

Country of Manufacture:
United States

Manufacturer:
Colt Firearms Company

Countries of Use:
U.S., Soviet Union, China, Spain, Austria, and many others

Period of Manufacture (approx.):
1893–1912

Period of Service (approx.):
1895–1920s

Primary Service:
Military and commercial sales

Primary Tactical Use:
Crew-served infantry

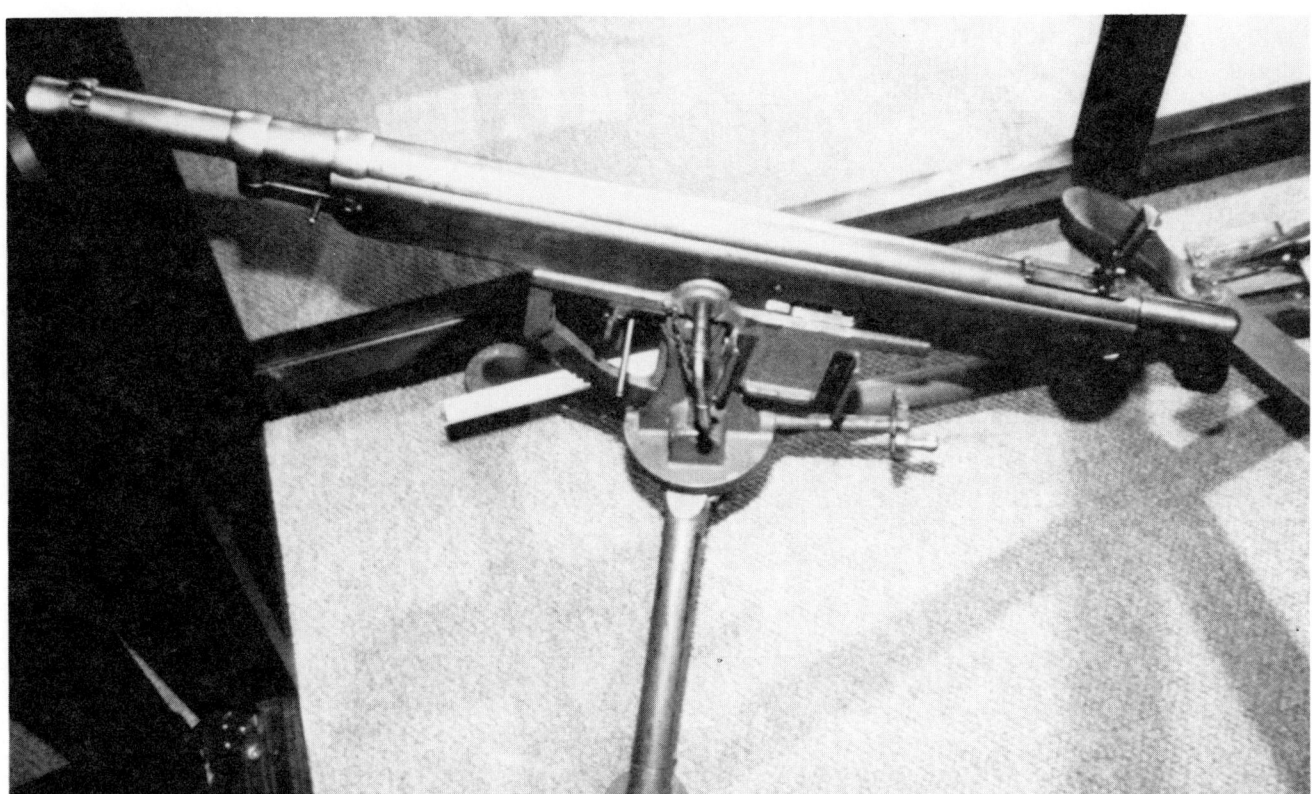

Colt-Browning M1895.

This Marlin machine gun (foreground) and Colt M1895 (rear) were gas-operated, stationary guns that were not very successful during their limited combat exposure. They can be considered John Browning's only real failures at automatic weapons design.

World War I. Though it seems they did not see actual combat, they were convenient for training.

The M1895 was Browning's last attempt at a gas-operated medium to heavy machine gun.

Chinn notes that the U.S. Army never officially adopted the M1895, though it procured quite a few in small lots. The original 1895 evaluation done by Army Ordnance was scathingly negative, amounting almost to a condemnation of machine guns in general, especially gas-operated versions. The army retained its Gatlings.

MARLIN M1914

Name:
Marlin machine gun (imported Colt-Browning)

Model:
M1914

Caliber:
7.62mm

Other Chamberings:
.30-06, .30-06 Krag, .303 British, 7x57mm, 7.65x54mm, and more

Overall Length:
40.5 inches

Barrel Length:
28 inches

Weight:
32.5 pounds

Type of Fire:
Full automatic

System of Operation:
Gas

Cyclic Rate (approx.):
500 RPM

Feed System/Ammunition Delivery:
250-round fabric belts

Country of Manufacture:
United States

Manufacturer:
Marlin-Rockwell Corporation

Countries of Use:
U.S. and other nations in small quantities

Period of Manufacture (approx.):
1914–1918

Period of Service (approx.):
1916–1930s

Primary Service:
Military, commercial export sales

Primary Tactical Use:
Individual or crew served

In an upgraded and slightly modernized form, the old Colt "Potato Digger" reentered production at Marlin for the Imperial Russian Government. Eventually, designer Carl Swebilius redesigned the entire mechanism, primarily for air use. The later 1917-1918 variant did away with the smooth but cumbersome articulated rod operating lever and added other improvements, though the guns looked something like the specimen shown here. Only the finned barrel visually distinguishes later guns from the original Colts. Once the United States entered World War I, production increased and caliber varieties were reintroduced.

The Champlin Museum's M1914 is one of the Russian-caliber guns, complete with scabbard and sheaths for the extra barrels, important accessories of the period.

Many Marlins are chambered for .30-06, and there were also 7mm export models.

I have fired these guns only in .30-06. While they are reliable, accurate, and treat brass well, even the heavy-finned barrel does not provide adequate cooling for long bursts. "Air cooling" is really cooling by luck and time; if there is inadequate circulation around a barrel, it's really no cooling at all. Short bursts and inadequate cooling are acceptable in a submachine gun or light machine gun, and in fact enforce a certain fire discipline that makes the guns more efficacious in tactical situations. Anything mounted on a tripod should maintain fixed lines of fire in the sustained role, or there's little purpose in dragging it around.

It seems fair to say that, at this stage in his career, John Browning had mastered operating mechanisms, but he was still working out some other details. As a result, though M1914s were accepted into service by Russia, Italy (in 6.5x52mm M91 chambering), and quite a few other countries, they took very little part in real warfare, before or during World War I. Tactically, they are heavy, tripod-mounted light machine guns. They're still fun to shoot since their accuracy in short bursts can amaze, especially with heavy, boat-tail match bullets. The U.S. Army procured quite a number of these guns in 1917 and thereafter, but regarded them only as training guns.

A Marlin M1914. This particular gun is one of two units once owned by the Arizona Ranger Battalion. The gun and all its accessories are serialized to match.

Still, the same basic gun body became the Marlin Aircraft gun. Because the slipstream and propeller supplemented cooling, the later gun, whose mechanism was completely redesigned, actually required a heater for operation above 8,000 feet in temperate conditions. Had this breech mechanism been combined with a good water-cooling system—awkward with a gas-operated gun—this gun's history might have been much different.

MAXIM M1904

Name:
Maxim heavy machine gun

Model:
M1904

Caliber:
.30-06

Overall Length:
44.2 inches

Barrel Length:
26 inches

Weight:
63 pounds

Type of Fire:
Full auto only

System of Operation:
Recoil

Cyclic Rate (approx.):
450 + RPM

Feed System/Ammunition Delivery:
Fabric web belt

Country of Manufacture:
Great Britain

Manufacturer:
Vickers, Son, and Maxim Ltd.

Countries of Use:
U.S.

Period of Manufacture (approx.):
Vickers: 1904
Colt: 1905–1907 (there may have been some commercial manufacture of similar guns until approximately 1915)

Period of Service (approx.):
1904–1918

Primary Service:
Military

Primary Tactical Use:
Crew served

Maxim M1904 heavy machine gun.

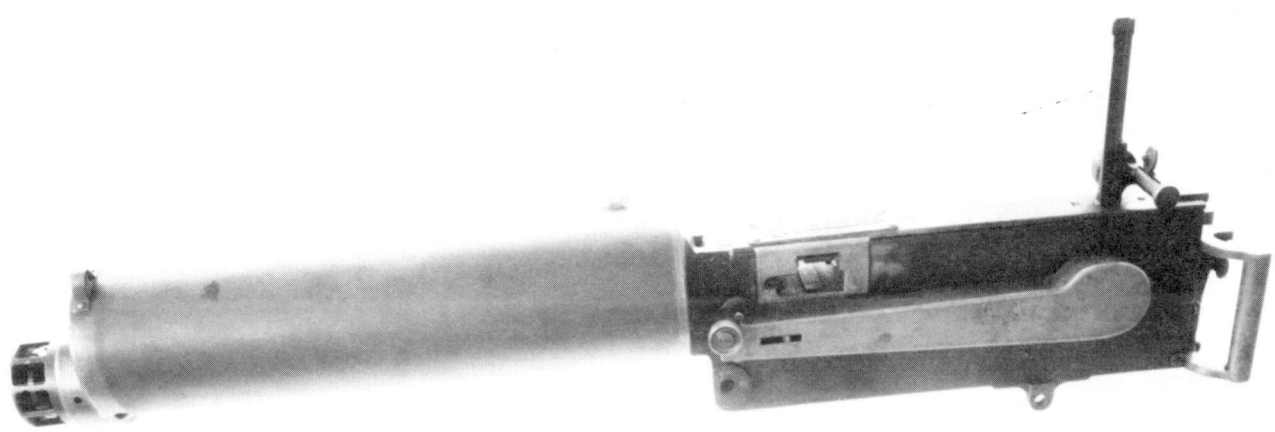

Maxim M1904 heavy machine gun.

Following a massive set of tests by the U.S. Army's Ordnance Board, the Maxim variant built by Vickers was selected and officially adopted as the U.S. Army's first "issue" machine gun. True, small quantities of others had been procured, and the Navy had adopted the Colt-Browning in 1896, but few people know that the Maxim was, for a time, an American gun. The first few apparently had unadorned muzzles. The last British-built guns and all the subsequent Colt production used the Vickers-style muzzle booster/"accelerator," intended to aid in extraction and boost cyclic rate about 20 percent by using muzzle blast against a tapered cone shim to speed the barrel on its rearward movement.

When World War I began for the United States in 1917, only 282 M1904s were in inventory. Vacillation had apparently retarded procurement, and Colt—having spent a good deal of money tooling for this weapon—appears to have sold the guns commercially between 1905 and 1915, before the more-refined Vickers M1915 entered production.

The authentic military guns are very rare, and British-built specimens are even more so. As few as three may still exist. This particular specimen was found in a haymow in Kansas, and was sold by the finder to J. Curtis Earl in 1968.

While a heavy weapon, even by the standards of World War I, the M1904 was the same reliable, quality weapon all Maxims were. Had it been produced in serious numbers, it might have prevented a great deal of the confusion and delay in machine gun policy in the early period of the Great War.

BENET-MERCIE

Name:
Benet-Mercie machine rifle

Model:
U.S. Navy Mark II Model 1 (same as U.S. Army M1909)

Caliber:
.30-06

Overall Length:
48.5 inches

Barrel Length:
25.1 inches

Weight:
27.6 pounds

Type of Fire:
Select, semiauto or full auto

System of Operation:
Gas

Cyclic Rate (approx.):
650 RPM

Feed System/Ammunition Delivery:
24- or 30-round feed strips

Country of Manufacture:
United States

Manufacturer:
Colt U.S.A.

Countries of Use:
U.S.

Period of Manufacture (approx.):
1909–1912

Period of Service (approx.):
1909–1918

Primary Service:
Military

Primary Tactical Use:
Light machine gun

This gun, an awkward but reliable design, is the U.S. version of the Light Hotchkiss used by France and England. This U.S. Navy variant is identical to the army's M1909. The army held only 670 of these guns at the beginning of U.S. participation in World War I.

An army expedition chasing Pancho Villa claimed it was unable to deploy this gun at night during Villa's raid on Columbus, New Mexico. Both army brass and the public refused to accept that this might be a training-related problem and blamed the gun, calling it the "daylight machine gun."

The feed strips can be loaded by feel; the gun can be similarly cocked and activated with the mode of

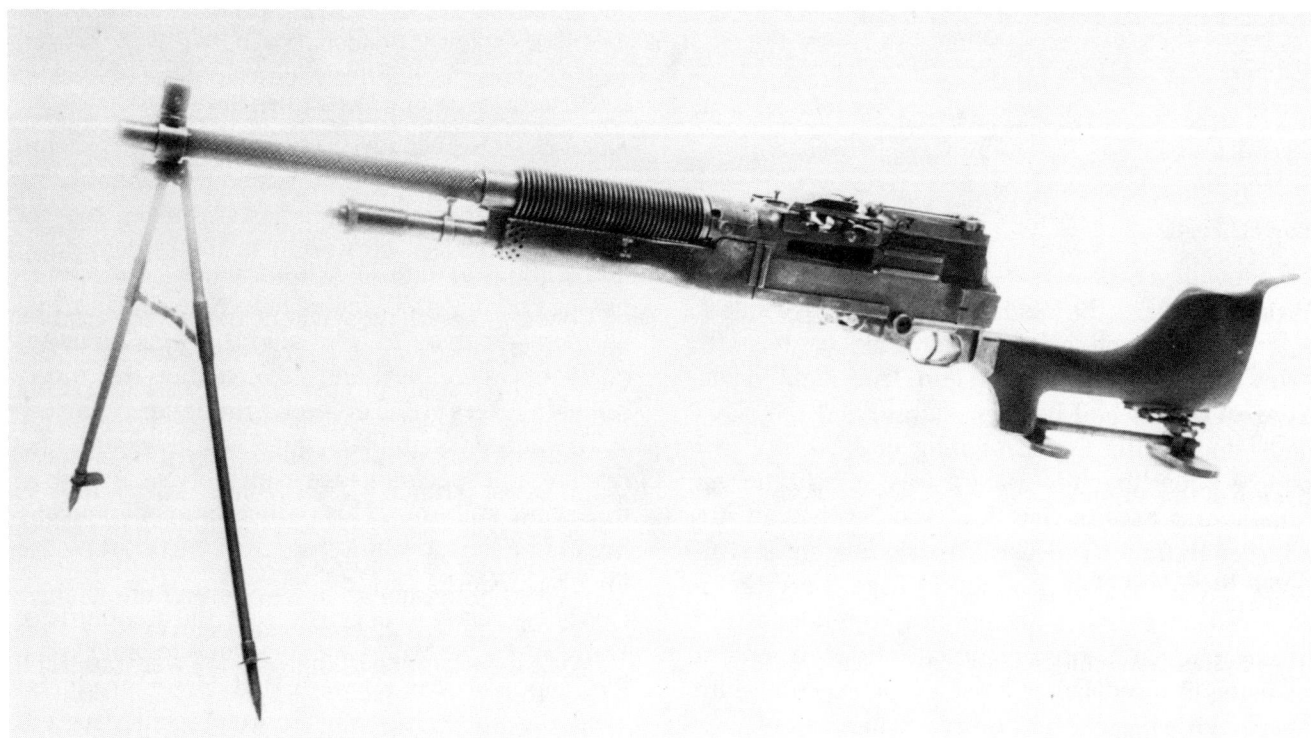

A U.S. Navy Mark 1. It is a rare gun.

fire set, though the cocking stroke is rather long. Neither the French nor the British had difficulties deploying this gun at night. But when the shooting started, U.S. troops were stuck with the Chauchat rather than this competent French design.

It should be noted that the navy never had any problems with this gun, and continued to use it on boarding and landing missions without incident.

Hotchkiss guns are not especially accurate, though these guns are better made and beautifully rifled. They might shoot better than the French guns, which I have fired only with old ammo. However, the action is fairly stable and reasonably gentle. The muzzle's heaviness, which makes the guns such a nuisance to lug from place to place, keeps them steady when firing. This means they hold target rather well.

The Benet-Mercie is a great gun only when compared to the Chauchat. It is credible and sturdy, though, which is more than can be said for the gun that replaced it. This may, in fact, be the first case in the history of automatic weapons—though by no means the last—when a competent, quality gun was replaced by an outright abomination.

VICKERS M1915

Name:
Colt-Vickers medium machine gun

Model:
Vickers 1915

Caliber:
.30-06

Overall Length:
44 inches

Barrel Length:
28.4 inches

Weight:
Gun: 34 pounds
Mount: 50 pounds

Type of Fire:
Full auto only

System of Operation:
Recoil (gas accelerated)

Cyclic Rate (approx.):
500 RPM

Feed System/Ammunition Delivery:
250- to 300-round fabric web belt

Country of Manufacture:
United States

Manufacturer:
Colt Firearms Company

Countries of Use:
Great Britain

Period of Manufacture (approx.):
1914–1918

Period of Service (approx.):
1915–1918 (the gun was rapidly replaced by Brownings after World War I; some may have seen limited postwar service)

Primary Service:
Military and commercial sales

Primary Tactical Use:
Crew served

Basically identical to the Vickers Mark I except that it fired the .30-06 U.S. cartridge, the M1915 Vickers was the second British machine gun to be adopted by the United States. The Vickers was a lightened Maxim executed to the very highest engineering standards. The articulated lock work and reciprocating system remained the same, and the ordinary operations a gunner employs were identical.

The water-cooled Vickers set many records for sustained fire versus stoppages in World War I. While British manuals list a considerable variety of stoppage sources, the guns worked superbly, provided a properly headspaced barrel was in place and adjusted and nothing was broken. The Vickers served the British army until 1968, and there have been barrels produced recently in the 7.62x51mm cartridge, indicating that someone (probably the British or a former colony) is still using the gun enough to have it converted to the more modern cartridge.

Conversions of the Vickers design are nothing new. As far back as 1911 and well into the 1930s, either conversions or new models were fabricated in 7.7mm Japanese (AVN's Type 97, 98, and 89), 7.65x54mm Mauser (Belgium, Argentina, others), 8mm Lebel (French M1909), 8mm (7.92x57mm JS) for Czechoslovakia, a 6.5mm for Italy as the Model 1911, and lots of 7x57mm conversions after World War I for Latin America. It was neither unusual nor especially difficult to convert the gun to the U.S. .30 caliber; in fact, much of this latitude was integral to the design.

The M1915 was the standard U.S. gun of more than twelve divisions shipped to Europe during World

Vickers M1915.

War I, though John Browning's gun was in what amounts to production-ready form by 1910 or so. The Army, however, expressed no interest. The government purchased 12,125 of these Vickers guns during the war, very few of which were on hand when the war started in 1917. Colt seems to have sold this gun commercially from 1915 until some time after World War I.

Part of J. Curtis Earl's purchase from the MGM collection, the gun shown here appeared in many feature films starring the likes of Clark Gable, Humphrey Bogart, Edward G. Robinson, Wallace Beery, and John Wayne.

A few of these guns remaining in inventory were sent to England to arm the Home Guard during the 1940 crisis. Because of their physical similarity to the British Vickers, lots of red and yellow paint was applied in the most conspicuous places to remind users that the guns were to be used only with the U.S. cartridge. The British guns were produced with both smooth and pleated water jackets, but almost all the U.S. guns used corrugated sleeves.

The British guns served in both world wars and with British forces in Korea.

LEWIS 1917

Name:
Lewis light machine gun

Model:
1917

Caliber:
.303 British

Overall Length:
50.5 inches

Barrel Length:
26.3 inches

Weight:
27.2 pounds

Type of Fire:
Full auto only

System of Operation:
Gas

Cyclic Rate (approx.):
500+ RPM

Feed System/Ammunition Delivery:
47- or 96-round drum magazine

Country of Manufacture:
United States

Manufacturer:
Savage Arms Corporation, U.S.A.

Countries of Use:
U.S., Great Britain, Holland, Belgium, and Japan

Period of Manufacture (approx.):
1911–1920s

Period of Service (approx.):
1914–1945 (see text)

Primary Service:
Military, commercial sales

The Lewis is one of those guns a casual observer with an engineering/mechanical background would swear could only be a calamity waiting to happen. Based loosely on a design by Samuel Maclean and O.M. Lissak and refined by retired Colonel I.N. Lewis, the guns depend on a series of complex interactions between gears, shafts, levers, arms, and gas gush, all of which seem to be potential sources of major problems. Furthermore, the gun's parts are precisely machined, finished to exacting specifications, and precisely mated to each other.

Fortunately, the Lewis gun was superbly well made. It had to be. Any slipshod craftsmanship on a Lewis would result in a nonfunctional device. Savage found this out between 1913 and 1916, when it had some difficulty converting the system to U.S. .30 caliber. The Lewis was never cheap. At a time when an automobile could be purchased for $500 or so, a 1916 Lewis carried a wholesale price of $1,000. However, in those early years, no one—probably not even Lewis himself—appreciated that those high machine and labor costs resulted in a piece of equipment that could last indefinitely.

In fact, a "new" Lewis, the Lewis .303 SS (Naval),

Lewis Model 1917 light machine gun.

was even introduced some twenty years after the weapon's formal production ended. It consisted of rebuilt guns that the British fitted with a new compensator/flash hider, short butt, and other fittings for antiaircraft and other uses from 1942.

This particular Lewis was purchased and ordered by General Presidente Pancho Villa during his border bandit days. Villa had worked for T.F. Miller Hardware in Clarkdale, Arizona, and through an intermediary, he ordered this and three other guns for shipment to Nogales, Mexico. The guns were confiscated before he could intervene.

Army Cavalry put these guns in storage, delivering them to Williams Field just before World War I. They were used there during World War II as guard guns. After that, two went to the Arizona National Guard, one to the Mesa Police, and one to the Phoenix Police. Earl acquired the specimen shown here after the National Guard disposed of it. The packing case, gun, drums, and accessories are from the original order. It has not been fired since J. Curtis Earl test-fired it. It is, therefore, not merely a rare gun with a story behind it, but it is in mint condition as well. It can currently be found in the Champlin Fighter Museum in Mesa, Arizona.

The Lewis ceased to be a first-line infantry gun shortly after the end of World War I, though the flexible aircraft guns were used in various applications until 1945. All variants of the gun were seen in combat by almost everyone on all sides during World Wars I and II, even by users who relied upon captured or commercially purchased pieces. This is because, even though the complexity of the Lewis was looked upon with some trepidation, especially the drum magazines, the guns proved to be accurate, very reliable, and far more durable than some of the guns that "replaced" them. Therefore, you will see them in all sorts of applications, in old photos, for example, long after they were replaced.

LEWIS .30 AIRCRAFT MACHINE GUN

Name:
Lewis aircraft machine gun

Model:
1917-1918

Caliber:
.30-06

Weight:
21.6 pounds

Type of Fire:
Full auto only

System of Operation:
Gas

Cyclic Rate (approx.):
600–650 + RPM

Feed System/Ammunition Delivery:
97-round drum magazine

Country of Manufacture:
United States

Manufacturer:
Savage Arms Corporation

Countries of Use:
U.S., Great Britain, Belgium, Japan, France, and Soviet Union

Primary Service:
Military aircraft

Primary Tactical Use:
Aircraft-mounted machine gun

Though many of I.N. Lewis' original Automatic Arms Company production prototypes had been prepared in the .30-06 U.S. chambering, it took some time before Savage was able to work out all the wrinkles in the feeding/ejection on an actual production basis. It probably mattered very little anyway, for General Crozier was convinced the gun would not and could not see U.S. infantry use. While the Lewis eventually worked fine in the U.S. loading and was taken into U.S. ground service via official and unofficial means, the air gun was one of the primary U.S. aircraft guns in both flexible and "over the wing" mountings. The Lewis was very difficult to synchronize. Drum magazines made side-by-side arrangements awkward, making the over-the-wing mountings far more convenient.

Lewis aircraft guns were sometimes converted from ground guns, though later guns like those shown feature slightly modified mechanisms. In many, the jacket was trimmed or dispensed with

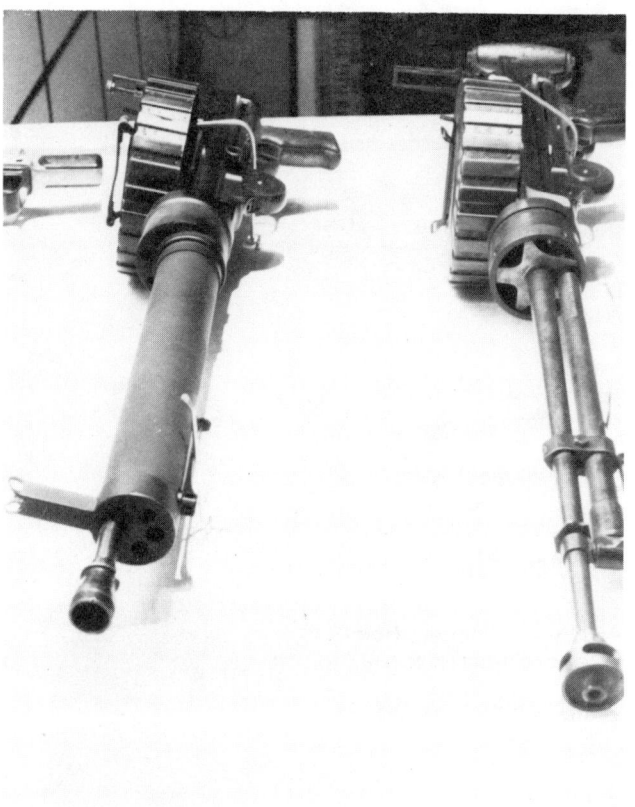

Lewis aircraft machine gun (right).

Detail of the Hazelton device on the Lewis aircraft machine gun.

altogether. A muzzle booster and sometimes a flash-hider were fitted to the aircraft guns, and the buttstock was usually replaced with a simple spade-type grip. The gas orifice was enlarged from .130 to .150 inches and stop, rebound, and feed pawl specifications and heat-treat were altered to hold up to the increased rate of fire. The muzzle booster, called the Hazelton device, and the other modifications boosted the rate of fire, generally reduced weight, and allowed the weapon to deal with increased stress and heat. These changes were also applied to French and British guns for similar service.

Allied guns of this vintage were issued quantities of the Buckham bullet, a yellow phosphorous pill whose incendiary qualities were nominal by modern standards. In British hands, it deprived Germany of flexibility in using its zeppelin fleet and destroyed a good many barrage and observation balloons. These lighter-than-air craft were very heavily defended, carrying lots of machine guns and often 20mm and larger cannon for defense. They were filled with hydrogen gas, though, and caught fire easily. The Lewis was the primary instrument of their destruction.

VICKERS M1918

Name:
Vickers aircraft machine gun

Model:
Model 1918 (Mark 1)

Caliber:
11mm

Overall Length:
44.19 inches

Barrel Length:
28.4 inches

Weight:
25 pounds

Type of Fire:
Full auto only

System of Operation:
Recoil

Cyclic Rate (approx.):
550 RPM (800–900 RPM in late M1918)

Feed System/Ammunition Delivery:
Fabric web belt

Country of Manufacture:
United States and its allies

Manufacturer:
Colt Firearms Company

Countries of Use:
U.S., Great Britain, France, and other Allied countries during World War I

Period of Manufacture (approx.):
1915–1918

Period of Service (approx.):
1915–late 1920s

Primary Service:
Military with aircraft modifications

Primary Tactical Use:
Cowl-mounted offensive aircraft machine gun

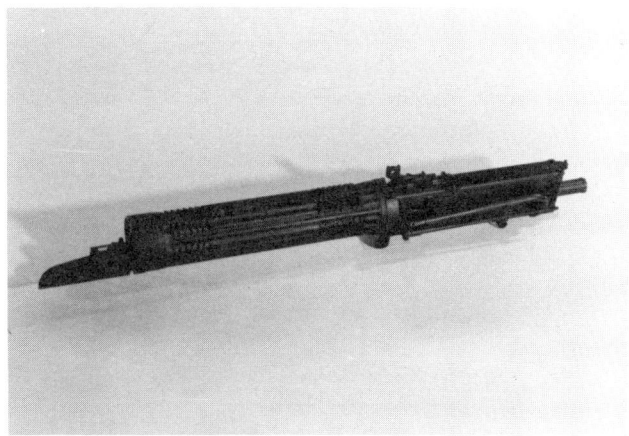

Vickers M1918 (Mark 1).

Detail of the muzzle booster on a Vickers M1918.

An exact, authorized copy of the British Aircraft Vickers, the Colt-made Vickers guns were supplied in all applications where the British weapon was standard. Many similar guns were also made in or converted to .30-06, especially after World War I when the 11mm cartridge went out of vogue.

The 11mm cartridge was designed around an old-fashioned rimmed case. Its trajectory was not especially flat, but the bigger bullet was deemed to have a better capacity for carrying incendiary compounds. It served much better in dealing with hydrogen-filled zeppelins and artillery spotter balloons.

What appears to be a water-cooling jacket is merely a sleeve, louvered to increase airflow around the barrel.

Note the synchronizer lines passing the fusee covers on two of these guns. These were hydro-mechanical retard mechanisms.

As with many other British and U.S. weapons of the period, the Russian Revolution of 1917 and the subsequent Treaty of Brest-Litovsk played a part in the weapon's availability. Colt had tooled for Vickers guns and was building them in the Russian 7.62x54Rmm loading for the air force when the revolution made the guns extraneous and shipments to Russia were embargoed. Since the rim and case length of the Russian rimmed cartridge are quite similar to the revised Anglo-French 11mm case, it was decided that Colt's production would be applied to the loading.

The Vickers case was similar to the French 11mm, differing only very slightly in bottleneck and rim; in fact, British ammunition could be used in French 11mm guns. For much of the war, this was not only done, but it was standard operating procedure. U.S.-Anglo ammo was known to be more reliable.

The M1918, externally identical to the Vickers, boosted the rate of fire to almost twice the British original because of the careful redesigning of the internals and muzzle booster.

Colt manufactured approximately 12,125 ground Vickers guns and 2,476 .30 Vickers Aircraft guns. At least 5,000 Vickers were produced from Russian guns in the 11mm caliber, probably many more.

MARLIN MODELS 1917 and 1918

Name:
Marlin aircraft machine gun

Model:
1917 and 1918

Caliber:
.30-06

Overall Length:
40.8 inches

Barrel Length:
27.9 inches

Weight:
22 pounds

Type of Fire:
Full auto only

System of Operation:
Gas

Cyclic Rate (approx.):
630 RPM

Feed System/Ammunition Delivery:
Fabric web belt

Country of Manufacture:
United States

Manufacturer:
Marlin Firearms Co., U.S.A.

Countries of Use:
U.S. and its allies

Period of Manufacture (approx.):
1917–1919

Period of Service (approx.):
1917–1930s

Primary Service:
Military aircraft machine gun

Primary Tactical Use:
Aircraft

The total number of 1918 Model Marlins (the bottom gun in the photo) produced under World War I budgets was 15,000; in contrast, 23,000 Model 1917s were produced. At war's end, twenty-two squadrons were wholly or fully equipped with Marlins. These guns were set up from their initial design stages for synchronizers, and the later model would easily accept either the Nelson on Constantinesco synchronizer gear.

The reliability and good reputation of this gun are interesting, for the base of this weapon is the eldest of all U.S. automatic guns, the ancient Colt M1895 "potato digger." This would not have been so had it not been for the considerable efforts of Carl G. Swebilius, who took the Colt-Browning, then manufactured at Marlin for the Russians, and adapted it to aircraft use.

First to go was the articulated arm operating lever. This was no easy task, for the knee action hinge provided gentle initial extraction. The remainder consisted of hundreds of small details of metallurgy and mechanics to produce a slender,

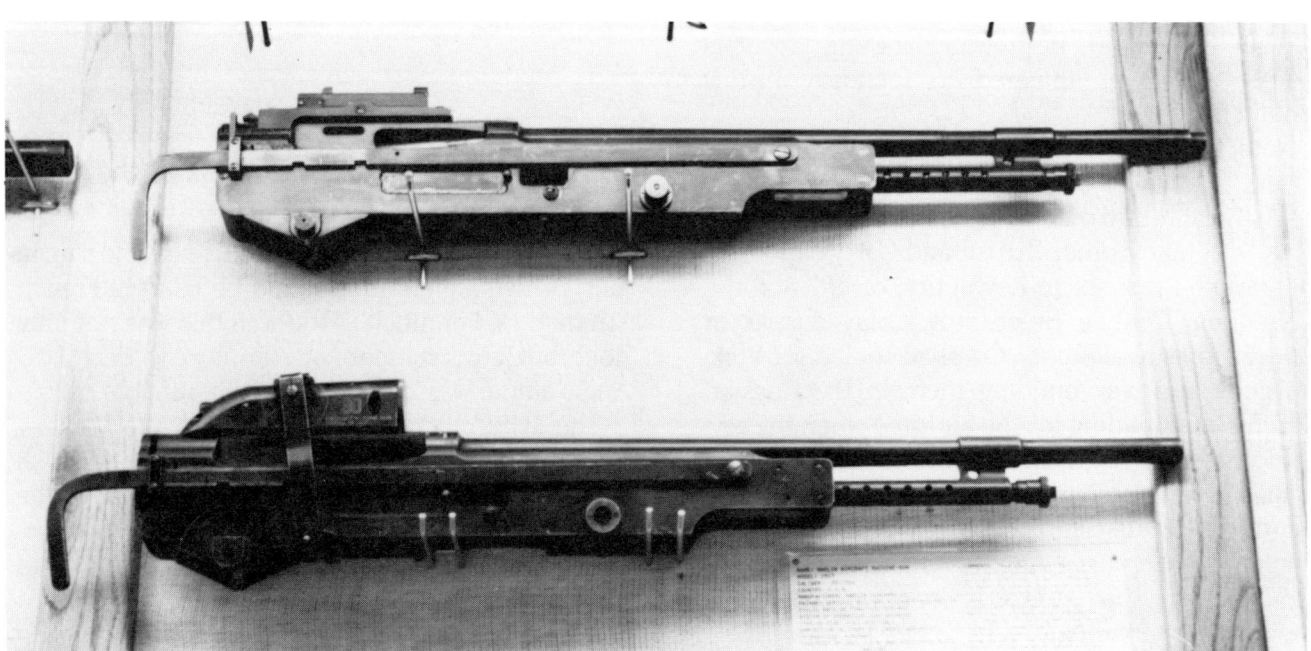

A Marlin aircraft machine gun Model 1917 (top) and Model 1918 (bottom).

A Marlin aircraft machine gun on a Tommy Morse Scout.

sturdy gun of very high cyclic rate for the time that was also easy to synchronize. The 1918 model was supplied with a trigger motor attached to the lock container and an adapter for connections with both the Nelson and C.C. Gear. These guns were the first guns to employ integral electric heaters.

One factor few writers mention in regard to this gun is that the narrow breech and barrel assembly made the gun easier to see past, an important factor in the World War I Scout aircraft. In fact, the guns often were mounted below and in front of the cockpit in order to leave the pilot's view totally unobstructed.

Initially regarded as little more than a convenient compromise, the Marlin probably was the best aircraft gun of the war.

Marlin tried to sell a ground version of the gun without much success.

BAR M1918

Name:
Browning light machine rifle (BAR)

Model:
M1918

Weight:
16.1 pounds

Manufacturer:
Colt, Remington, and others

Special Note:
See BAR M1918A2 for complete tabular data

This is the original version of the Browning Automatic Rifle (BAR). It actually did see considerable action at the very end of World War I. The M1918 was quite a bit lighter than later versions, and because it was intended for "walking fire," no bipod was used. Most of these guns were later modified with the bipod, though pictures reveal WWII GIs often discarded the bipods.

The original flash hider was a simple tube, making the gun eight-tenths of an inch shorter than the 1918A2.

Some of these original guns were still in stock when substantial quantities were converted to the 7.62mm NATO cartridge and are generally called T34s.

The Browning Automatic Rifle was not the most light rifle-caliber automatic weapon of either world war, but it was the most mobile. It was issued at the fire team level rather than at squad level, meaning that there were always two guns in tactical situations where a similar British unit had only one Bren. Therefore, the BAR has to be viewed as a brilliant success in performing the role for which it was designed—making sure that small units could move swiftly and attack sharply.

Most M1918 guns were converted to M1918A2 standard before, during, or after World War II. It isn't an elaborate conversion, though many of the original, beautifully blued, commercial-quality guns were parkerized, a process that diminished their aesthetic appeal.

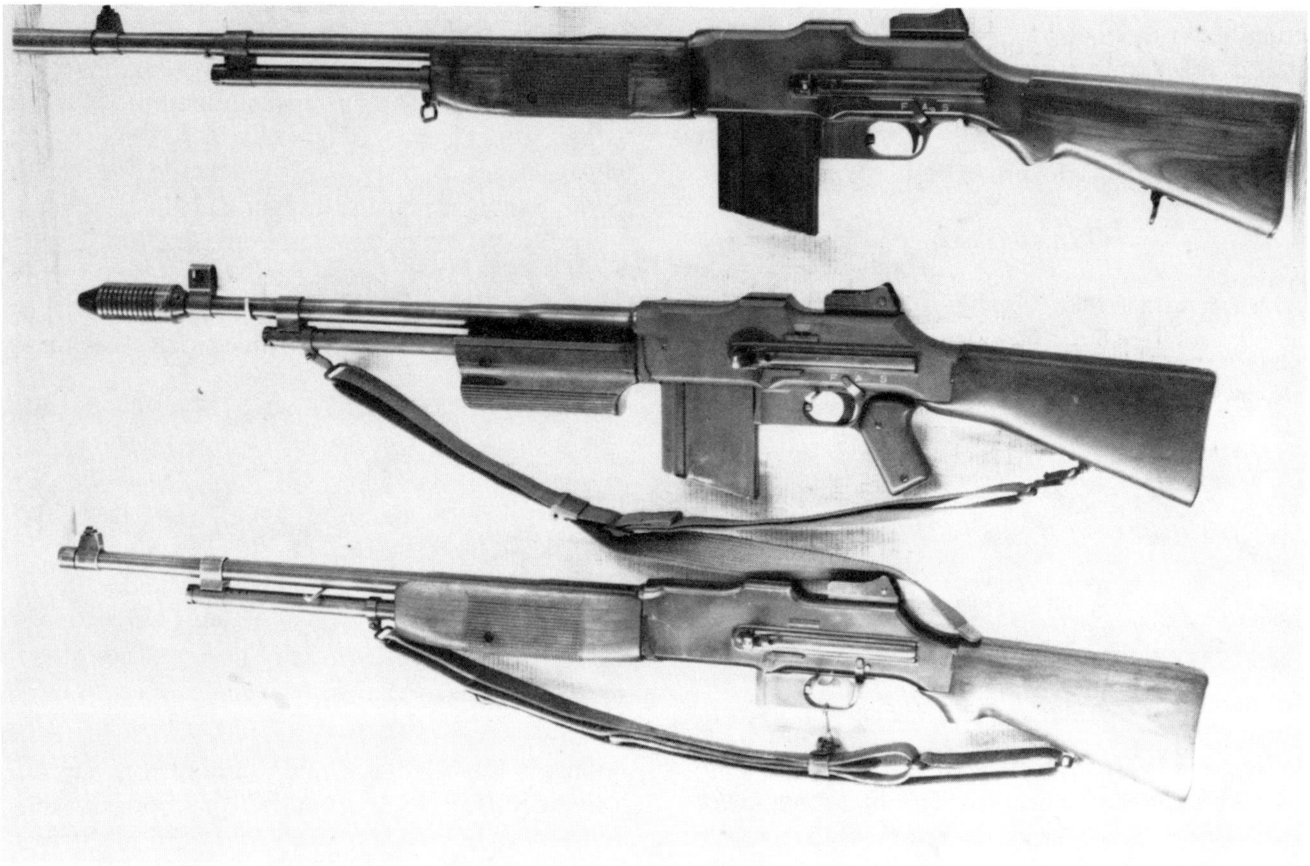

Colt BARs: M1918 (top), Monitor (center), and M1919 (bottom).

BAR M1919

Name:
Browning Automatic Rifle

Model:
1919

Manufacturer:
Colt (Hartford)

Special Note:
See BAR M1918A2 for complete tabular data

Colt and other companies produced a variety of commercial and export guns after World War I, most of which were failures owing to the glut of surplus guns on the market. Except for the flash hider, the gun shown here is an M1918 BAR.

Colt also produced and devised a quick-change system similar to FNs late Model 30, marketing it as the R75A. Some of those models found their way into U.S. service early in World War II.

Some of these weapons were selective fire, while

BAR M1919.

others used the usual two rates of automatic fire. Fit and finish were superior to those of most military guns, and wood stocks seem to have been from commercial selected blanks.

All commercial BARs are extremely rare.

COLT MONITOR

Name:
Colt light machine rifle

Model:
Monitor

Overall Length:
41 inches

Barrel Length:
18.5 inches

Weight:
16.3 pounds

Manufacturer:
Colt

This BAR variant was Colt's attempt to market a civilian version of the military rifle, based loosely on the short Model 1922 "cavalry" BAR. Colt was tooled to build the BAR and felt constrained to make some use of the machinery. Very few of these guns were built. Though it was hoped the Monitor would sell to law enforcement and perhaps foreign governments, there was little demand for such a piece. Some criminals, however, did like the gun.

The Cutts-style shotgun-configuration Lyman compensator was intended to suppress recoil. However, it tended to blast to the sides and rear, making the gun uncomfortable to shoot. The blast also obscured the sights.

The Monitor is one of the most rare and sought after of all automatic weapons. Probably only a half dozen or so are known to collectors. The one shown here is in mint condition, having only been test-fired by previous owners.

I have fired this particular weapon, and found recoil to be at the usual gentle BAR level. However, the direction of blast, especially under dusty conditions, inspires even the strongest of men to close his eyes or develop a self-protective flinch. This might improve slightly were special loads developed with fast-burning powders especially for this rifle, but the gun may be too valuable for much experimentation.

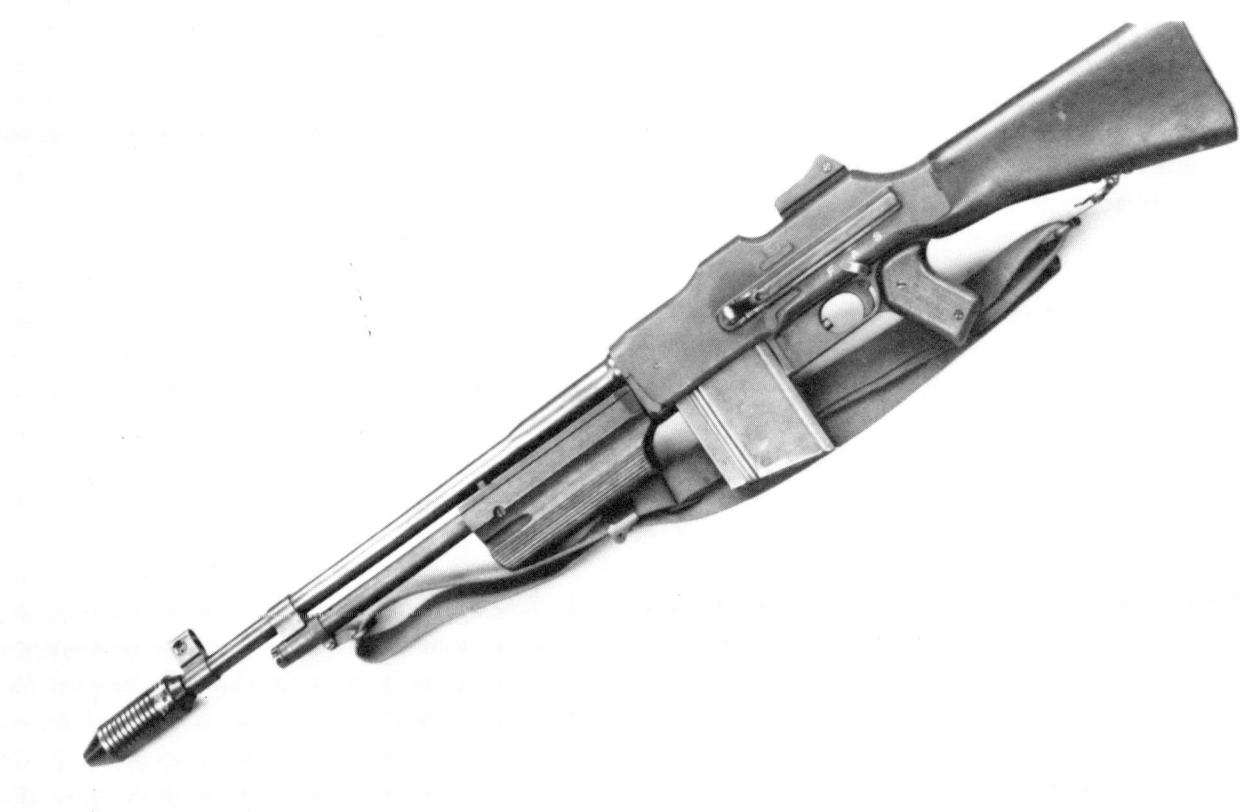

Monitor.

BAR M1922

Name:
Browning Automatic Rifle, cavalry model

Model:
Model 1922

Caliber:
U.S. .30-06

Other Chamberings:
Some exports in 7mm

Overall Length:
41.2 inches

Barrel Length:
18 inches

Weight:
19.2 pounds

Type of Fire:
Selective

System of Operation:
Gas

Cyclic Rate (approx.):
550 RPM

Feed System/Ammunition Delivery:
20-round staggered box

Country of Manufacture:
United States

Manufacturer:
Colt and others

Countries of Use:
Primarily U.S. and Latin America, but exported in small quantities worldwide

Period of Manufacture (approx.):
1922–1925

Period of Service (approx.):
1922–1930s

Primary Tactical Use:
Troop automatic weapon

The M1922 BAR was supposed to be the cavalry equivalent of a squad automatic weapon, but its main contributions were to the export business since the M1922 was produced under license in Belgium. While it did not sell well, it led to the Model D, the M1918A1, another short-lived variant, and the Monitor.

Muzzle blast form the 18-inch barrel was fairly stiff, but recoil was no worse than that of a standard BAR. This gun passed on its selective-fire capability and ill-placed bipod to the M1918A1. Should you wonder what then happened to this gun and the M1918A1, take a close look at some World War II action photos and you'll realize a lot of what appear to be M1918A2s are earlier guns fitted with later furniture. Generally, only the odd middle band can be spotted.

In a 1964 visit to a major Army Reserve/National Guard armory at an active facility, I noted several converted M1922 and M1918A1 receivers mixed in with other 1918A2 guns. They retained their blued finish in several cases and mostly retained their rather nice wood. Then fitted with standard 24-inch barrels, they retained their selective-fire capability. Two were marked "T34A2" and engraved "7.62mm" above the ejection port. The same notation was painted on the buttstock on both sides. Chances are, these particular guns have since been "demilitarized" or passed on to some Latin American dictator under the Military Aid Program.

Original, unmodified M1922 guns are extremely rare and valuable.

BAR M1918A2

Name:
Browning Automatic Rifle

Model:
M1918A2

Caliber:
.30 U.S./M1906

Overall Length:
47.8 inches

Barrel Length:
24 inches plus flash hider

Weight:
19.4 pounds

Type of Fire:
Selective-fire rates

System of Operation:
Gas

Cyclic Rate (approx.):
300–450 RPM (slow)
500–650 RPM (fast)

Feed System/Ammunition Delivery:
20-round box magazine

Country of Manufacture:
United States

Manufacturer:
Colt Patent Firearms

Countries of Use:
U.S. and its allies

Period of Manufacture (approx.):
1918–1950s

Period of Service (approx.):
1918–present

Primary Service:
U.S. and Allied infantry, mobile fire

Primary Tactical Use:
Fire-team level

It's a tribute to John Browning's genius that the BAR is still one hell of a weapon when compared with most any weapon of similar size, even seventy years after its inception. Constantly compared with squad automatic weapons and light machine guns like the Bren, the BAR suffers somewhat, for it is not and was never intended to be a light machine gun. It was incorporated at a much lower level than, for example, the Bren, supporting three to five riflemen who carried the superb infantry rifle of the period, the M1 Garand. It was always intended for walking fire, with some limited semistationary capability, for which the A2 series bipod was added.

Many tactical historians credit the BAR with the aggressive tactics used by the U.S. infantry during World War II. It was sufficiently accurate for use as a sniper rifle at great range and was more mobile than the Bren or anything the Germans or Japanese had in numbers (except, of course, whatever BARs they had access to). Each infantry squad in combat could field *two* guns.

Adopted just prior to World War II, the M1918A2 may be distinguished from all earlier models by the muzzle-end location of the bipod. The cone-type flash suppressor is typical of issue until about 1944. Many later guns deleted the carrying handle and/or used a bar-type flash hider. The specimen shown here is a conversion from an early M1918. Later on, a plastic fore-end was introduced. This unit retains old-style fittings and furniture.

While obsolete in U.S. service for almost all purposes, U.S. Navy stocks still list a quantity of T34 1918A2 units. With the magazines modified slightly at the rear and having a shorter follower, these guns accept the 7.62x51mm NATO cartridge adopted in 1957. The BAR is a durable and reliable weapon whose main drawback was its expense.

If some old soldier recalls selective-fire and pistol-gripped BARs and everyone tells him he's crazy, he's not. Many nonstandard BARs wound up being marked M1918A2, including commercial and export guns bought "off the shelf" and converted to approximations of the standard gun. Not many of these have found their way to private hands. Even when they have, they're often dismissed as "cobble jobs," which is only partly true.

I have found that BARs respond to about the same selection of ammo I run through my match M1

BAR M1918A2.

Firing a BAR M1918A2.

Garands. I especially had good luck with Speer and Hornady boat-tail hollow points of 168- and 190-grain weights. The guns have zero difficulty with these bullets; as with the M1, they shoot tighter groups than with 150-grain ball ammo. Some of Hilton LaZarr's handloads, using 51.58 grains of 4350 with the 190-grain slugs, developed a nice and even 2,500 fps, performing brilliantly out to 600 yards (which was as far as I could shoot from where we were firing). The 168-grain concoctions were not as crisp beyond 400 yards but shot tighter groups closer in. The BAR was loaded with 43.38 grains of 4895 for about 2,530 fps; 52.3 grains of 760 produced similar results with the 168-grain rounds, 49.4 with the 190-grain. I preferred the ball powders with the BAR primarily because the residue in the gas system is easier to clean and the cook-on adhesion is less profound.

The BAR is not picky at all about bullet length, unlike many magazine-fed guns. I ran just about everything in the Federal and Winchester lines from 125 grains and up, most of IMI's Samson stock, a few rounds of the much-sought-after RWS TIG, and about a truckload of surplus ammo. No jams through any of the BARs, and no bad performance, either. It would be wise for anyone shooting a .30-06 automatic of any kind to immediately gobble up all the surplus ammo he can get since the cartridge is falling into obsolescence in military use and there won't be much surplus around after 1990.

BROWNING M1919A6

Name:
Browning light machine gun

Model:
1919A6

Caliber:
.30-06

Overall Length:
53 inches

Barrel Length:
24 inches

Weight:
32.5 pounds

Type of Fire:
Full auto only

System of Operation:
Recoil

Cyclic Rate (approx.):
550 RPM

Feed System/Ammunition Delivery:
Web belt, 250-round capacity

Country of Manufacture:
United States

Manufacturer:
Saginaw Steering Gear Division of General Motors and others

Countries of Use:
U.S. and its allies in major quantities; most of the world using in smaller quantities. Obsolete in U.S. service except for limited naval and reserve stock.

Period of Manufacture (approx.):
1941–1946

Period of Service (approx.):
1942–1950s

Primary Service:
Military

Primary Tactical Use:
Crew served and individual

The M1919A6 was an unsuccessful attempt to field a genuine light machine gun. Poorly balanced, the weapon handles clumsily. Most of the weapons still in service at the end of World War II were converted to M1919A4 units.

Once positioned with some stability, however, the weapon did have greater sustained fire capability than the BAR.

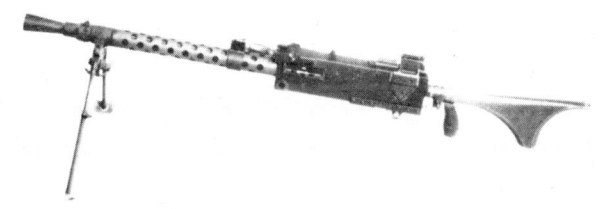

Browning M1919A6.

JOHNSON MODEL 1941

Name:
Johnson light machine gun

Model:
1941

Caliber:
.30-06

Overall Length:
42 inches

Barrel Length:
22 inches

Weight:
12.5 pounds

Type of Fire:
Select, semiauto or full auto

System of Operation:
Recoil

Cyclic Rate (approx.):
450–750 RPM

Feed System/Ammunition Delivery:
20-cartridge single-column magazine

Country of Manufacture:
United States

Manufacturer:
Johnson Automatic, Inc.

Countries of Use:
U.S.

Period of Manufacture (approx.):
1941–1944

Period of Service (approx.):
1941–1945

Primary Service:
Military

Primary Tactical Use:
Individual

Melvin Johnson's light machine gun was the only issue light machine gun used by the United States during World War II. Featuring a quick-change barrel, variable rate of automatic fire, a 20-round magazine that could be recharged from stripper clips without removal from the gun, automatic fire from an open bolt and semiautomatic from a closed bolt, and a side mounting for the magazine that kept it from dragging in the dirt, the Johnson was a splendid weapon. Popular with the marines and Army Rangers who used it, it was procured only in the comparatively small quantity of 5,000 units.

While there have been many adverse comments published over the years concerning the Johnson, the worst that may truly be said about it is that it may have been a little too lightly supported in the barrel area. Other than that, its main weakness was that it came along after the BAR was popular and in general issue. The magazine is a trifle awkward for carrying purposes, but this is largely a matter of growing accustomed to the weapon. The short recoil system vibrated more than the gas system of the BAR, but it became a problem only at the "high" rate in long bursts.

The gun was copied exactly by the Israelis in a gun they called the Dror; in spirit and features, the German version was the FG42.

Johnson Model 1941 light machine gun.

Detail of the Johnson Model 1941.

The gun received a favorable report from the Ordnance Department at the end of the war, with the suggestion that it might be a good idea to convert it to belt-feed.

Perhaps the gun was on the market a little too early. By the early sixties, when the M14 was having difficulty and the M60 was being adopted, the Johnson could have filled a niche or two.

It's been years since I've fired a Johnson and, owing to the rarity of the gun, I am not sure I will ever do so again. Very accurate, it performed exceptionally well at the slow rate. It does not treat brass as gently as the BAR, but it doesn't rip it up, either.

THOMPSON SUBMACHINE GUN

Name:
Thompson submachine gun

Model:
M1921, M1928, M1928A1, M1, and others

Barrel Length:
10 inches on all models

Cyclic Rate (approx.):
475–900 + RPM

Manufacturer:
Colt, Savage, and Auto Ordnance

Special Note:
See specific models for further tabular data.

The splendid and beautiful "Midas" Thompson submachine gun, now in the J. Curtis Earl Collection of the Champlin Fighter Museum in Mesa, Arizona.

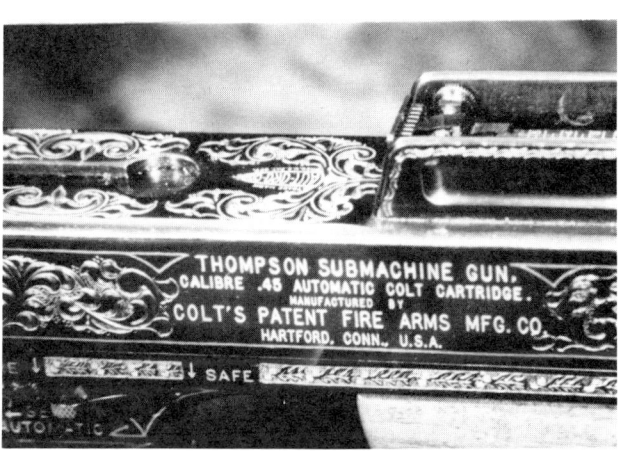

Detail of the "Midas" Thompson submachine gun.

This Savage production prototype 9mm gun is serial number S-1. Obviously not a handmade shop job, there must have been an order or the promise of an order for such a gun to be made, considering the tooling costs necessary. The gun combines features of the M1 and M1928 guns with a new magazine.

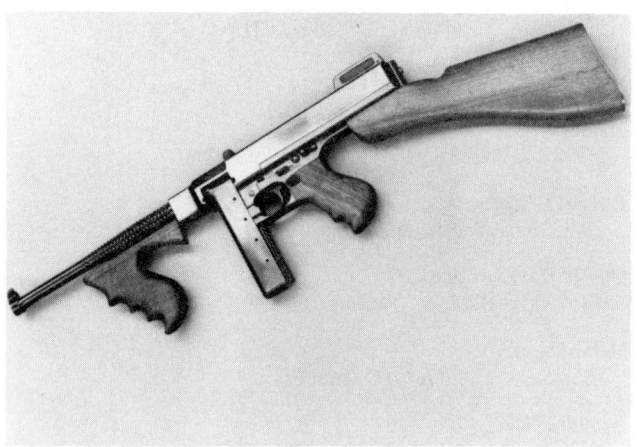

A Thompson M1921 that was assembled after the war.

Thompson M1928 Navy model.

An extremely rare Thompson M1927 semiautomatic carbine.

The Thompson submachine gun has always occupied a special place in the hearts of collectors and the public. Like most people, I have ambivalent feelings about the guns. I can think of eight or ten perfectly good reasons to reject it, starting with the fact that it's too complex, has always been too expensive, and is too heavy. Yet, when I consider buying an automatic weapon, the purchase that comes to mind is the Thompson.

The birth of the Thompson was a result of John Tagliaferro Thompson's project to develop a weapon which, had it been ready and working in time, might have become the world's first assault rifle. Along the way, the former Ordnance Board general acquired rights to the Blish lock, an H-shaped bronze wedge device that used the differential friction factors of dissimilar metals to provide delay in a blowback mechanism. Many criticize this device, often going so far as to describe how they were able to throw the little piece away and still use the gun. As Chinn points out, however, the lock on models 1921 and 1928 acts to moderate cyclic rate.

Because of its mechanical force transfer function and the way the dovetails in the receivers are cut, "experts" who claim to have removed the device and used the gun are participating in some sort of fantasy, for as any 1921 or 1928 model owner who has tried it knows, the action locks up *totally* with the lock removed. Neither the actuator nor the bolt can be moved at all. The oiler could perhaps be discarded, but definitely not the Blish lock. Savage experimented with new machining techniques and a

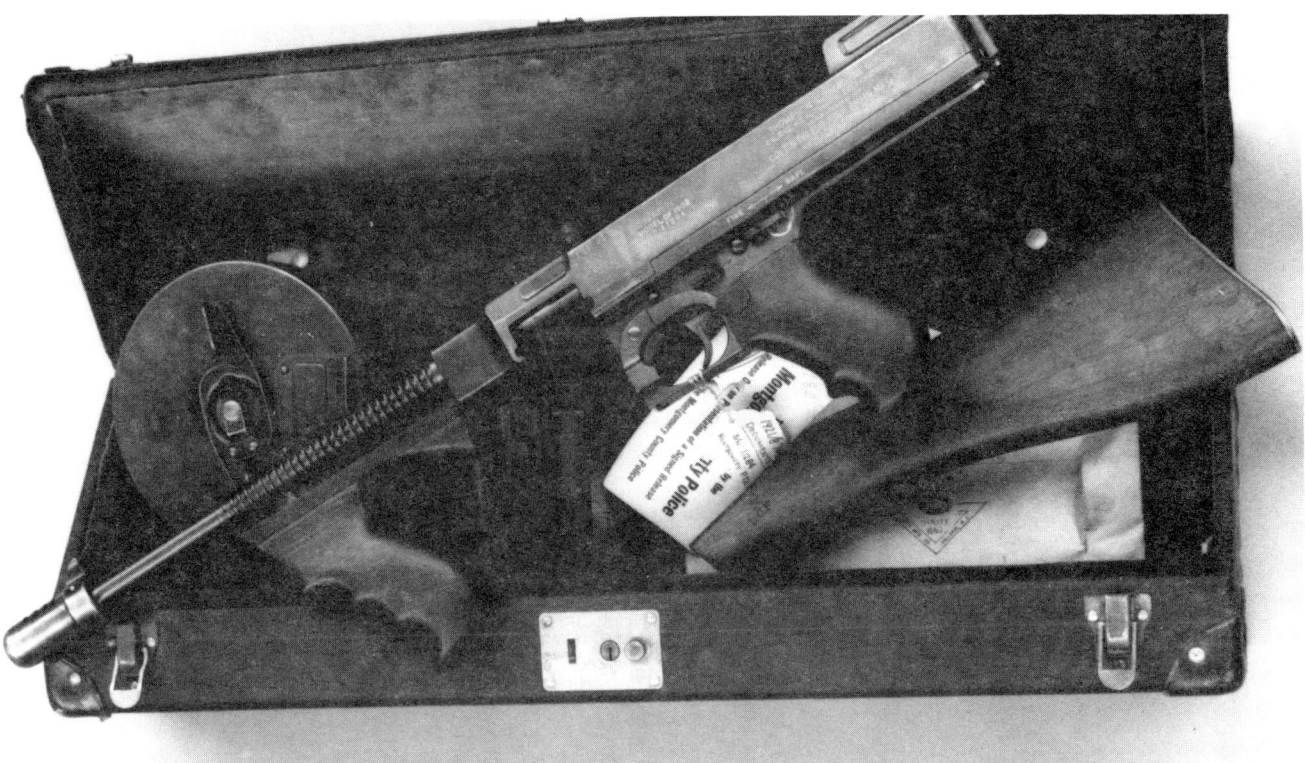

A cased FBI M1921-8.

Rare 21-8 Thompson that was reconverted to 1921 specs.

new bolt, ultimately deriving the M1 guns that were entirely new, to make a Model 1928 gun that operated on straight blowback without the lock. Doing so entailed a lot of work and basically a new receiver; there was essentially little point to the exercise except developmentally. Such guns no longer exist.

Thompsons may be conveniently divided into the following groups:

1. *"You Can't Get 'Ems."* Included in this group are the Warner-Swasey-built prototypes, the T2 and BSA prototypes, the Savage 9mm guns, all Thompson's tape-fed (belt-feed) prototypes, the largely fictional M1923 military guns, and other units made in extremely small quantities.

2. *Model 1921 guns.* There were a little over 15,000 of these made only by Colt and only in 1921. These are beautiful guns. Apparently, final markings were applied by Auto Ordnance; nineteen years later, re-marked variants were still being delivered.

Barrel, trim, fore-end, actuator, and compensator details will vary according to delivery time and customer specification, but *all* Colt-marked guns are or were originally M1921 guns.

Subgroups can seemingly be infinitely divided, but other than the actual commercial Model 1921 guns and trim variants, subtypes include the following:

A. Standard Model 1921s, with and without compensators (A and AC suffixes);

B. Model 1927s, semiautomatic-only guns but otherwise 1921s. Easily converted to full auto, they are short-barreled with detachable stocks, so they must be registered;

C. Military 1928 guns, usually called the "Navy" models. They almost always have horizontal foregrips and a new actuator and buffer to slow cyclic rate. Often blued and parkerized, they show the original markings overstruck. They are usually called 21-8 guns by collectors.

3. *Model 1928A1 guns.* These include guns indicative of a general trend toward cheaper trim items and the elimination of the finned barrel. They have adjustable sights and oddments in checkering. They were mostly equipped with horizontal foregrips. The Model 1928A1s were mostly built by Savage, though Auto Ordnance acquired some production capability during the war and subcontracted some work to deliver the "AO" prefixed serial number guns. Many were completed or modified postwar, including some "28-1" guns. Savage Model 1928A1s were retrofitted after the war to some local specification by fitting Model 1921 actuator/buffer parts.

4. *Postwar guns.* These include guns made by Auto Ordnance beginning about 1975 till about 1986. There were many problems with the Model 1928s thus produced, especially early on when a few machining errors were made, and even later with some accessories, such as the 50-round drums.

5. *M1 and M1A1 guns.* This is a new design sharing only the barrel and fore-end with the original. These all have smooth barrels—though the old finned unit will fit. The magazine catches did not originally include, nor was the frame group cut for, drum magazines. Many of the guns, however, were cut and modified for drum applications, most likely long after their military service and most likely for police service. Almost all M1-series guns were built by Savage.

In a way, the Thompson is the cause of the 1934 and 1938 national and federal firearms acts. The gun arrived on the market at exactly the wrong time. In 1921, anyone who was reequipping an army could choose from lots of surplus guns. The South and Midwest were experiencing tough economic times during Prohibition, despite the national boom. Thus, owing largely to a need to rob banks and discourage competition in the beer and booze business, Thompson's "trench broom" wound up sweeping the streets of Chicago rather than the fields of Flanders. Gangster were mainly interested in the firepower of the gun and used it as often to intimidate as to actually kill. Incidentally, many of the early Thompsons shoot much faster than the 800 to 850 rounds-per-minute rate cited in most texts, and one can only guess whether wear, individual modification, or variation in fit account for this rate.

Hollywood movies built entire fantasies around the "Tommy Gun," giving the impression that any crook more sophisticated than a pickpocket felt naked without one. However, the fictional/fantasy business inspired political terrorists of the right and left all over the world, and several scandals involving separatist movements, especially the IRA, and would-be dictators of various stripes further besmirched the gun's reputation among more legitimate circles. The fact remained, however, that the same virtues that made the gun popular with thugs were handy in military and police situations.

Thompsons are very rugged guns. When shot with good ammunition, they can deliver excellent accuracy. I shot mainly with Winchester and Federal match ammo, as well as Zero's semiwadcutters, all of which fed from stick mags in the Model 1921s. The shorter rounds caused problems with late 1928s and got genuinely annoying using drums or the M1-series guns. That's because they slop around as the gun is fired, and take odd feed angles for which the guns were not designed. IMI-Samson's high-velocity load was especially fun to shoot, fed well, and operated all guns close to their maximum rate of fire.

The Thompson is the most distinctive automatic weapon ever made. Nothing else looks like it, though the Eagle and Ingram guns of some years ago tried desperately to ape the gun's lines, with schlocky results. Even the Chinese copies only vaguely resemble the original. One can argue details of the Thompson's innards, design, and weight, but whoever decided on the gun's final external configuration (probably John T. Thompson himself) had the eye and aesthetic judgment of a fine artist. That look is why Thompson guns are so expensive. Except for the Model 1921 and rare variants, the Thompsons are really not as rare as the market makes them seem.

The Thompson saw use all over the world, but mostly in small quantities until World War II. It was robust and nearly immune to water intrusion, though sand could cause considerable consternation. Used carefully, the big-bulleted .45 round was dead accurate to roughly 200 to 250 yards and a bit longer in semiautomatic fire. After that, though, the big 230-grain bullet drops like a stone. The .45's armor-piercing capability was always poor, even with special ammo, as was its trajectory. This matters little to civilians, but it can cause emergencies in military environs. Therefore, other calibers for the submachine gun were preferred by most countries where the impact of a single hit was not as important as the gun's controllability and versatility.

For those who are using Thompson guns in actual defense today (and there are very few such people), I recommend a mix of Winchester Silvertips and IMI-Samson high-velocity "carbine" rounds in a 30-round magazine. I've yet to run into a Thompson that won't feed both, and it gives the user a good combination of expansion and penetration/range loadings.

Many of the guns in this array are from the superb J. Curtis Earl collection at the Champlin Fighter Museum in Mesa, Arizona, where twenty units are on display, including the rare and beautiful Midas Thompson that's engraved by Earl C. Bieu. The 9mm is also from that splendid group. Several shots included here depict guns that were once in my collection, while others are from Marty Mandall's shop and several small collections.

THOMPSON M1921A

Name:
Thompson submachine gun

Model:
1921A (early)

Cyclic Rate (approx.):
850 + RPM

Special Note:
See M1928A1 for other tabular data.

This is the original commercial version of the Thompson submachine gun. Colt only made 15,000 receivers, all in 1921, and perhaps another odd thirteen to fifty overruns. Any Colt-marked gun was originally part of this lot, though it may have been re-marked to conform to another specification. When initially introduced, there was no Cutts Compensator; those devices began to arrive in 1926.

This variant, with the finely finished barrel fins and high-gloss commercial blue, is fairly typical of the Prohibition era "Chicago Pianos," subject of the Helmer book, *The Gun that Made the Twenties Roar.* The quick detachable buttstock made for easy carriage under a coat or in a violin case. Said one club owner on the Lake Michigan shore in referring to violin-toting "customers" entering his establishment during the speakeasy days of harsh competition amongst rum-runners, "When a bunch o' guys walked in with violin cases, I sure as hell hoped they was the band."

Thompson M1921A.

Thompson M1921A with 100-round drum.

The negative publicity from the free-and-easy days of bootleg liquor and machine-gun murders did the Auto Ordnance Corporation no material good at all. By 1939, the company still had many of the original 15,000 guns on hand. The IRA had been caught smuggling some Thompsons to the scene of various hot spots. Though the FBI, post office, navy, Treasury Department, many police agencies, and others bearing legal and illegal credentials had purchased the guns in small quantities, not enough of them were sold to keep the Auto Ordnance Company firmly in the black.

Colt apparently supplied the guns unassembled and unmarked to Auto Ordnance, for the markings went through gradual changes long after Colt delivered the entire batch. The marking and lettering shown in the photo are of the earliest style.

Only about 1,500 Model 1921s remain in U.S. civilian hands. No one knows how many unregistered, government-owned, or foreign Thompsons still exist, but there is virtually no chance they will ever be on the legitimate U.S. market again.

Colt was paid $45 per gun. Remington cut the wood, and the sights came from Lyman. The total cost of the guns to Auto Ordnance once assembled and finished was probably around $75 to $100. Today, almost any complete M1921 brings about $2,000; superb specimens like the one shown command much, much more.

THOMPSON M1928A1

Name:
Thompson submachine gun

Model:
1928A1 (British)

Caliber:
.45 ACP

Other Chamberings:
Savage Arms Corporation

Type of Fire:
Semiauto and full auto

System of Operation:
Delayed blowback

Cyclic Rate (approx.):
600 RPM

Feed System/Ammunition Delivery:
Various box and drum magazines

Country of Manufacture:
United States

Manufacturer:
Savage Arms Corporation

Countries of Use:
Great Britain

Primary Service:
British military

Primary Tactical Use:
Individual

When stocks of the original Colt-built receivers began to dwindle in 1939 and 1940, Auto Ordnance approached Colt about new production. Colt expressed no interest, nor did Savage at first. Eventually both companies put tools and jigs back to work that had been in storage since 1921. The guns were not as lavishly finished or machined as the Model 1921s, but they worked well.

The British were the largest customers of the Model 1928A1s at that time, preferring the old-style vertical foregrip they had become accustomed to from the small earlier purchases they had made of Model 1921s and 1928s. They added swivels on the forward grip and the top of the detachable buttstock. Many of the early British 1928A1s contained oddments of leftover Colt and commercial parts

Thompson M1928A1 (British).

that Auto Ordnance had apparently had on hand for nineteen years.

This specimen carries a complete set of British proofs, indicating it saw actual service with British troops during World War II.

THOMPSON M1

Name:
Thompson submachine gun

Model:
M1

Caliber:
.45 ACP

Type of Fire:
Semiauto and full auto

System of Operation:
Blowback

Cyclic Rate (approx.):
600 RPM

Feed System/Ammunition Delivery:
Box magazine only

Country of Manufacture:
United States

Manufacturer:
Savage Arms Corporation

Countries of Use:
U.S. and many countries worldwide

Period of Manufacture (approx.):
1942–late 1940s (Savage ceased production in 1945, but Auto Ordnance was still assembling guns much later)

Period of Service (approx.):
1942–1950s (some guns are still in service in U.S.-controlled countries and with law enforcement agencies)

Primary Service:
Military contracts

Primary Tactical Use:
Individual

Original M1s are quite rare since they were replaced in production by the M1A1 shortly after their manufacture (the M1A1 used a fixed firing pin). Though physically similar to the M1921 to 1928 guns, the M1 is an entirely different mechanism of straight blowback variety.

As with all Thompson guns, the M1 could use any Thompson barrel whether or not the M1 had fins. The M1, however, was virtually always delivered with no fins and no compensator. The fancy Lyman sight had by this time been dropped.

The M1 was still heavy and bulky, and was still considered too expensive. Until Auto Ordnance was caught under wartime price control/profit restrictions, it continued to bill the U.S. government the same price for the simplified M1/M1A1 guns as for the much more elegant M1928A1s.

Thompson M1.

THOMPSON M1A1

Name:
Thompson submachine gun

Model:
M1A1

The M1A1 Thompson was the final modification of the Thompson submachine gun. The floating firing pin was eliminated, and the striker was machined into the bolt face.

Government procurement price on the last M1A1 guns from Auto Ordnance was $44.85 in 1944 and 1945, including spares, cleaning kit, and magazine. This contrasts with the $209 per unit charged in 1939 for Model 1928s and 28A1s.

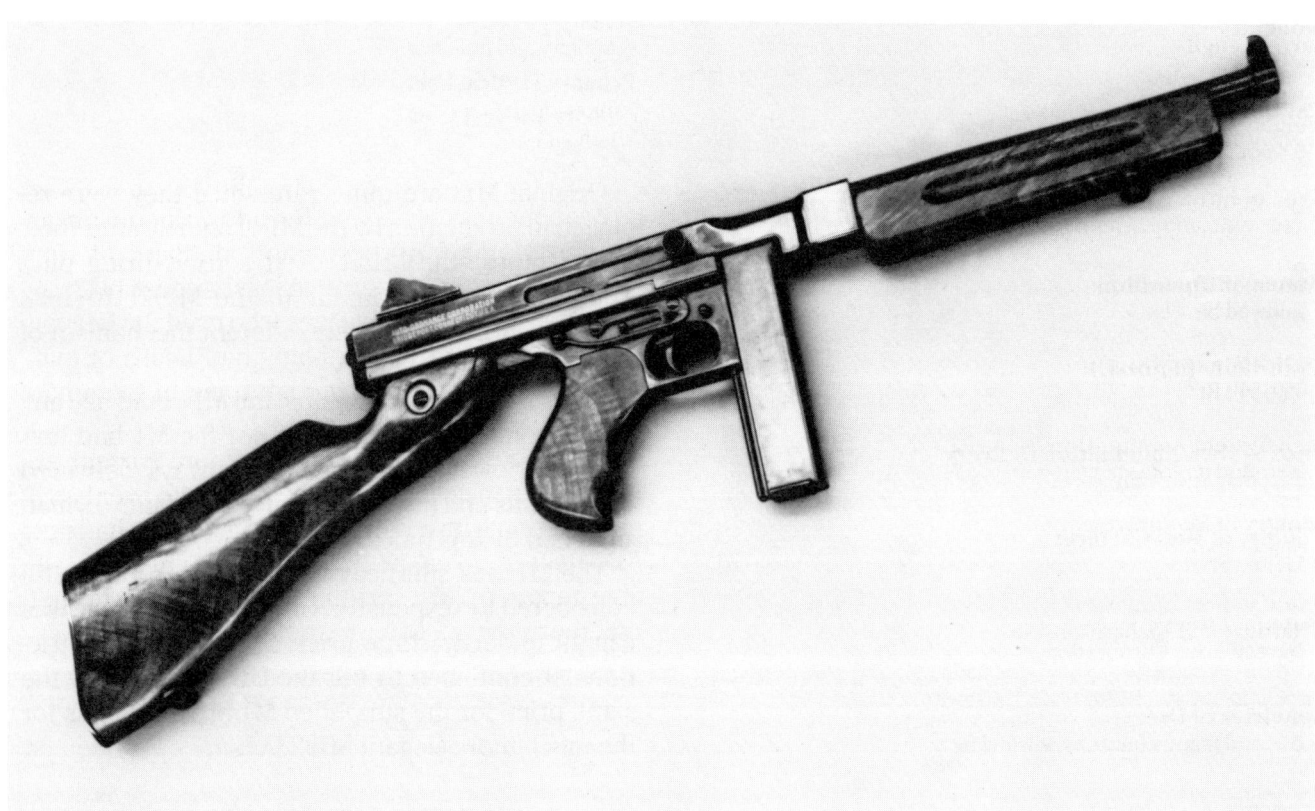

Extremely rare presentation Thompson M1A1.

Rare Thompson M1A1 "tanker" with steel reinforced fore-end.

REISING M50 (MILITARY)

Name:
Reising submachine gun

Model:
M50

Caliber:
.45 ACP

Overall Length:
35.75 inches

Barrel Length:
11 inches

Weight:
6.8 pounds

Type of Fire:
Select, semiauto or full auto

System of Operation:
Delayed blowback

Cyclic Rate (approx.):
450–550 RPM

Feed System/Ammunition Delivery:
20-round double staggered magazine or 12-round magazine

Country of Manufacture:
United States

Manufacturer:
Harrington & Richardson, U.S.A.

Countries of Use:
U.S. and others

Period of Manufacture (approx.):
1942–1946

Period of Service (approx.):
1942-1945 (military)
1942–present (civilian)

Primary Service:
Military and police sales

Primary Tactical Use:
Individual

Weapons maker Eugene Reising was converting the Reising M50 to production standard at Harrington & Richardson until at least August 1942.

I've talked to many marines who used the Reising during World War II, and many had heard of malfunctions with the gun, though none of them had ever actually had one. Nor have I.

I asked J. Curtis Earl, who has more current experience than anyone I know, whether he ever had a malfunction with a Reising and was told he had not. As a matter of fact, he had never even heard a reliable report of M50 malfunctions, despite the fact that the gun has a bad reputation for reliability.

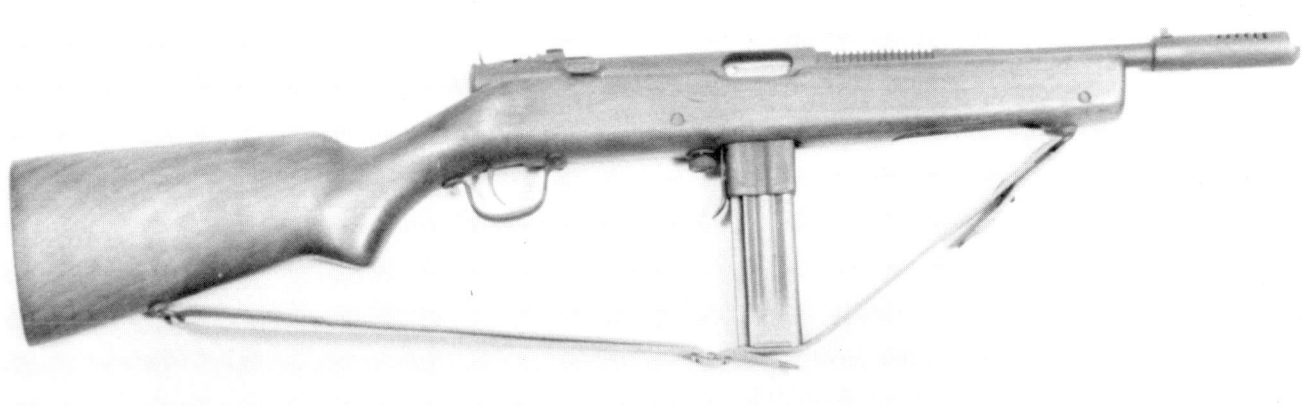

Reising M50 (military).

Unlike most collectors, I've had some serious experience trying to keep Thompsons working under adverse conditions. Thompsons *do* stop working when sand is introduced into their mechanism, but Reisings do not because their bolt mechanism just doesn't allow sand near any important parts. The Reising may have had some glitches because its activating handle was under the fore-end, especially if it rusted on its internal working surfaces. The Thompson isn't very moisture-sensitive.

Despite stories of unreliability, the Reising is definitely a superb submachine gun if kept reasonably clean. It shoots at a good, moderate rate from a closed bolt, not much of a problem with submachine guns with a maximum 20-round magazine capacity where heat doesn't built up to very high temperatures. There is little clearance in the bolt groove, but there is also little likelihood that a significant amount of dirt will get into the Reising's action.

"Experts" often condemn the weapon as "too complex," but a schematic reveals that the Reising is far less complicated than a lot of weapons of similar size with better reputations. The magazine is a potential problem source, for it is a staggered column with a narrow, single-feed well in the 20-round incarnation. The 12-rounder is a single-column type. Yet there seem to have been few reported magazine problems.

An unusual safety is incorporated in the bolt retarding mechanism. The firing-pin rear projects slightly from the center of the cylindrical bolt. There is a clearance hole formed in the hammer cylinder. Thus, if the bolt does not rise into its locking detent in the receiver's top, the piece cannot fire since the hammer is prevented from reaching the firing pin.

REISING M50 (CIVILIAN)

Name:
Reising

Model:
50 (Civilian)

The Reising has an excellent reputation as a civilian weapon, so much so that a semiautomatic version similar to the selective-fire variant shown in the photo was marketed for some time with a longer barrel. The primary difference between this piece and the standard military weapon is the finish, which on this variant is gloss blue on all metal parts and oil and varnish on the wood.

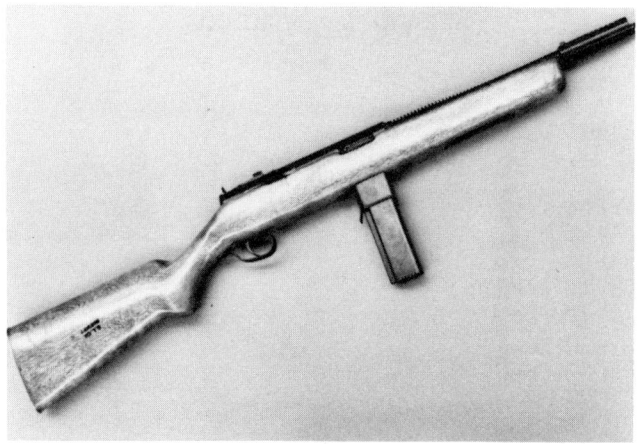

Reising M50 (civilian).

For the collector or nostalgia buff who wants an operating submachine gun, the false rumors about the Reising are in fact an *advantage,* since the guns—which are really quite rare—are sold at an artificially low price.

REISING M55

Name:
U.S. Reising submachine gun

Model:
55

The Reising Model 55 is the only variant of the H&R produced gun to do away with the compensator. A hard wire stock replaces the buttstock of the Model 50, though the mechanisms are basically identical.

The weapon was actually quite popular with Marine Raiders, airborne units, and Army Rangers, and was far more accurate than the M3 without being much bigger.

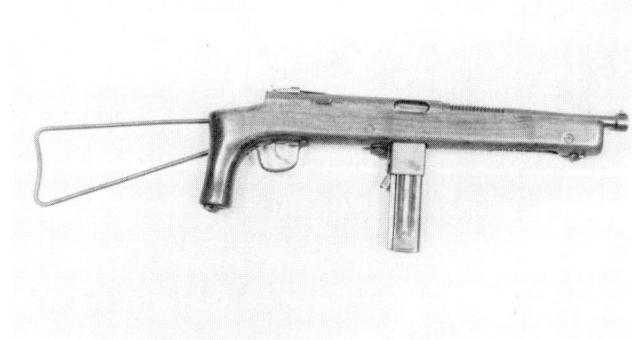

Reising M55 submachine gun.

UNITED DEFENSE SUBMACHINE GUN MODEL 42

Name:
United Defense submachine gun

Model:
Model 42

Caliber:
9mm Parabellum

Overall Length:
32.3 inches

Barrel Length:
11 inches

Weight:
9.15 pounds

Type of Fire:
Selective fire

System of Operation:
Blowback

Cyclic Rate (approx.):
700 RPM

Feed System/Ammunition Delivery:
40-round double, 20-round box magazine (back to back)

Country of Manufacture:
United States

Manufacturer:
Marlin Firearms

Countries of Use:
U.S. and Great Britain

Period of Manufacture (approx.):
1942–1944

Period of Service (approx.):
1942–1945

Primary Service:
OSS (Office of Strategic Services), MI5/6, and other clandestine operation units

Primary Tactical Use:
Individual

Of all the firearms allegedly designed, built for, and used in clandestine operations, the United Defense Model 42 is one of those that seems to have seen no other use. The Model 42 has been pictured as having been used in Adriatic, Aegean, Asiatic, and Northern European intelligence operations in both U.S. and British hands, but virtually nowhere else.

Designed by Swedish engineer Carl Swebelius around 1938 and originally set up for both the U.S. .45 loading and the European 9mm round, the Model 42's mechanism was complex and expensive to build, but was designed from its inception for durability and reliability. The bolt actuating handle was a slide that did not move with the bolt, sealing off the bolt's channel and keeping out dirt.

Since the gun arrived not too long after the Thompson's adoption, after arrangements had been made to produce the simplified M1928A1, and after research on the M3 was already well underway, only 15,000 Model 42s were built. Almost all have disappeared. The specimen included here is probably the finest of all remaining M42s.

The weapon had a considerable reputation for accuracy. It was superbly built and finished, was made of the finest steels, and was detail-machined like a first-quality commercial hunting weapon. There were single 20-round magazines, but photos of the period indicate they saw little or no use. The Dutch appear to have used a small quantity of the M42s in the East Indies in 1942; espionage and UDT (Underwater Demolition Team) personnel in the Philippines also reportedly used these guns.

United Defense submachine gun Model 42.

M2 CARBINE

Name:
Carbine .30

Model:
M2

Caliber:
.30 carbine

Overall Length:
35.6 inches

Barrel Length:
18 inches

Weight
5.5 pounds

Type of Fire:
Selective fire

System of Operation:
Gas

Cyclic Rate (approx.):
600 RPM

Feed System/Ammunition Delivery:
15- and 30-round boxes

Country of Manufacture:
United States

Manufacturer:
Plainfield Machine Company

Countries of Use:
U.S. and its allies

Period of Manufacture (approx.):
1941–present

Period of Service (approx.):
1941–present (now obsolete in U.S. service)

Primary Service:
Military and police units, and civilian

Primary Tactical Use:
Individual

M2 .30 carbine.

The Williams M1 carbine design had barely reached field units in 1942 before men set to work with files to convert the handy little weapon to fully automatic fire. Late in the war—most authorities say about 1944—a slightly beefed-up version with a selector switch began to arrive along with the first 30-round straight magazines. Later, the currently popular banana-shaped unit began to be issued.

The M1 and M2 carbines do not use the .30-06 full-powered rifle round. Instead, they use a straight-tapered, mid-range round that looks much like a pistol cartridge. The carbine was originally in-tended to replace the pistol in all applications, though it never did so. It was a handy piece, similar in concept to the assault rifle. Giving more range and stability than the submachine gun, it did so without the bulk of a rifle or machine gun. The carbine was very popular late in World War II and throughout the Korean conflict.

Though long out of production for military use and long out of issue even to reservists, the carbine is still produced for the civilian commercial and law enforcement markets.

Folding-stock versions and carbines set up for the infrared sniperscope (M3) were also manufactures. Most commercial guns are of the semiautomatic M1 variety.

We ran lots of Federal American Eagle ammo through the carbines, as well as ample stocks of Chinese surplus and Winchester's "USA" rounds. I must confess that I have never really liked the carbine and now like it even less. That said, I've owned many of them. The gun is very heat-sensitive. Handy as it is, accuracy—what little there is—deteriorates rather rapidly when bursts are used. We got excellent results with all this ammo in semi-automatic fire and with handloads using Hornady and Speer 100- to 110-grain round-nosed bullets. Bolts slipped off operating rods on two guns when used in automatic fire, and another M2 sent its extractor flying. Though these military guns were over forty years old, the carbine's problems are design-related. Even though the gun is still handy, if one wishes to spend the time and trouble to acquire an automatic weapon, there are many better weapons than the M2s (though not many cheaper ones) designed for full automatic fire.

M3 SUBMACHINE GUN

Name:
M3 submachine gun ("Grease gun")

Model:
M3

Caliber:
.45 ACP

Overall Length:
Stock extended: 29.8 inches
Stock retracted: 22.8 inches

Barrel Length:
8 inches

Weight:
8.15 pounds

Type of Fire:
Full auto

System of Operation:
Blowback

Cyclic Rate (approx.):
350–500 RPM

Feed System/Ammunition Delivery:
30-round staggered box magazine

Country of Manufacture:
United States

Manufacturer:
Guide Lamp Division of General Motors

Countries of Use:
U.S. and client countries

Period of Manufacture (approx.):
1942–1950s

Period of Service (approx.):
1943–present

Primary Service:
Military

Primary Tactical Use:
Individual

M3 submachine gun.

and much easier to service than the big, complicated Thompson. It is worth noting, however, that it was not as durable as the Thompson, which it wasn't intended to be, though it was not fragile, either.

The M3 and M3A1 both have the annoying habit of spraying the user with lubricant, fouling, or unburnt powder from time to time. Sights are crude. Seldom anyone's choice, it does not like ammunition shorter than standard hardball.

M3A1 SUBMACHINE GUN

Name:
Submachine gun

Model:
M3A1

Manufacturer:
Guide Lamp Division of General Motors

If the M3's tinny construction and crank-type cocking device seemed crude to U.S. troops, the M3A1 must have seemed the final step toward absolute junk, especially after the rather posh Thompson began to disappear from service. To cock the M3A1, one inserts his finger into a groove on the bolt itself and yanks rearward. The firing pin was built into the bolt, riding on guide rods, to save even more fine machine work. An oil bottle was tucked into the pistol grip, a magazine tool built into the retractable buttstock, and, as with the M3, conversion capability to 9mm was built in from the beginning.

Oddly, the 9mm capability saw little use until fairly recently, when NATO police/security units and some tank crews in Europe were issued "as new" M3A1s in 9mm. Such guns were technically

When the M3 first reached U.S. units overseas in late 1943 and early 1944, it was not well received. There was a time when no one would use the M3 if he could get *anything* else. It looked cheap, which it was. Literally a U.S. Sten equivalent, the M3 was designed to accept a 9mm conversion kit. The gun was cocked with a crank, and it did look like a "grease gun," a term that troops using this gun immediately applied to the M3.

The gun's reputation was not helped by the realization that it was made by firms not previously involved in war procurement plans. It was mostly made by a firm whose previous business was auto lamps.

Most of the negative stories about the M3, though, are just fiction. The gun was quite reliable

M3A1 submachine gun.

Cocking procedure for the M3A1.

declared obsolete in the sixties.

An extremely effective silencer was built for these guns, and a flash hider was introduced toward the end of World War II. The M3A1 actually was issued before the end of that war, though it was not common until the Korean War.

The M3A1 is quite uncommon in civilian collections since very few of them that were delivered under the Military Aid Program can be reimported. Not many were released stateside. There may be as few as a dozen in civilian hands.

COLT-BROWNING M1919

Name:
Browning water-cooled machine gun

Model:
1919 Colt

Caliber:
.30-06

Overall Length:
38.5 inches

Barrel Length:
24 inches

Weight:
Gun: 32.6 pounds
Mount: 54 pounds

Type of Fire:
Full auto only

System of Operation:
Recoil

Cyclic Rate (approx.):
550 RPM

Feed System/Ammunition Delivery:
Fabric web belt

Country of Manufacture:
United States

Manufacturer:
Colt Patent Firearms Mfg. Co.

Countries of Use:
U.S.

Period of Manufacture (approx.):
1919–1920s

Period of Service (approx.):
1919–?

Primary Service:
Commercial and military sales

Primary Tactical Use:
Crew-served infantry weapon

Colt had set up and was producing Browning M1917 guns when World War I ended. The company did not deliver many, since it was busy with many other infantry and aircraft gun projects. After the war, Colt introduced the M1919 as a commercial version of the M1917 gun in an effort to capture foreign markets. Law enforcement was not interested in a heavy gun in this caliber, and the export market was flooded with surplus, refurbished guns at bargain prices. Consequently, very few Model 1919s were made, though Mexico did procure some in 7mm caliber.

The guns pictured are a matched, consecutively numbered pair and are two of the three 1919s known to be on display in the entire United States. The guns are mounted on the 1919 tripod, a modified version of the 1917 tripod, which may be more rare than the gun itself.

Colt-Browning M1919.

The M1917 on which these guns are based is almost as rare as the Model 1919 since from the twenties on, the original guns were modified with top cover changes and a reinforcing stirrup to strengthen the plates. They were mostly brought up to M1917A1 standard and re-marked.

That the Brownings were used during World War I only in what Chinn calls "a meaningless show of force" after September 26, 1918, reflects not a lack of procurement funds, but a lack of vision on the part of Army Ordnance. The design was battle-ready between about 1910 and 1912. Had guns not been procured in large numbers, even a nominal procurement and adoption would have allowed manufacturers to tool for the machine guns. The U.S. Army, however, spent far more of its money on new saddle and tack gear and designs for horsed cavalry between 1899 and 1915 than on machine guns.

Several unit histories of the late war suggest strongly that the Brownings in France were brought forward but never truly fired in anger. Val Browning's notes also imply French use of the gun at that time. The German army by that time was severely demoralized owing to the failure of the big Spring Offensive and various broken supply promises. German troops tended to vacate areas around fixed enemy positions, and at times moved so fast that fresh U.S. infantry had trouble following them. U.S. army troops were on the offensive, and the BAR saw considerable use in these late spurts. There was seldom time in the helter-skelter of rapid advance to even set up heavy machine guns, let alone use them in their traditional covering fire role. There were lots of tanks around, providing rolling cover fire.

Down to its wooden grips and exposed brass, these 1919 guns mirror the original 1917 model.

BROWNING M2 HEAVY BARREL

Name:
Browning heavy machine gun

Model:
M2 Heavy Barrel

Caliber:
.50

Overall Length:
65.2 inches

Barrel Length:
45 inches

Weight:
Gun: 84 pounds
Ground mount: 44 pounds

Type of Fire:
Full auto only

System of Operation:
Recoil

Cyclic Rate (approx.):
550 RPM

Feed System/Ammunition Delivery:
Disintegrating steel belt

Country of Manufacture:
United States

Manufacturer:
Kelsey-Hayes Wheel Co., Plymouth, Michigan, and many others

Countries of Use:
U.S. and most of the Western world

Period of Manufacture (approx.):
Late 1920s–present

Period of Service (approx.):
Late 1920s–present

Primary Service:
Military

Primary Tactical Use:
Crew-served heavy machine gun designed to be used on tripods, heavy-mounted bases in vehicles, or aircraft mounts

It is a tribute to John Browning's design and production genius that, more than sixty years after his death, several of his designs are still in full-scale production. Browning's designs were straightforward, fairly simple, and very sturdy. There was little reliance upon ultrafancy metals, tricks of machining, and impractical but ingenious applications of bizarre devices offering some unnecessary "com-

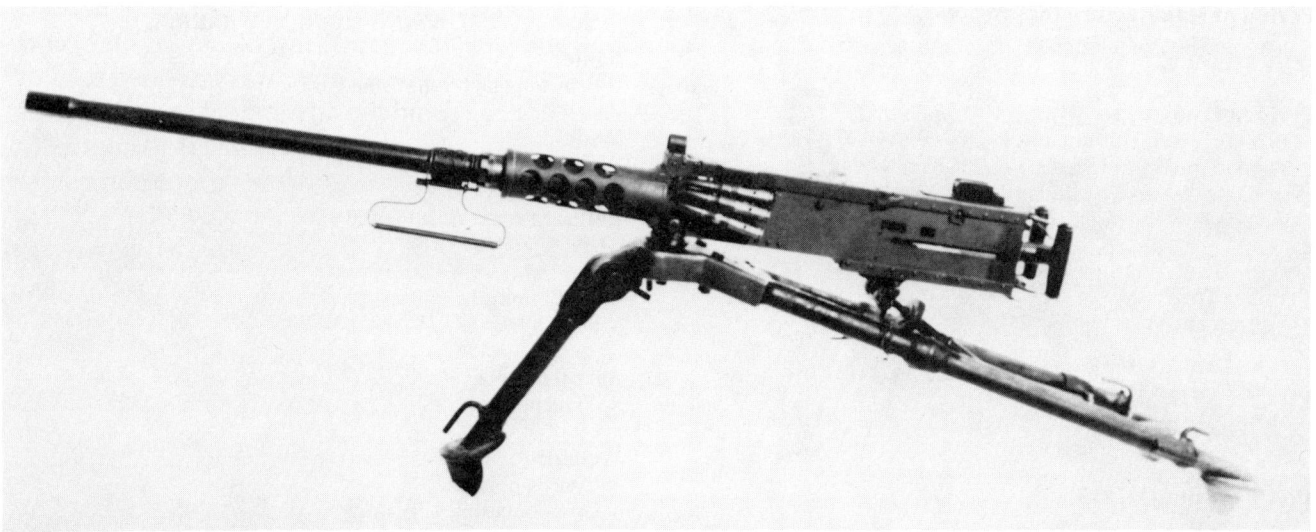

Browning M2 Heavy Barrel.

fort" function that in the end caused only malfunctions. He was a master of mechanical simplification.

In the late 1970s, the M2 caliber .50 series was "replaced" in some applications by a "far more sophisticated" design, the M85. The M85 saw almost no service, cost millions in research, and is in the process of being replaced by the gun it was designed to replace, the by-now ancient M2 Browning.

The ubiquitous nature of the .50 M2 Heavy Barrel is a profound tribute to the soundness of its basic design. Beefed up with a heavy sleeve that served as a barrel support and heat sink, the barrel enlarged and lengthened, the M2 HB replaced the lighter, original M2 as the infantry company level gun. Though there have been sight, trim, ammunition, and small internal modifications over the years, there is no tactical difference between an early 1930s version and one built today.

These guns are the standard infantry and vehicular gun in so many countries that it would be impossible to list them all. The trajectory of the original 1918 cartridge is not as flat as some military authorities would like, but the punch of the 709-grain bullet is both handy for thin-skinned vehicles and intimidating against infantry. The Soviet DShK and UB series 12.7mm rounds shoot flatter and use a heavier bullet, but are issued in nowhere near the numbers of the M2Hb. They seldom accompany ordinary Soviet infantry.

The most critical adjustment on the gun is headspace. In the M2 series, barrel removal is unnecessary to secure correct chamber to bolt relationship.

Turret versions of the M2 HB, some of World War II vintage, are also still in issue. Such versions are used mostly on multiple mounts on vehicles.

BROWNING M2 BASIC and AIRCRAFT

Name:
Browning heavy machine gun

Model:
M2 (basic and aircraft)

Caliber:
.50 U.S.

Overall Length:
56.25 inches

Barrel Length:
36 inches (some versions use other lengths)

Weight:
61 pounds in most common versions

Type of Fire:
Fully automatic (selective fire on spotting guns only)

System of Operation:
Recoil

Cyclic Rate (approx.):
600 + RPM in some "basic" versions
750–900 RPM in speeded-up aircraft versions

Feed System/Ammunition Delivery:
Disintegrating link belts of varying length according to installation

Country of Manufacture:
United States and others

Manufacturer:
Many commercial companies and U.S. arsenals

Countries of Use:
Worldwide

Period of Manufacture (approx.):
1928–present

Period of Service (approx.):
1928–present (This gun has been used for many purposes. Made in the United States, Belgium, and England in so many versions, the above tabular data may be construed to include only the most common aircraft versions extant.)

Primary Tactical Use:
Aircraft and vehicle mounts, primarily antiaircraft

The original M2 was a collaboration between Colt and the Rock Island Arsenal, among other companies. The "basic" receiver was intended to allow reversible feed and the adjustment or replacement of the bolt, springs, and mechanisms to control firing rate. In its original form, the ground gun quickly disappeared in favor of specialized variants, but all versions used what was in essence a common receiver.

The aircraft "basic" could be tripped electrically

Browning M2 guns were used with a variety of aircraft and antiaircraft mountings.

The U.S. Boeing B-17 bomber carried as many as fourteen .50 M2 aircraft guns.

A Browning M2 basic on display tripod. The P-40 plane in the background carried six M2 machine guns.

The Champlin Museum's F-86F Sabre jet displays the weapons bay, holding six .50-caliber M2 aircraft machine guns. Note the antisway clips, introduced to keep the belts from tangling in each other.

or by mechanical plunger or conventional trigger. Fixed and flexible versions could be converted back and forth in the field without using special tools. Heaters for high-altitude applications could be added.

The M2 .50 design stressed high-quality internal finish and weight reduction (both gross weight and the weight of reciprocating internals).

BROWNING M2 ANTIAIRCRAFT MACHINE GUN

Name:
Browning very heavy AA machine gun

Model:
M2 Antiaircraft

Caliber:
.50 U.S.

Overall Length:
66 inches

Barrel Length:
45 inches

Weight:
Gun with water: 121 pounds
Mount: 401 pounds

Type of Fire:
Fully automatic

System of Operation:
Recoil

Cyclic Rate (approx.):
600+ RPM

Feed System/Ammunition Delivery:
Canister of belts/linked belts

Country of Manufacture:
United States

Manufacturer:
Colt and others

Countries of Use:
U.S. and its allies

Period of Manufacture (approx.):
1920s–late 1930s

Period of Service (approx.):
1920s–1945

Primary Service:
Military

Primary Tactical Use:
Usually crew-served antiaircraft and heavy local defense

This was the standard heavy antiaircraft machine gun for single mounts between the world wars, showing up intermittently on ships until quite some time after World War II. Like 20mm cannon, it was to knock down airplanes with very few shots. The gun had superb sustained fire characteristics, but multiple mounts of air-cooled .50s worked even better since the rate of fire of any single gun was too low. Obviously, however, the gun was devastating when the gunner got the range and lead right since he could continue to punish his target for a long time due to its water-cooling feature. The gun was a superb fixed-base antipersonnel weapon, as the Japanese discovered in the Wake Island and Philippines campaigns. Navy gunboats in China engaged in many small actions after 1937 also experienced its effectiveness.

Guns similar to this one saw action in films like *Tora, Tora, Tora* and *Midway*. A similar but lighter gun known as the M1921A1 was also produced. It bears similarity to the Champlin Museum's MG52A, which also was designed with the M3 AA mount in mind.

As time went by, the word "very" disappeared form the "very heavy" designation in most stenciling, but the gun didn't lose any weight. Its jacket contained channeling to keep the water circulating, and in some stationary installations where power was available, auxiliary pumps were in inventory to keep cool water flowing through the jacket. Such pumps seem to have been seldom used.

While many nations used aircraft and vehicle guns of .50 caliber and larger, only the United States issued and used such a gun for ordinary infantry in great numbers. It added power and great range to the infantry repertoire. Shooting at a mile was not unknown with the .50, especially this version. A scope sight, now very rare, was often seen in use with U.S. .50 caliber guns in the interwar period. A new scope model for the current versions of the gun may soon be in issue, for the .50 in its M2/M3 basic and M2 Heavy Barrel forms has recently been returned to production to replace the M85.

The big Browning M2 antiaircraft on its 400 + pound M3 mount with tripod.

BROWNING MG52A

Name:
Browning heavy machine gun, water-cooled

Model:
MG52A

Caliber:
.50 U.S.

Overall Length:
56.5 inches

Barrel Length:
36.25 inches

Weight:
Gun without water: 79 pounds
Quadripod mount: 88 pounds
AA mount: 401 pounds

Type of Fire:
Automatic only

System of Operation:
Recoil

Cyclic Rate (approx.):
500 RPM

Feed System/Ammunition Delivery:
Fabric or disintegrating link belt, 250-round or interconnected

BROWNING MG52A (continued)

Country of Manufacture:
United States

Manufacturer:
Colt

Countries of Use:
Latin America

Period of Manufacture (approx.):
1919–1920s

Period of Service (approx.):
1919–present

Primary Service:
Commercial, military export

Primary Tactical Use:
Sustained fire, fixed base

John Browning's original M1918 ("M1") gun never saw official U.S. service. An enlargement of the M1917 caliber .30, it was not as refined as it might have been, largely because most of the designer's time was spent with the cartridge, which was based loosely upon a German 12.7mm antitank round. However, since the basic unit was satisfactory, Colt added a few refinements and sold the MG52 series of commercial guns worldwide. Second in the series, the MG52A is a rare gun. Some M2 feed cover improvements and the flip-flop capability of the actuating handle were incorporated into the series.

Since it was several years before the United States or Fabrique Nationale of Belgium exported any M2s or its variants, military establishments seeking a U.S.-style .50 caliber machine gun bought the MG52.

The single-base "quadripod" mount is a sustained-fire unit, and is also very uncommon.

Some MG52As are still in service in Latin America, where their sustained-fire capability and size are used as impediments to armed attacks on various presidential palaces.

The U.S. military M1921 series was similar to the MG52A. Had the M2 series not been developed in the late 1920s to early 1930s, a gun very similar to the MG52A might have become the heavy-caliber infantry machine gun of the United States rather than the M2 basic/M2 HB series of World War II fame.

Browning MG52A.

Browning MG52A.

BROWNING AN M2

Name:
Browning .30 general purpose light machine gun

Model:
AN (Army-Navy) M2

Caliber:
.30-06

Other Chamberings:
All standard rifle cartridges

Overall Length:
39.19 inches

Barrel Length:
24 inches

Weight:
23 pounds

Type of Fire:
Automatic

System of Operation:
Recoil

Cyclic Rate (approx.):
850–900 RPM (some guns could deliver 1,000–1,350 RPM)

Feed System/Ammunition Delivery:
Linked metallic belt

Country of Manufacture:
United States

Manufacturer:
Many

Countries of Use:
United States

Period of Manufacture (approx.):
1928–late 1940s

Period of Service (approx.):
1928–1950s (probably much later outside major countries)

Primary Tactical Use:
Fixed and flexible aircraft; some antiaircraft use

Externally similar to the 1919A4 ground guns, the vehicular and aircraft M2/AN M2 guns were quite different internally. They used high polish, special springs, and lighter parts in a manner similar to the M2 .50 to produce a higher cyclic rate, which was valuable in aircraft and antiaircraft roles.

One still sees the guns and their commercial Colt MG37-38 versions on multiple mounts since they require only rather more frequent barrel changes when regularly used.

By the middle of World War II, however, rifle-caliber aircraft and antiaircraft guns had been almost entirely replaced by heavier weapons.

Browning AN M2.

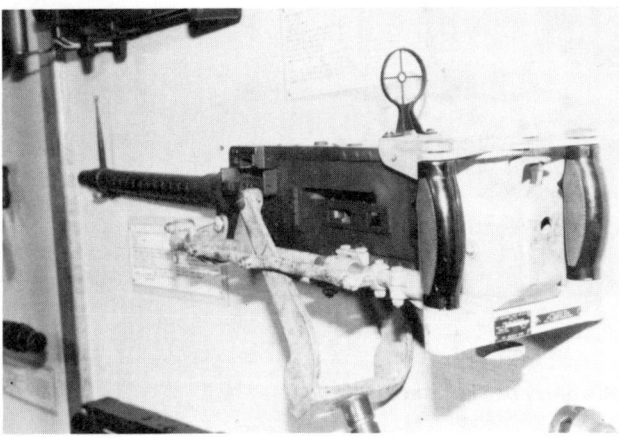

Browning AN M2.

BROWNING M1917A1

Name:
Browning .30-caliber water-cooled machine gun

Model:
1917A1

Caliber:
.30-06

Overall Length:
38.5 inches

Barrel Length:
24 inches

Weight:
Gun with water: 41 pounds
Mount: 53.2 pounds

Type of Fire:
Full auto only

System of Operation:
Recoil

Cyclic Rate (approx.):
550–600 RPM

Feed System/Ammunition Delivery:
250-round canvas web belt

Country of Manufacture:
United States

Manufacturer:
Government arsenals and private firms

Countries of Use:
U.S. and its allies

Period of Manufacture (approx.):
1936–1947 (Many M1917s were modified to M1917A1 standard in the 1930s before new production began. Other Browning variants were converted to the water-cooled standard after the weapon was out of front-line service, primarily for infiltration courses at training facilities.)

Period of Service (approx.):
1936–early 1960s; longer outside U.S.

Primary Service:
Crew-served infantry weapon

Primary Tactical Use:
Crew served

Two of the M1917A1 guns shown here are from the Champlin Museum and, like the museum's M1919s, are a matched pair of Brownings. Consecutively numbered, one has been painted black to represent Colt's 1930s to 1940s commercial guns, which were generally finished in that manner. Most wartime Browning 1917A1s were olive drab.

The M1917A1 was the standard sustained-fire, rifle-caliber heavy machine gun of World War II. The wooden pistol grip of the World War I original has now been replaced by an all-metal assembly. A new bottom plate, belt-feed lever, improved cover latch, sight for newer ammunition, cover catch hold open, tripod, steam tube assembly, gland setup, stirrup reinforce, and recoil plate in the face of the bolt were fitted to all new production guns and retrofitted to many of the original World War I guns. These changes were intended to make the gun more durable and relatively free from service headaches.

As with most Brownings, the headspace adjustment remained the most important adjustment on the gun. Too loose an interface between the bolt and chamber left the cartridges partially unsupported and would cause case damage and jams due to swelling in the chamber. Failure to extract would therefore result. Excessively tight headspace would not allow cartridges to fully seat in the chamber, and rounds would not fire at all. Checking and adjusting the headspace are, however, straightforward procedures, and testing merely involves ob-

Browning M1917A1.

serving the bolt's movement in its tract forward, confirming the condition by attempting to move the bolt with the extractor raised. Any free movement indicates excessive headspace.

The water-cooled gun was preferred for infiltration courses and defensive, sustained-fire applications long after it was out of general service. Rock Island Arsenal even converted some of the subsequent 1919A4 guns to the water-cooled configuration in the late 1950s.

All the belt-fed Brownings are reliable, sturdy, and accurate. The M1917A1 is the most accurate and reliable of all the rifle-caliber guns since the water-cooled guns are supported firmly on both ends of the barrel and virtually cannot get as hot. The tripod mounts are sturdier than the M2 unit used on the M1919A4.

One of the guns shown here is a converted M1917 on a 1917 mount.

BROWNING M1919A4

Name:
Browning light machine gun

Model:
1919A4

Caliber:
.30-06

Overall Length:
41 inches

Barrel Length:
24 inches

Weight:
Gun: 31 pounds
Tripod: 14 pounds

Type of Fire:
Full auto only

System of Operation:
Recoil

Cyclic Rate (approx.):
550–600 RPM

Feed System/Ammunition Delivery:
Fabric web belt, 250-round capacity

Country of Manufacture:
United States

Manufacturer:
Saginaw Steering Division of General Motors and other companies

Countries of Use:
U.S. and all allies and NATO countries

Period of Manufacture (approx.):
Mid 1930s–late 1950s

Period of Service (approx.):
Mid 1930s–present

Primary Service:
Military and commercial foreign sales

Primary Tactical Use:
Crew served

Evolved from the M1917 and M1918 Browning Aircraft gun, the 1919A4 was a somewhat heavier barreled, more robust version of a tank gun. Its introduction into U.S. service was as a sort of general-purpose light machine gun. Whereas the M1917A1 water-cooled gun was generally used at the company level or higher, the 1919A4 was often vehicle-mounted. M2 tripods were issued with each gun and, in some cases, a single platoon controlled three or four guns. Considerable attention was paid developing a light but flexible low tripod mount.

The 1919A4 is still in use throughout much of the world. The U.S. Navy retains a large quantity that have been converted to the 7.62x51mm NATO round. Known as the Machine Gun 7.62 NATO Mark 21 Model O, the guns are fitted with a prong-type flash suppressor. The Canadians employ a very similar gun called the C1. These guns have also been exported and given away under the Military Aid Program (MAP), both in their original configuration and other calibers. Fabrique Nationale in Belgium built and sold the Browning M1919A4 and most other Browning designs worldwide.

While the United States did not lavish great amounts of money on radical designs between the

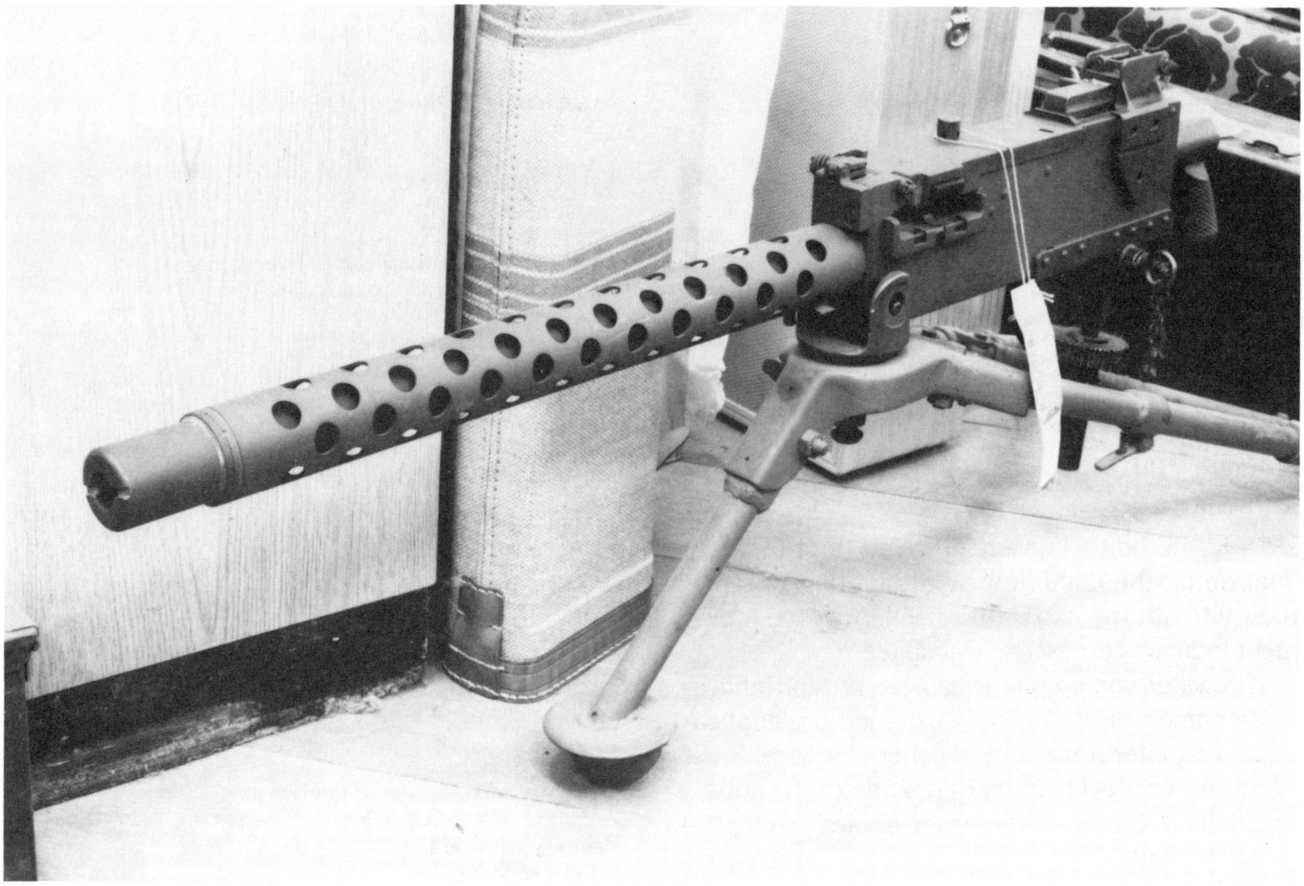

Browning M1919A4.

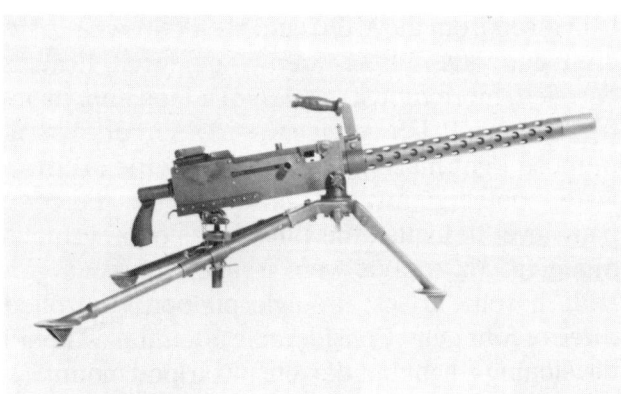

Browning M1919A4.

world wars, considerable research was devoted to developing maximum efficiency from designs based upon John Browning's two key infantry tripod guns. For example, the M37 tank machine gun for fixed-vehicle applications is essentially a 1919A4 gun with a feed-group capability of the ANM2 aircraft guns so that it can be fed conveniently from either side. By contrast, the Germans expended much research on their machine guns, never having quite enough to cover all contingencies. The Japanese copied whatever came along that seemed to work well, leading to several incompatible guns of different calibers in similar applications.

The first air-cooled infantry machine gun of sustained-fire capability to be accepted into regular army service, the M1919A4 had a basic mechanism identical to the M1917A1.

BROWNING M3 HEAVY MACHINE GUN

Name:
Browning heavy machine gun (aircraft)

Model:
M3

Caliber:
.50

Overall Length:
57.25 inches

Barrel Length:
36 inches

Weight:
68.75 pounds (with recoil adapter/booster)

Type of Fire:
Full auto only

System of Operation:
  Recoil

Cyclic Rate (approx.):
  1,100 + RPM

Feed System/Ammunition Delivery:
  Disintegrating steel link belt

Country of Manufacture:
  United States

Manufacturer:
  Various military contractors

Period of Manufacture (approx.):
  1944–1960s

Period of Service (approx.):
  1944–present

Primary Service:
  Military

Primary Tactical Use:
  Any vehicular or aircraft mount where high cyclic rate of fire is desired, primarily aircraft

Early prognostications that the machine gun would encounter mechanical and lubrication difficulties due to cold at altitudes proved correct. Cocking systems, lubricants, parts clearances, and heater installations were modified on the .50 guns, and fighter altitude performance improved. Muzzle boosters and high-speed bumpers that speeded up reciprocating parts were also employed on the M3 Brownings to boost the rate of fire.

Three M3s shown here are the starboard installation on the Champlin Museum's F86F. Gases that tended to build up in jet aircraft and then lead to explosive mixtures were given special attention in this installation, as was the cocking mechanism. World War II experience revealed that belt movement under g-forces caused more stoppages than any other single factor. The ammunition chutes were therefore given special attention, with an eye toward limiting the movement of the belts.

Under some circumstances, the rate of fire of the M3 series could be boosted to almost 1,300 rpm.

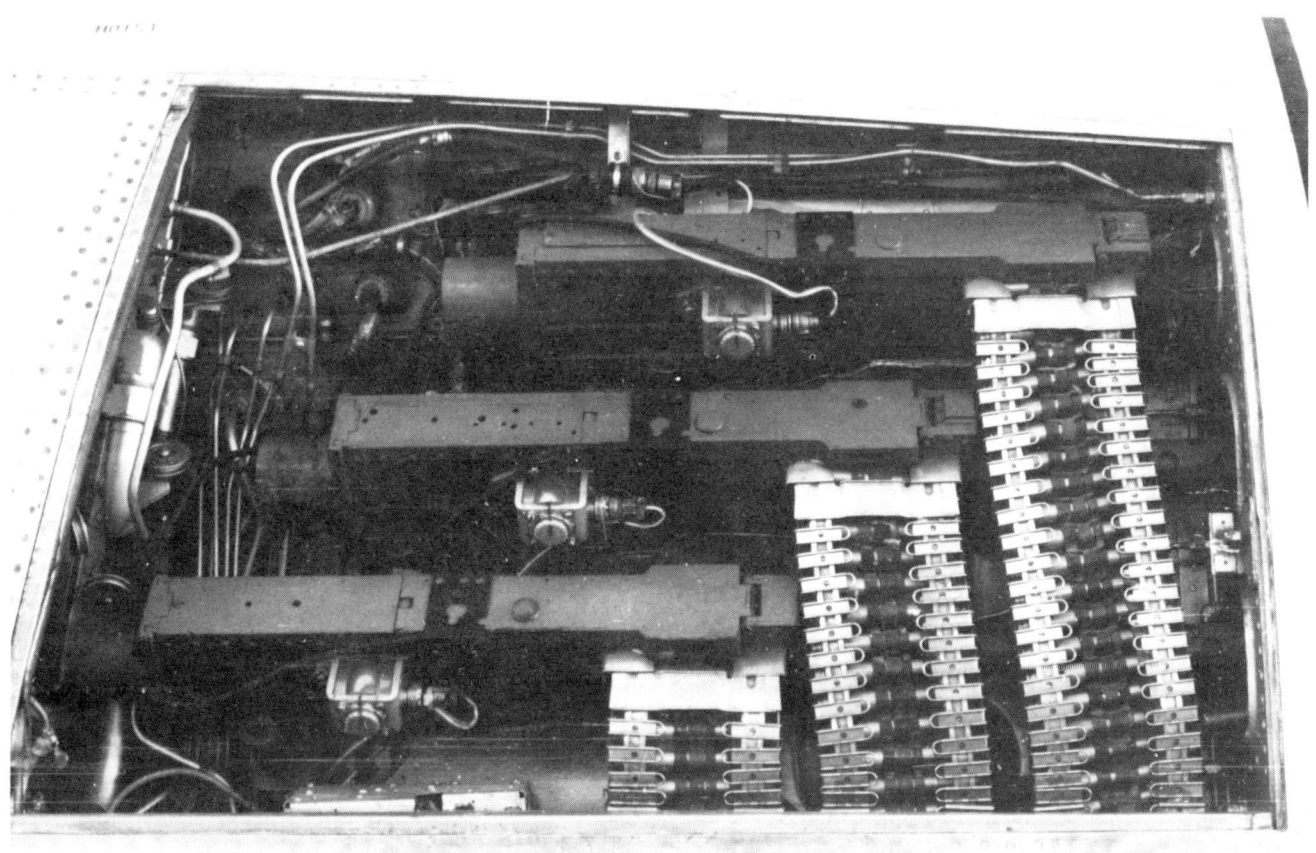

Browning M3 heavy machine guns.

INGRAM M6

Name:
Ingram

Model:
M6

Caliber:
.45 ACP

Overall Length:
37.2 inches

Barrel Length:
9 and 16 inches

Weight:
Standard version: 7.8 pounds
Long version: 8.3 pounds

Type of Fire:
Selective fire (by trigger pressure)

System of Operation:
Blowback

Cyclic Rate (approx.):
600 RPM

Feed System/Ammunition Delivery:
30-round box magazine

Country of Manufacture:
United States

Manufacturer:
Police Ordnance Company

Countries of Use:
U.S., Latin American countries

Period of Manufacture (approx.):
1949–1952

Period of Service (approx.):
1949–present

Primary Service:
Police and paramilitary units

Primary Tactical Use:
Police and paramilitary

Gordon B. Ingram designed the Ingram M6 to fire a variety of cartridges, including the 9mm, .38 ACP/Super, and .45 ACP, of which the latter was by far the most popular. Ingram formed the Police Ordnance Company with three veterans in 1949, and the company folded around 1952.

A bolt-actuated trip applies positive actuation of semiauto or full-automatic sear action. All parts are fabricated with a minimum of milling and machine tool use. Many parts are made from standard industrial stock (the receiver, for example, is made from conventional seamless tubing). The gun worked satisfactorily, but it looked shabby when compared to other guns available for the same price or less on the surplus market.

Ingram designed several M6 variants and spin-offs long after the Police Ordnance Company ceased to exist.

The 16-inch barrel was devised for a semiautomatic version of the gun, but it also provided a considerable increase in velocity on the automatic gun.

A variety of trim and fixtures was available. However, the attempt to visually emulate the Thompson with Sten M3-type guts made the gun look like a cheap substitute for a Thompson, rather than a new, improved, or updated gun. Like the Thompson, it was introduced at the worst possible time, right after major demobilization and when all types of high-quality surplus guns were available at cheap prices.

Ingram M6.

U.S. M14

Name:
Rifle

Model:
M14 (civilian), M14A1 (military and SWAT), M1A (civilian)

Caliber:
7.62x51mm NATO (.308 Winchester)

Overall Length:
M14: 44.14 inches
M14A1: 44.7 inches

Barrel Length:
22 inches

Weight:
M14: 8.7 pounds
M14A1: 13 pounds

Type of Fire:
M14: semiauto only
M14A1: selective fire

System of Operation:
Gas (Garand system)

Cyclic Rate (approx.):
675–750 RPM (modified M14A1: 575 + RPM)

Feed System/Ammunition Delivery:
20-round box magazine

Country of Manufacture:
United States, its allies, and client countries

Manufacturer:
M14: Smith of Mesa, Arizona
M14A1: H&R

Countries of Use:
U.S. and MAP (Military Aid Program) recipients

Period of Manufacture (approx.):
1957–1964

Period of Service (approx.):
1958–present

Primary Service:
Individual infantry and sniper

Primary Tactical Use:
U.S. combat infantry

On its best day, the M14 couldn't do what it was supposed to do, which was to replace each and every firearm in the 1950s military arsenal from the pistol to the BAR, including the motley collection of M1919A6 and other "light" machine guns. Based upon the excellent Garand system, the M14 was lightened, particularly in the front, and adapted to full-automatic fire.

There was no way the U.S. military would buy some "freaky-looking" foreign rifle such as the plastic-trimmed, straight-line stocked FAL, with which the M14 was compared for years. These "comparisons" were often rigged until tests (often irrelevant to actual use) were devised whereby the M14 could slide by and be "the winner." Even when fitted with a heavy barrel and front-end doodads available for the M15, the M14 was a terrible automatic weapon. It did not even come close to the standard FAL in performance and the dimensions were far from the superior performance evinced by quality FAL-HB guns.

The gun cost the taxpayer millions of dollars in phony research and contrived "experiments," producing the worst automatic weapon in U.S. service since the Chauchat. The M14 had the shortest first-line service of any U.S. service rifle, a mere eight years of panicky attempts to modify the system to a usable weapon with full-automatic capability.

In contrast, Beretta produced the BM59 on a basically unmodified M1 receiver in about ninety days at a cost of only a few thousand dollars in research. No country except for the United States ever paid cash for M14s; other users either captured, received, or purchased the M14s with MAP funds. The FAL, which produced a positive trade/payments balance for Belgium, saw use in almost the entire Western world at one time or another. Many countries still use the FAL.

Most M14s ended their days with their selectors secured in the semiautomatic position. The gun, even in the M14A1 variant, jumps, jiggles, and climbs far too rapidly for sane automatic use. Ironically, the FG42, condemned by many as a ridiculous weapon, actually handles better in automatic fire despite the fact its design predates the M14 by fifteen years.

That said, however, one must remember that the M14 is a modified Garand, with the forward handguard removed, gas cylinder slid back, and receiver lightened. A quick-detachable, 20-round staggered box magazine can be added. Weight savings are marginal, but the rigidity and basic quality of the semiautomatic rifle remain. For that reason, the M14 produced by Smith Enterprises is the *only* semiautomatic rifle covered in this book. A superb rifle, the M14's fully automatic capability is not worth the cost of the switch. The Smith is a civilian-market gun, which is fortunate because no other M14s will be released to civilians.

The H&R rifle shown here is an interesting gun.

The M14 is basically a simplified Garand, but the receiver was lightened and shortened, making recoil arc and violence more severe.

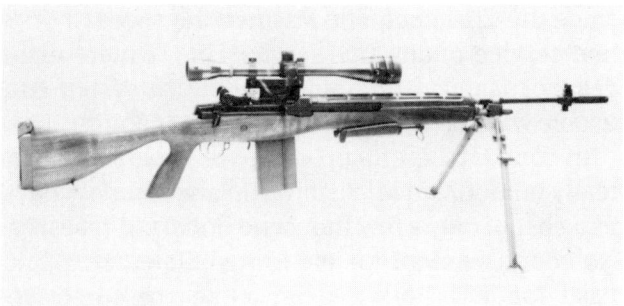

U.S. M14 with bipod.

Released to a small-town police agency in the 1960s under one of the Nixon administration's so-called "anticrime" measures, it began life as a standard H&R M14 with a TRW barrel. However, the barrel made it extremely inaccurate. With me supplying the prodding, a SWAT team commander converted the piece from a useless hose-pipe, bullet-spraying device suitable only for scaring unarmed civilians to a less-than MOA (minute of angle) target rifle with a moderately useful automatic capability.

An extra-heavy Kreiger match-grade barrel replaced the mint, but useless, original, immediately putting the rifle on the mark. Oversize and overweight National Match operating rods were culled until we found a rod that was heavier and tighter. An oversize operating rod tab was fitted. Tiny weights were added to the new "HRA" bolt, which was then carefully headspaced to the new barrel. Springfield Armory in Geneseo, Illinois, supplied the M14A2 stock, which was steel- and hard-epoxy bedded. The trigger was smoothed, but neither the two-stage pull nor the final release weight was modified. Since the rifle could already shoot better than its sights, a B-Square scope mount and powerful but inexpensive optic were added. The cyclic rate is

still too high for BAR-like shooting at 575 rpm or so, but it is far better than a "stock" rifle. In semiautomatic fire, this hybrid is devastatingly accurate, and the heavy barrel helps keep the rifle on target.

All these modifications involve too much work and planning to make what was supposed to be a production selective-fire all-purpose weapon into a combination MOA sniper rifle/fully automatic noisemaker.

M14s and their clones with GI bolts and ejectors will often shed them when used with ammo other than of military 7.62mm specification, owing to slight differences in rim geometry. A polish job will quickly solve the problem.

Match-preparing even a fully automatic M14 is a good idea. Actually shooting one in full-automatic fire is largely a waste of time and perfectly good ammo, unless one can exercise exceptional self-control.

M16

Name:
Assault Rifle

Model:
M16

Caliber:
5.56mm (.223)

Overall Length:
39 inches

Barrel Length:
20 inches

Weight:
6.35 pounds

Type of Fire:
Selective fire

System of Operation:
Gas

Cyclic Rate (approx.):
700–800 RPM

Feed System/Ammunition Delivery:
20- or 30-round box magazine and others

Country of Manufacture:
United States

Manufacturer:
Colt

Countries of Use:
U.S. and patron countries

Period of Manufacture (approx.):
1950s–present

Period of Service (approx.):
1963–present

Primary Service:
Military and law enforcement

Primary Tactical Use:
Individual

The M16 was designed by Eugene Stoner in the 1950s to provide a light and effective fully automatic weapon usable out to about 200 yards. Rights to manufacture the AR-15, which is what the M16 was originally called and is still called in its commercial incarnations, were sold to Colt in 1959. The U.S. Air Force adopted the weapon in 1962 and 1963, while the other armed forces followed the limited air force adoption by 1966 and 1967. It is a simple, uncontested fact that no other country has purchased the controversial M16 from their own tax funds; users outside the United States acquired them solely with funds provided under MAP.

Ammunition in the 5.56mm loading has undergone almost constant revision from its early days in an attempt to obtain more accuracy deep downrange and more power at all ranges. These efforts have been largely unsuccessful. Since the rifle sells on the international market for four times the price of the Soviet-designed AK series—and doesn't move too well—justifying the rifle's adoption and its price is somewhat difficult. This is especially so since many infantrymen who were issued M16s in Vietnam acquired AKs because of its greater reliability. On the plus side, the rifle is far better in fully automatic fire than the M14, which it replaced.

As in the Swedish Ljungmann system, gases in the M16 impinge directly upon the bolt, meaning that the weapon is powder-sensitive and demands careful and regular cleaning. Early in its life, U.S.

troops were sent afield with the M16 without proper cleaning supplies after having been told the weapon would not require cleaning. M16A1 rifles have the added forward-assist actuating handle and closed flash suppressors. A new variant has been produced with a heavier barrel, supposedly bringing accuracy to an acceptable level out to 400 yards under calm conditions.

COMMANDO ASSAULT RIFLE

Name:
Commando assault rifle/submachine gun

Model:
M16/XM177/CAR-15

With a total extended length of 31 inches and a compressed length of 28 inches, the "Commando" is a cross between the traditional submachine gun and the newer, light-caliber, small-bore "assault" rifle of limited range. As such, it is less controversial than the M16, its parent rifle, since its small size and high cyclic rate are handy in isolated and cramped quarters. The handy telescoping butt is more rigid than a folding stock yet shorter than a full-length unit. The 10-inch barrel reduces velocity and thus range, which is acceptable in a secondary weapon.

Weight unloaded is about 6.5 pounds.

As with its predecessor, the use of plastic and aluminum has been maximized. The same optical sights as those employed on the M16 may be used.

CAR-15.

AWC markets the M-22 and Project C Suppressors for the Armalite/Colt AR-15 and its derivatives. Mounted on the CAR-15, the rifle is still smaller than an ordinary AR-15. (Photo courtesy of AWC Systems Technology.)

M16 assault rifle.

S&W MODEL 76

Name:
Smith & Wesson submachine gun

Model:
76

Caliber:
9mm

Overall Length:
31.9 inches

Barrel Length:
8.75 inches

Weight:
7.1 pounds

Type of Fire:
Full auto only

System of Operation:
Recoil

Cyclic Rate (approx.):
700 RPM

Feed System/Ammunition Delivery:
30-round staggered magazine

Country of Manufacture:
United States

Manufacturer:
Smith & Wesson, U.S.A.

Countries of Use:
'U.S. (civilian) and others (police agencies)

Primary Service:
Commercial and military sales

Primary Tactical Use:
Individual law enforcement submachine gun

S&W Model 76.

A stamped, welded, very low-cost submachine gun for law enforcement, the S&W Model 76 was not a success. Only a few thousand were made, which are now mostly found in private collections.

I have attempted to test these guns twice. Both times I have suffered serious breakdowns, horrible jams, and potentially dangerous damage. I have no interest in trying again.

RUGER MINI-14

Name:
Mini-14 Assault Rifle

Model:
AC-556K

Caliber:
5.56mm

Overall Length:
37.25 inches

Barrel Length:
18.5 inches

Weight:
6.5 pounds

Type of Fire:
Selective fire with 3-shot burst control

System of Operation:
Gas

Cyclic Rate (approx.):
700 RPM

Feed System/Ammunition Delivery:
20- and 30-round staggered box magazines

Country of Manufacture:
United States

Manufacturer:
Sturm-Ruger and Co., U.S.A.

Countries of Use:
U.S. and Latin American countries

Period of Manufacture (approx.):
1970s–present

Period of Service (approx.):
1970s–present

Primary Service:
Commercial law enforcement sales

Primary Tactical Use:
Police and paramilitary

This version of Ruger's very successful Mini-14 series was intended to give law enforcement handy yet inexpensive selective-fire capability in the .223/ 5.56mm loading. The gun sells for almost $200 less than the M16A1/HB, and will generally outshoot that rifle.

The action of the rifle, commercially available as a semiautomatic, is a miniaturization of the military M14 for the .22 U.S. Army cartridge. A scope sight is easily fitted to these selective-fire rifles, and there are many aftermarket accessories available.

AR-18

Name:
Armalite Assault Rifle

Model:
AR-18

Caliber:
5.56mm (.223)

Overall Length:
38 inches

Barrel Length:
18.25 inches

Weight:
6.75 pounds

Type of Fire:
Selective fire

System of Operation:
Gas

Cyclic Rate (approx.):
750 RPM

Feed System/Ammunition Delivery:
30-round box magazine (20-round units are also available)

Country of Manufacture:
United States

Manufacturer:
Armalite Corporation

Countries of Use:
U.S. and Great Britain

Period of Manufacture (approx.):
1970s–present

Period of Service (approx.):
Late 1970s–present

Primary Service:
Police and military

Primary Tactical Use:
Individual

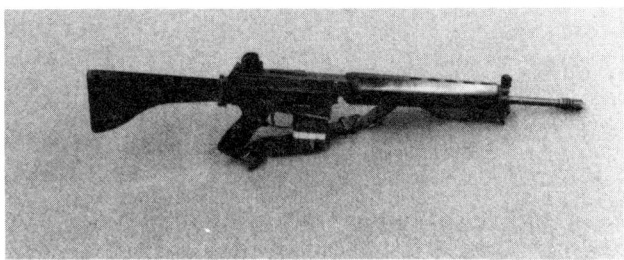

AR-18.

Currently under field-testing in Great Britain and adopted to replace the L1A1 (FAL) in some applications, the U.S.-designed AR-18 may become the standard weapon of much of the Western world. It is also manufactured in England by Sterling Armaments.

While the 5.56mm ammunition limits the range, hitting power, and penetration of this lightweight assault rifle, these drawbacks are considered acceptable in automatic fire.

Similar in some respects to the AR-15/M16, the AR-18 is quite different in its detailing. The newer rifle uses robust steel stampings in place of the alloy forgings prominent in the M16 family. The design has been simplified to aid maintenance and facilitate cleaning, and the rifle is intended to be stronger and more reliable than the M16. Civilian and police versions are available in semiautomatic only.

Recent tests indicate the AR-18 is far more reliable than the M16. The U.S. Army tested the rifle and came up with similar results, but expressed no interest in adopting it.

MAC-10

Name:
MAC

Model:
10

Caliber:
9x19mm

Overall Length:
10.5 inches (stock folded)

Barrel Length:
5.75 inches

Weight:
6.3 pounds

Type of Fire:
Selective fire

MAC-10 (continued)

System of Operation:
Blowback

Cyclic Rate (approx.):
900–1,100 RPM

Feed System/Ammunition Delivery:
20-, 30-, and 40-round box magazine

Country of Manufacture:
United States

Manufacturer:
Military Armament Corporation and other companies

Countries of Use:
U.S., El Salvador, and others

Period of Manufacture (approx.):
1972–present

Period of Service (approx.):
1972–present

Primary Service:
Police, paramilitary, and guard units

Primary Tactical Use:
Individual

Despite its regular appearance in films and television series, the MAC-10 has acquired a moderately poor reputation lately because there are many illegal "bootleg" and sloppy legal and illegal conversions on the market. A considerable number of guns manufactured out of tolerance are on the market at very high prices. In some cases, it is difficult to establish the MAC-10's manufacturer or date of production since someone seems to have made guns from reject Military Armament Corporation parts after the company went out of business. The gun is still being made.

A standard MAC-10.

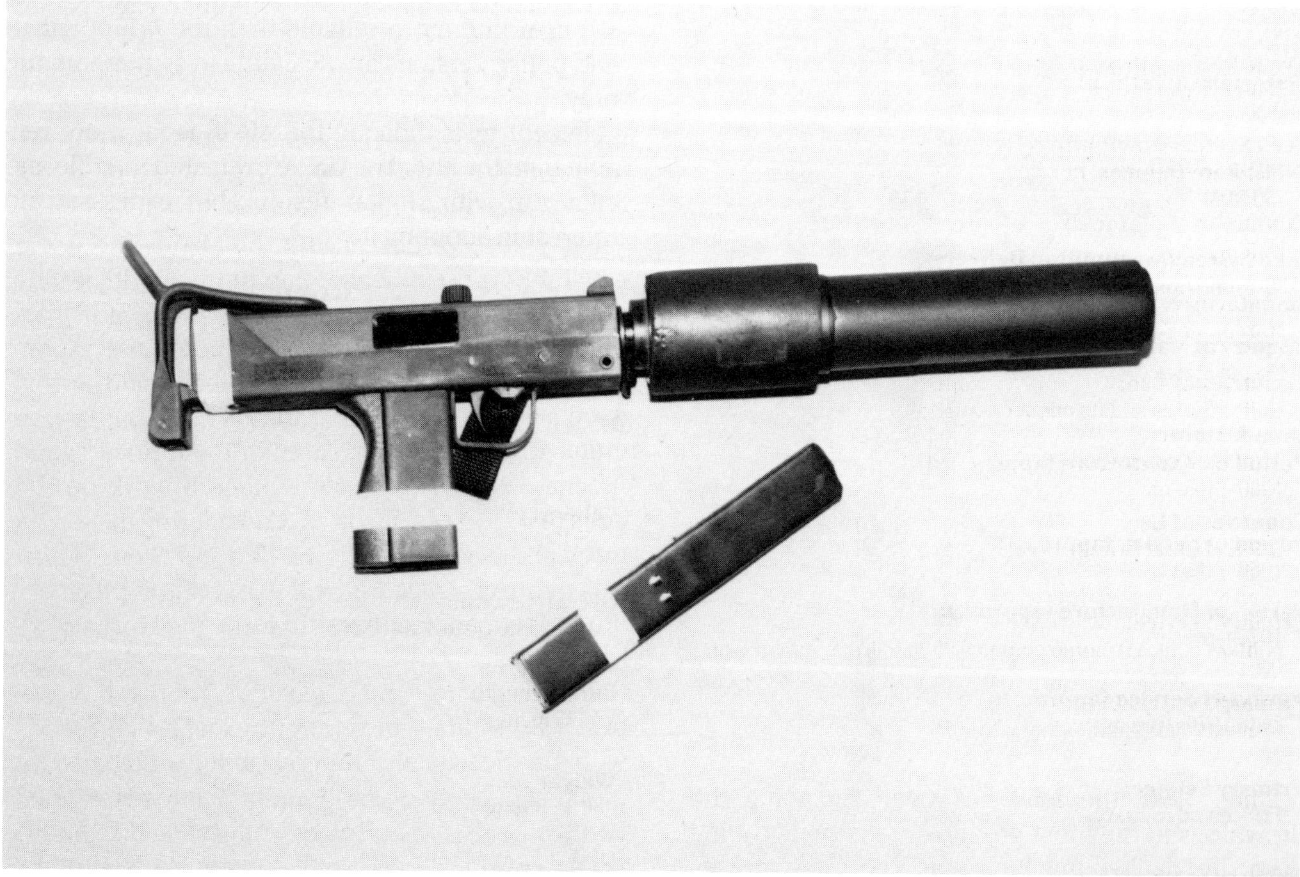

A suppressed MAC-10.

Properly made MAC-10s are quite reliable, though not very accurate. An entire family of silencers and suppressors has been designed for them. The guns have seen some military use in specialized applications where firepower is convenient and larger weapons either couldn't be carried or couldn't be moved around.

M60

Name:
U.S. machine gun, general purpose

Model:
M60

Caliber:
7.62mm NATO

Overall Length:
43.75 inches

Barrel Length:
25.5 inches

Weight:
23 pounds

Type of Fire:
Full auto only

System of Operation:
Gas

Cyclic Rate (approx.):
550 + RPM

Feed System/Ammunition Delivery:
Disintegrating steel link belt

Country of Manufacture:
United States

Manufacturer:
Maremont Corporation, U.S.A.

Countries of Use:
United States and its client countries

Period of Manufacture (approx.):
1960–present

Period of Service (approx.):
1960–present

Primary Service:
Military contract, some commercial law enforcement use

Primary Tactical Use:
Crew-served or individual weapon

Since 1960, the M60 has been replacing the Brownings in the most ground applications calling for a rifle-caliber machine gun. The weapon uses the German FG42 operating system and the MG42 feed setup, and has bits and pieces of MP44- and MG34-inspired lines and furniture. However, the M60 costs at least four times the price of commercial MG42/59s and has proven to be somewhat clumsier to handle in terms of barrel change and use from fixed positions. Many old veterans and firearms buffs believe the United States would have been better advised to merely adopt the FG42, which in fact was tried in .30-06 during World War II.

The M60 was the first real U.S. general purpose machine gun. On early versions, a gas cylinder and bipod had to be attached to each barrel and therefore changed with each and every barrel, each and every time. A special asbestos mitten had to be furnished with the gun for such changes. These factors raised the cost of the system even higher. Newer guns still require careful handling when conducting barrel changes, but a handle has been provided and the gas cylinder is no longer attached.

Barrels for these guns are lined with hard polymer/metal (stellite) for the first six inches of the chamber, with the remainder chromium-plated. Stellite is a nonferrous, polymer-bound amalgam of cobalt, chromium, molybdenum, and tungsten, the purpose of which is to minimize wear and erosion. It has the ancillary effect of limiting chemical and atmospheric corrosion as well.

Since this weapon has become standard "armament" in some movies, it is worth noting that gas-operated machine guns can be either terminally dangerous or extremely unreliable when fired in a water-filled condition.

Many people suggest that the M60 is the worst general purpose machine gun in the world, if they don't assign that distinction to the HK 21. Still, it's a pretty decent gun, though it's much more expensive than the MG42 would have been and not as good a gun as the MG42 or the FN MAG. But to give credit where it is due, Maremont and Rock Island Arsenal (Illinois) have done superb work on the guns that I've seen and fired. Considering the touchiness and fragility of the FG42 gas system, which was never designed for heavy use, it is a great tribute to the manufacturers that the gun works at all in heavy use.

The gun is not ammo-sensitive, though it works best with military brass. I got exceptional results with American Eagle (Federal) ammo and had a lot of fun with Norma's 168-grain match loads. Among surplus loads, some British stuff marked L2A2 RG (Redway-Green) and some Indian loads shot almost as well as the match ammo.

An M60 on a tripod. (Photo courtesy of RIA.)

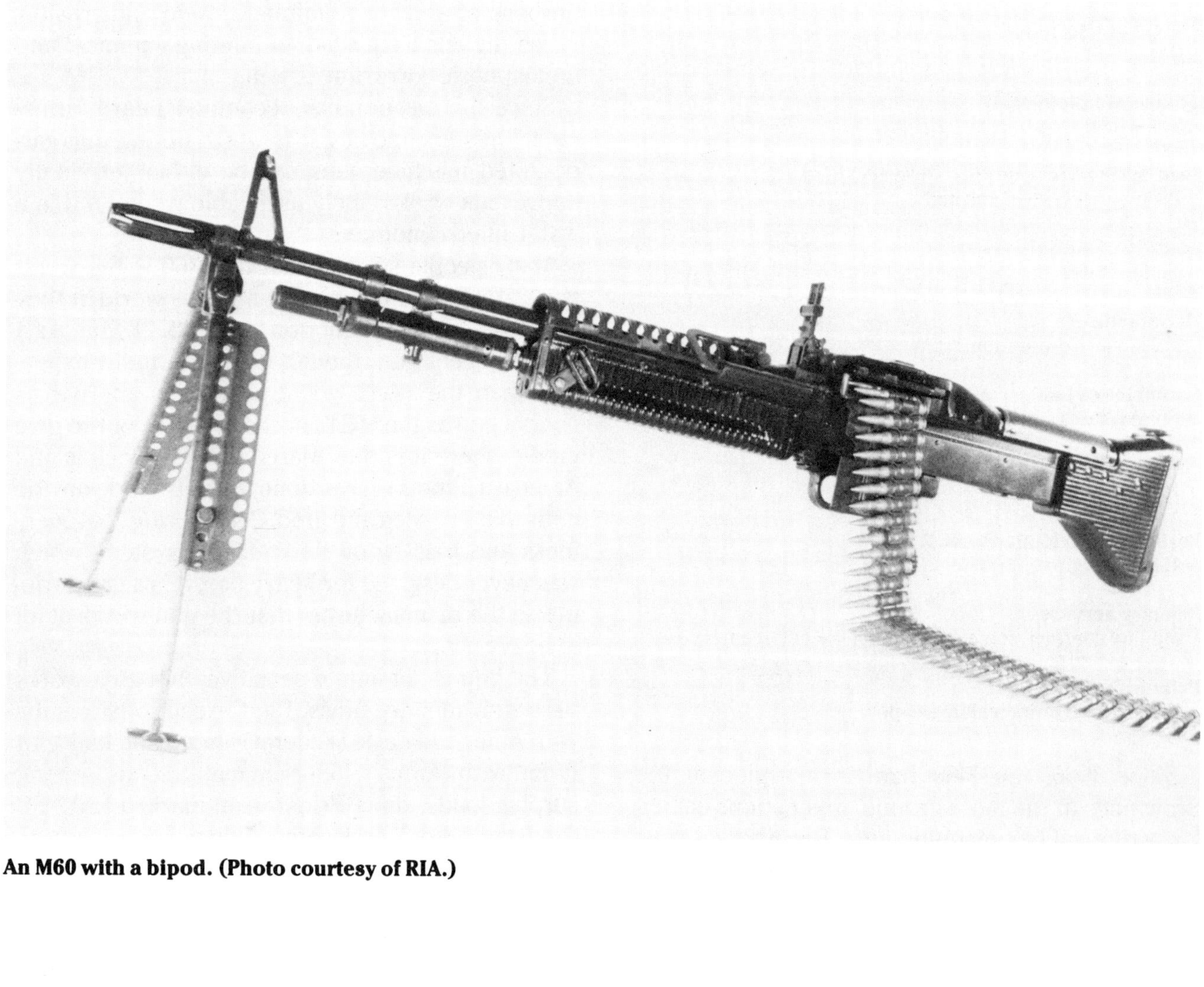

An M60 with a bipod. (Photo courtesy of RIA.)